WEST ST.
MADISON
LOCUST ST.
NORTH
JEFFERSON ST.
WASHINGTON ST.
PRAIRIE
FRONT ST.
EAST LOCUST ST.
WOODARD ST.
MC LEAN ST.
EVANS ST.
OLIVE ST.
CLAYTON

To Mother -
Christmas 1982
Love,
Phylis

30—

HISTORY
OF
McLEAN COUNTY

THE ILLUSTRATED

Dr. Cyrenius Wakefield residence, East Washington Street, Bloomington, 1852
The earliest known exterior photograph of a McLean County subject

HISTORY

OF

McLEAN COUNTY

COMMENTARY BY
DON MUNSON

EDITED BY
MARTIN A. WYCKOFF
&
GREG KOOS

Transactions of the McLean County Historical Society, VIII.
1982

The Illustrated History of McLean County

This book was composed at Circle Type Corporation,
printed at Illinois Graphics Incorporated,
and bound at the Pantagraph Printing and Stationery Company,
all of Bloomington, Illinois

Original photographs copied and artifact photography by
Camera Craft of Bloomington

Text editing by James Keeran, *The Pantagraph*

Library of Congress Cataloging in Publication Data

Main entry under title:

The Illustrated History of McLean County

(Transactions of the McLean County Historical Society; v. 8)
1. McLean County (Ill.)—History—Pictorial works.
2. McLean County (Ill.)—Description and travel—Views.
1. Munson, Don, 1941-
II. Wyckoff, Martin., 1950-
III. Koos, Greg, 1949-
IV. Series.

F547.M16I44 1982 977.3′59 82-14833
ISBN 0-943788-00-5

Designed by Greg Koos and Martin A. Wyckoff

Table of Contents

Bloomington Band, ca. 1910

This volume is respectfully dedicated to

N. Elmo Franklin
President, McLean County Historical Society
1978 - 1982

And the Members of the Board of Directors
who served with him.

David Ashbrook
Sue Baumgart
Dorothy Benjamin
Jim Bicket
Marvin Bower
John Bowles, III
David Davis, Jr.
Eunice Foskett
*Eugene Funk
Howard Gravett
Timothy Ives
Alfred Kemnitz
Edward Jelks
Judy Markowitz
Elizabeth Masters
Richard Middleton
Gene Paxton
Donald Raycraft
*Wayne Rogers
E. William Rolley
Roberta Ropp
Harriett Rust
Sam Stern
Irving Tick
Mrs. Arthur Williams
Leonard Wochner
Walter Wright

*Past President McLean County Historical Society

PREFACE

There are many ways of looking at a photograph. The most obvious is viewing the central subject. Much may be learned, however, by studying the other things that just happen to be in the picture. The image below is an excellent example. Seemingly a straightforward street scene, careful analysis reveals a wealth of information, even to the extent that it was a windy day! We invite you to give the same attention to all the photos contained in this book, and to view the past as it appeared when it was the present.

1. Decorative cornice, now removed
2. Wagon with steamer trunks might be on its way to a hotel
3. Original doorway has now been removed
4. Popcorn wagon
5. Crowd gathered (for what?)
6. Streetcar tracks
7. Mr. Livingston on a windy day
8. A horseless carriage (note crank and steering tiller)
9. Advertising bicycles via parking rack
10. Mother and son shopping
11. Electric carbon arc street lamp
12. Big store window!
13. Old National Bank building
14. Before air conditioning, awnings kept the sun out, and the rooms cooler
15. Withers Public Library is now missing
16. Storage vault under sidewalk
17. Laundry wagon
18. Wooden watch advertising jewelry store
19. Barber shop signs

100 West Washington Street, 1904

1. THE FIRST SETTLERS

We measure the tenure of the white man's occupancy of McLean County by mere decades. United States ownership of the land is a comparatively recent development.

Various groups of Indians had, in fact, lived here for thousands of years—since the end of the last ice age.

Late Paleolithic Holcombe point, found in Dale Township

The Paleo Indians arrived in McLean County as the glaciers were retreating—about 8,000 B.C.

It was the "new stone age" period of Illinois occupancy, and the landscape resembled Northern Canada's in the 1980s—spruce forests and bogs. The Paleo Indians subsisted by hunting small game.

Weapons were made for thrusting and jabbing—mostly smaller animals, but occasionally the mastodon, moose and giant beaver.

The Paleo Indians roamed the McLean County area for about 3,000 years.

Central Illinois, 15,000 B.C.

THE ARCHAIC PERIOD

Gradually warmer weather characterized the next 6,000 years—the Archaic Period. The ice disappeared and the Archaic Indian hunters supplemented their food supply by gathering nuts, berries, herbs and roots. Many of the great animals that had existed with the Paleo Indians became extinct.

The Archaic Indians began to use the axe and the atl-atl (spear-thrower), and their artistic talents became evident in some of the tools they fashioned.

Grooved axe

"Lost Lake" blade

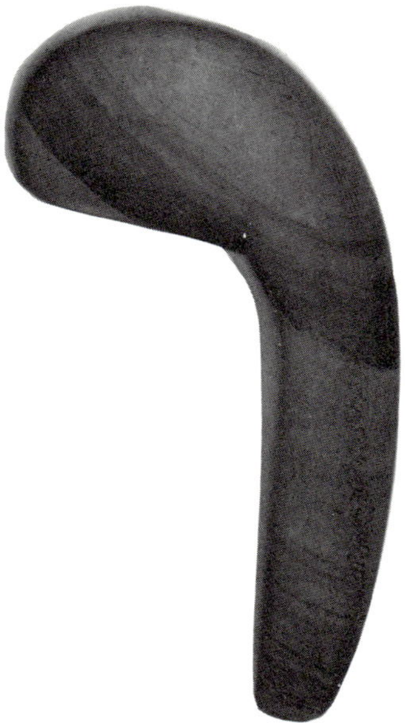

Atl-atl weight

Chert knife,
found in Bloomington Cemetery

Animals hunted by the Archaic Indians

THE WOODLAND AGE

By the end of the Archaic period—about 1,000 B.C.—the McLean County climate was much as it is today. It was the early-to-middle Woodland Period—from 1,000 B.C. to 500 B.C.—when agriculture appeared here. The Woodland Indians grew corn, beans and squash, and hunted buffalo and deer.

Accumulated wealth allowed the Indians more time for personal adornment and artistic production.

Religion became more sophisticated, as evidenced by the burial and ritual mounds found throughout the Midwest.

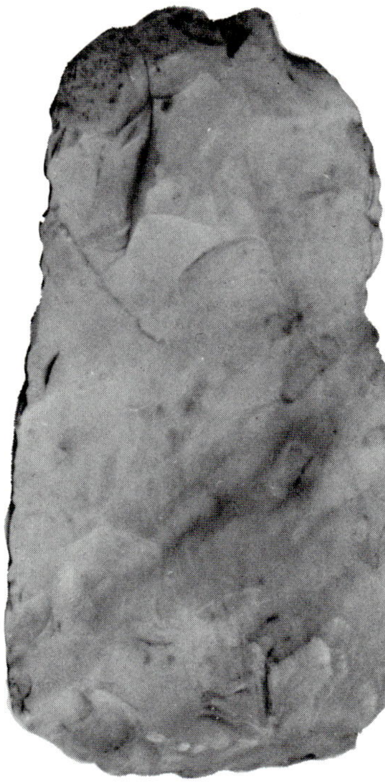

Chert hoe

**Stone pipe,
found in Lawndale Township**

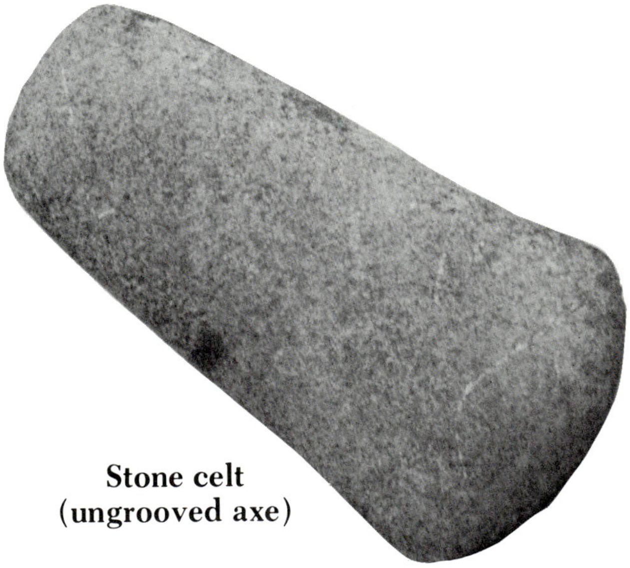

**Stone celt
(ungrooved axe)**

**Projectile points
The forms are an expression
of the culture of the makers**

THE MISSISSIPPIAN CULTURE IN

The years before the white man arrived —1,000 A.D. to 1,500 A.D.—are called the Mississippian Period, a time when nearly 30,000 Indians resided near Cahokia, Illinois. Smaller numbers of less sophticated Mississippian Indians lived in what is now McLean County.

They engaged in agriculture and hunted for the first time with bow and arrow. But the artistic production of the Mississippians didn't equal that of the Woodland Indians.

Corn became a more important crop and settlements became more permanent.

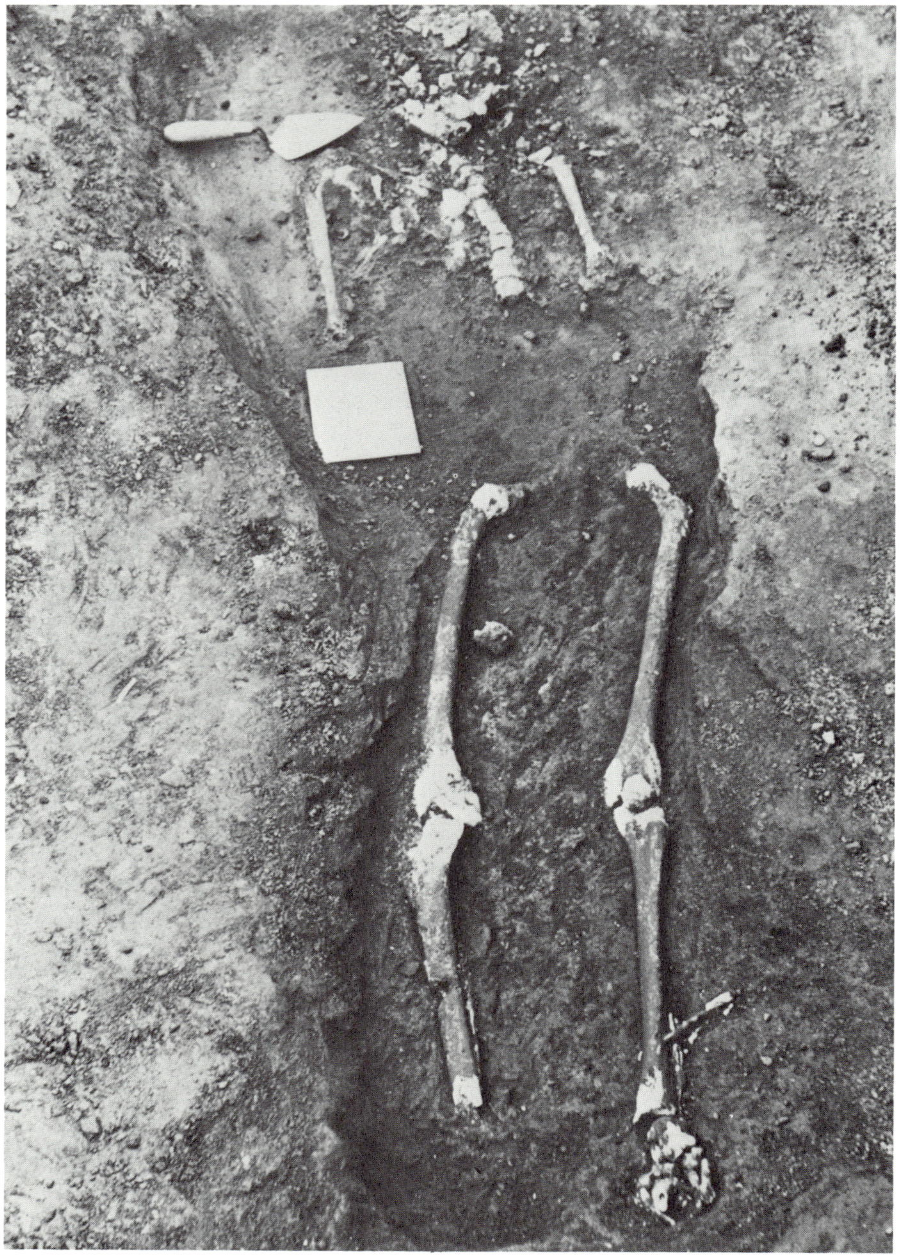

Excavated remains

"Madison" projectile points

Bone awls

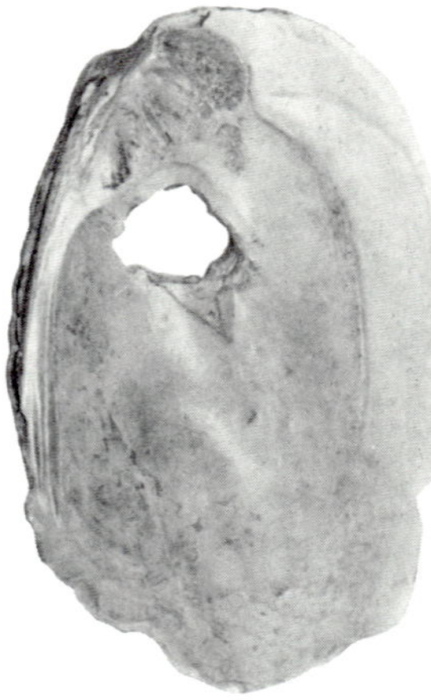

Mussel shell hoe

Clay pot

McLEAN COUNTY

The Noble-Wieting Site

As early as 1900 excavations were being made at a small mound in Randolph township. In the 1960s further work was undertaken by Fred Brian of Illinois Wesleyan University.

The most extensive investigation was conducted by Dr. Edward Jelks of Illinois State University in 1972. Much has been learned from this site about daily life in McLean County 700 years ago.

It was a permanent village occupied by a small group of Mississippian Indians for a period of 60-90 years. They lived primarily on deer and elk, but did raise some corn, beans and squash. There may have been a central plaza north of the burial mound. The village flourished around 1200 A.D., making it truly one of McLean County's first settlements.

Setting out for the dig

Excavating the Noble-Wieting Site, 1972

EUROPEAN CONTACT: THE HI

ORIC PERIOD

French map of North America, 1745

THE ARROWSMITH QUESTION

Soon after their first contact with the French in Wisconsin, the Fox Indians began a series of running battles with them that peaked, possibly near Arrowsmith, in 1730. The French were aided by contingents from several allied Indian tribes, and they surrounded the 1,000 Fox warriors and families, holed up in a hastily-built fortified encampment.

After a siege of 23 days, the Fox tried to slip away during a middle-of-the-night thunderstorm. But the cries of the Fox children alerted the French, who overtook the retreating Indians the next day. Only 50 of the Fox survived.

McLean County Academy of Science at Arrowsmith Site, 1934

William Brigham identifying his site, 1943

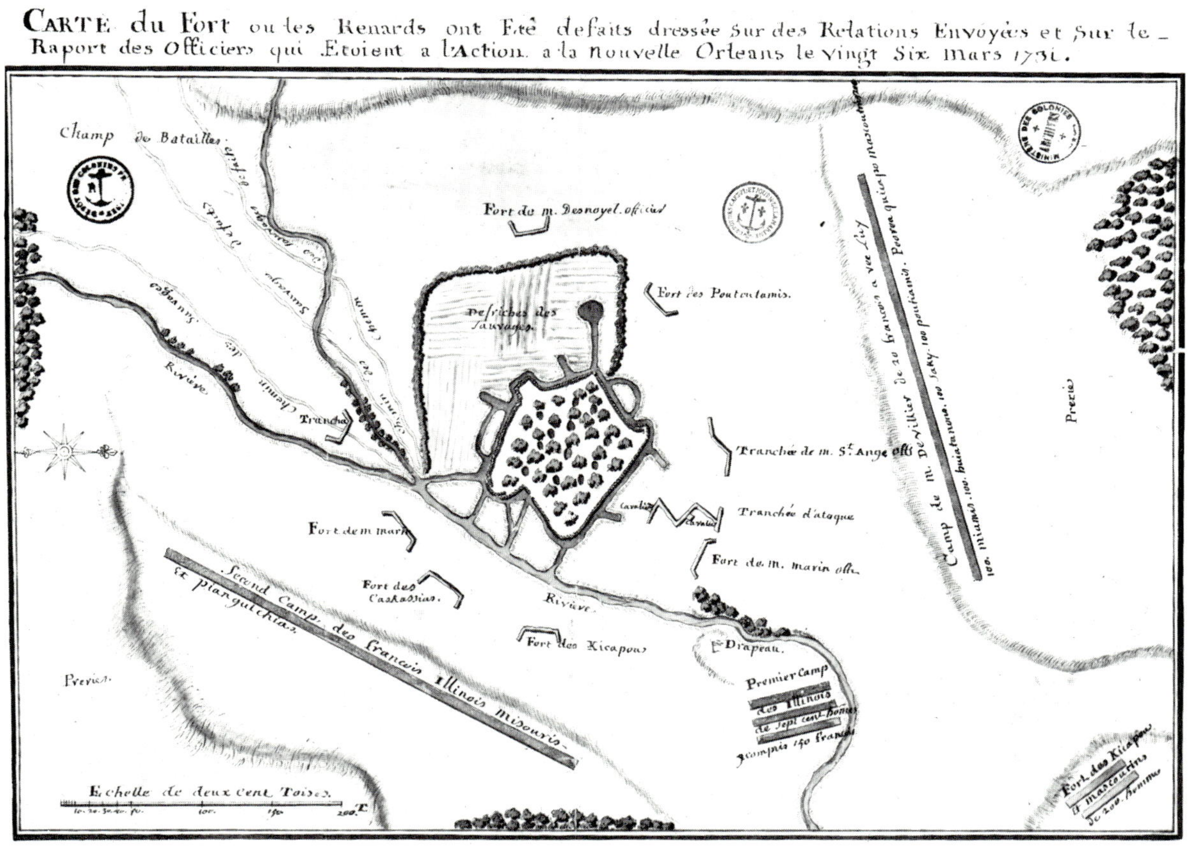

French Map of the Fox fort, made at New Orleans, 1731

Musket balls from the site

The Fox-French encounter was 92 years before the first white settlement in McLean County, and historians disagree over the location of the otherwise well-documented battle at the Fox fort, Etnataek. But the many bullets of the period uncovered near Arrowsmith, along with some evidence there of pits and trenches matching French descriptions, were used by McLean County historian William Brigham to support his interpretation that the battle took place near the headwaters of the Sangamon River.

THE KICKAPOOS

The Kickapoos became one of the Midwest's mightiest Indian nations after their migration here from Wisconsin in the early 1700s.

They built their grand village at the edge of the area's largest timber, near the present town of Ellsworth.

Bark-covered winter hut

White settlers arriving a century later honored them by calling it Old Town Timber, after the Indians' "old town."

The Kickapoos built a fort a half-mile east of their village about 1752—22 years after the French defeated the Fox—and it stood until 1813.

Major Zachary Taylor's men, engaged in a punitive expedition against the Indians that year, were driven back to Cheney's Grove by a prairie fire started by the Kickapoos. But several months later, Colonel Bartholomew, who would later become one of McLean County's most prominent citizens, approached the Kickapoo fort, found it abandoned, and burned it.

Kickapoo war club

Kickapoo summer houses

HOW THEY LIVED

The Kickapoos fought often and effectively. When both the British and the Colonists sought their help during the Revolutionary War, the Kickapoos accepted favors from both but supported neither.

They engaged in hostage-diplomacy, holding in their fort in McLean County several whites they captured during the War of 1812.

The men hunted larger game—without horses until the late 1700s—and the women prepared the food and clothes, hunted small game, tended the gardens, and built the bark-covered huts.

Items such as those seen here were obtained from white traders either as gifts or as barter. All were found in McLean County.

Iron hoe

Knife blade

Scissors

Trade axe

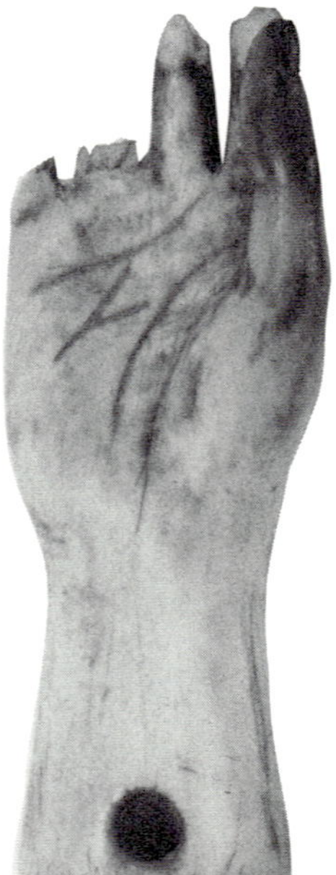

Carved bone hand

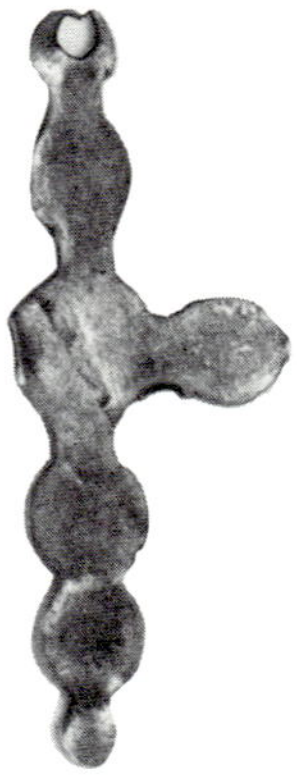

Silver cross

Gun cock

Iron arrow point

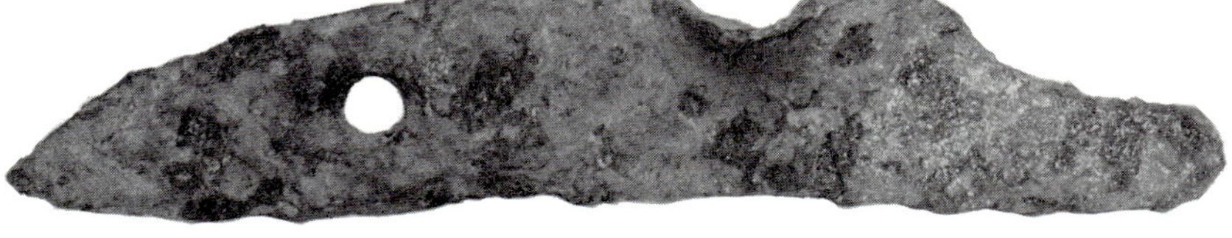

Gun lock plate

KICKAPOO REMOVAL

White settlers spilled into Illinois after the War of 1812, and the United States government forced the Kickapoos to move west of the Mississippi. Treaties were signed in 1819, giving the Indians compensation in return for their lands east of the river. Their fate was placed in the hands of General William Clark, Superintendent of Indian Affairs.

But many of the Kickapoos were reluctant to leave—Chief Machina among them. Machina first threatened early white settlers in McLean County in 1822, then existed with them, making some friends.

Machina moved on to Livingston County in 1829, and to Kansas soon after.

William Clark

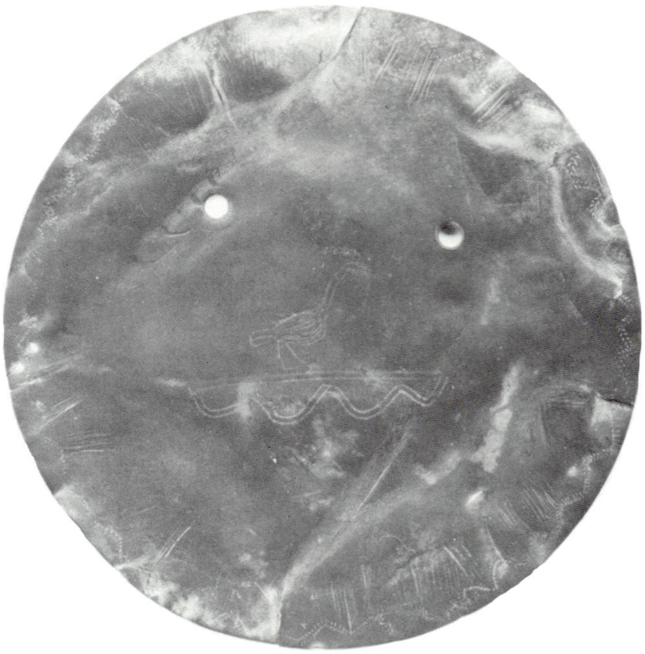

Brass amulet

A'h-tee-wat-o-mee, a Kickapoo woman

Machina, a chief of the Central Illinois Kickapoos, refused to believe their land had been sold to the whites. When told of the treaty, he replied, "Damn quick putting black upon white."

Machina

Trade kettle

KANNEKUK

Machina joined Kannekuk, the Kickapoos' "prophet." Kannekuk had been influenced by Methodist and Catholic missionaries and while his followers didn't accept Christianity, they did adopt into their doctrine many of the principles of the Old Testament.

Kannekuk introduced a prayer stick, carved with symbolic characters, and led his people in a temperate life. In 1833, he led his "Praying Kickapoos" to the reservation near Fort Leavenworth, Kansas, where he later married Machina's daughter.

Kannekuk

Prayer stick

"My friends, where are your thoughts today? Where were they yesterday? Were they fixed upon doing good? Or were you drunk and tattling, or did anger rest in your hearts? If you have done any of these things your Great Father in Heaven knows it. His eye is upon you. He always sees you and will always see you. He knows all your deeds. He has knowledge of the smallest transactions of your lives."

— KANNEKUK
July 17, 1831

THE KICKAPOOS IN KANSAS

The Kickapoos settled down to a more permanent lifestyle on the reservation. Their numbers diminished, and so did their territory.

The traditional and Praying Kickapoo were represented, and discipline was strong in each of them. Order for the Praying Kickapoo was kept by the Regu-

Wahkwahpoakuk

lators, the "whippers" of the Kannekuk's church.

And among those punished was old Machina, who killed a Delaware Indian after an argument. Machina was sentenced to 120 lashes, but members of his tribe took most of the whipping for him.

McLean County historian Milo Custer visited the Kansas reservation in 1906 and 1911 and hired a photographer. The portraits he brought home reflect a people who called McLean County "home" less than a century before.

Mkopahmah (Bear Chief)

James Allen & his wife, a Sac/Fox woman

Kawkeasauqua
(great grand-daughter
of Machina)

Nubya Eshnoqua
(Daughter of Machina)
Born in Illinois, 1824

Keepoakwa

Jack Masquat (Nenawa) Willie Whitewater (Ktukpea) Little Simon (Nenasak)

Weeweenas Kaukeasauqua Neepakum

BAND
KICKAPOO BAND, KICKAPOO
UPPER ROW; (1), Mrs. Elm; (2),
Lewis, LOWER TWO ROWS; (1), Reuben
(3), Frank Masquat, (K.), (4),
(Iowa); (6), Susan Masquequa,
(8), Minnie Wawawsuk, (K.); (9)
(K. & Fr.); (11), Madeline Lasley,
(13), Lucy Masquat, (K. dec.),
Love, (clerk of the school); (16),

ROWN COUNTY, KANSAS, 1905.
---; (3), Mrs. Hattie Love; (4),Miss
en,(K.); (2), O. C. Edwards, (Supt.)
upuis, (Iowa); (5), Eddie Deroin,
John); (7), Louis Wawawsuk, (K.);
Tesson, (Iowa); (10), Sophie Cadue,
& Fox), (12), Rosa Kawkeeka, (K.);
rank Dupuis, (Iowa); (15), Arthur
nk Kawkeeka, (K.).

EPILOGUE

Cock Turkey

Some attempt was made by both the Indian and the white man to accomodate the other, but the ways of life simply were not compatible.

Various Indian tribes hunted, fished and lived in McLean County for more than 16,000 years. But the game was disappearing and the times were changing.

Within a decade of the arrival in McLean County of the first white settlers, the Indians had all moved west.

Thomas Orendorff

". . . At one time an Indian, called Turkey, came to Mr. Orendorff and gave him warning that Machina would kill him; but no attempt was made to put such a threat into execution . . ."

— Prof. E. Duis
The Good Old Times in McLean County
1874

2. The White Settlers

It was an independent, hardy group of farmers—most of them Scotch-Irish—who first settled McLean County in the early 1820s.

Most of them were illiterate, but there was little for them to read about this area anyway. Few of them knew exactly where they were going or if there would be churches or schools ahead. But enough of them who happened by Blooming Grove were motivated to stop. By 1830, the grove became the most thickly-settled spot between Vandalia and the Wisconsin line.

John Patton was typical of the early arrivals. He and his family spent their first winter in an unchinked cabin, then took over an abandoned Indian hut near the present town of Lexington the following spring. When the Indians returned, Patton made peace with them and secured their help in raising his own cabin in June, 1829—the cabin that stands to this day in Lexington's park.

Patton Cabin, Lexington, Illinois

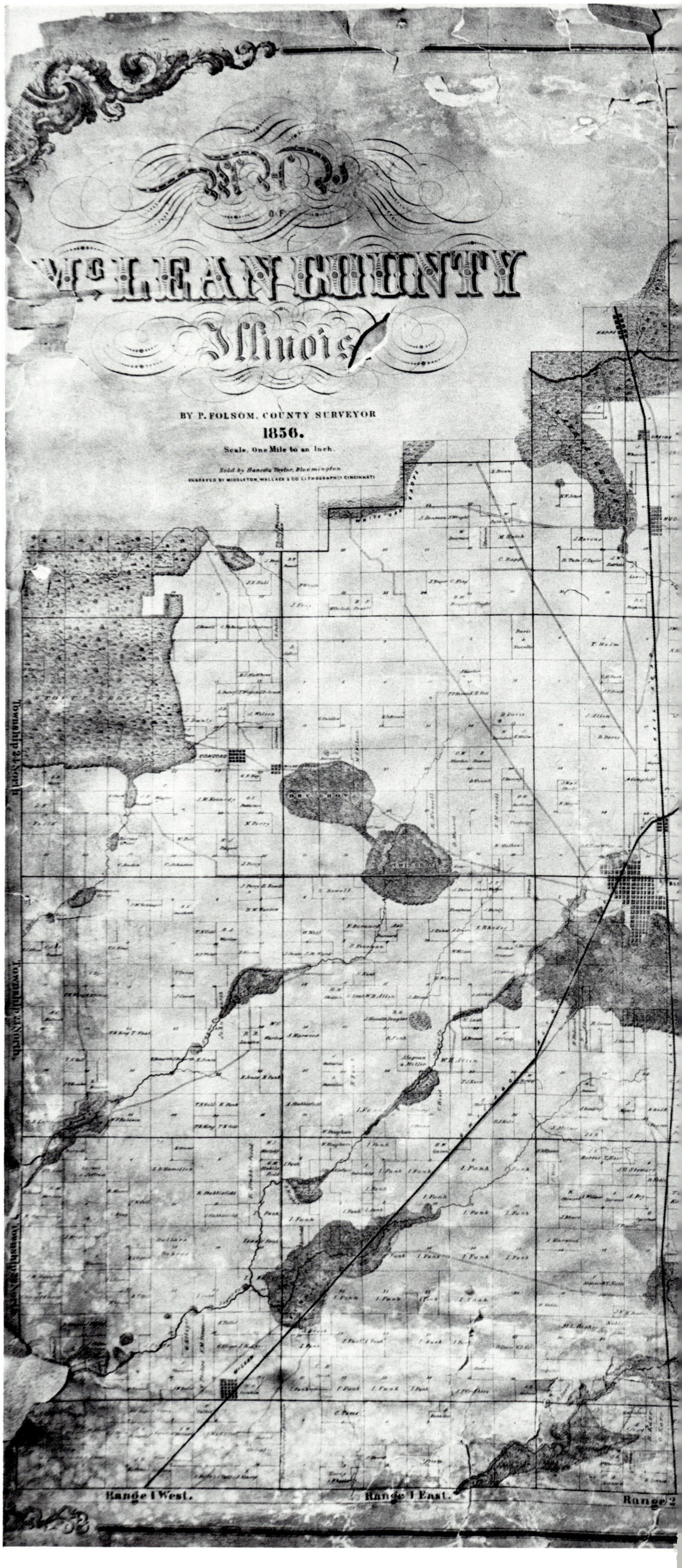

". . . The land is as rich as I could wish and the greatest depth of soil I ever have seen. All the different kinds of grain and vegitables grows to the greatest perfection . . ."

— William Brown, 1830

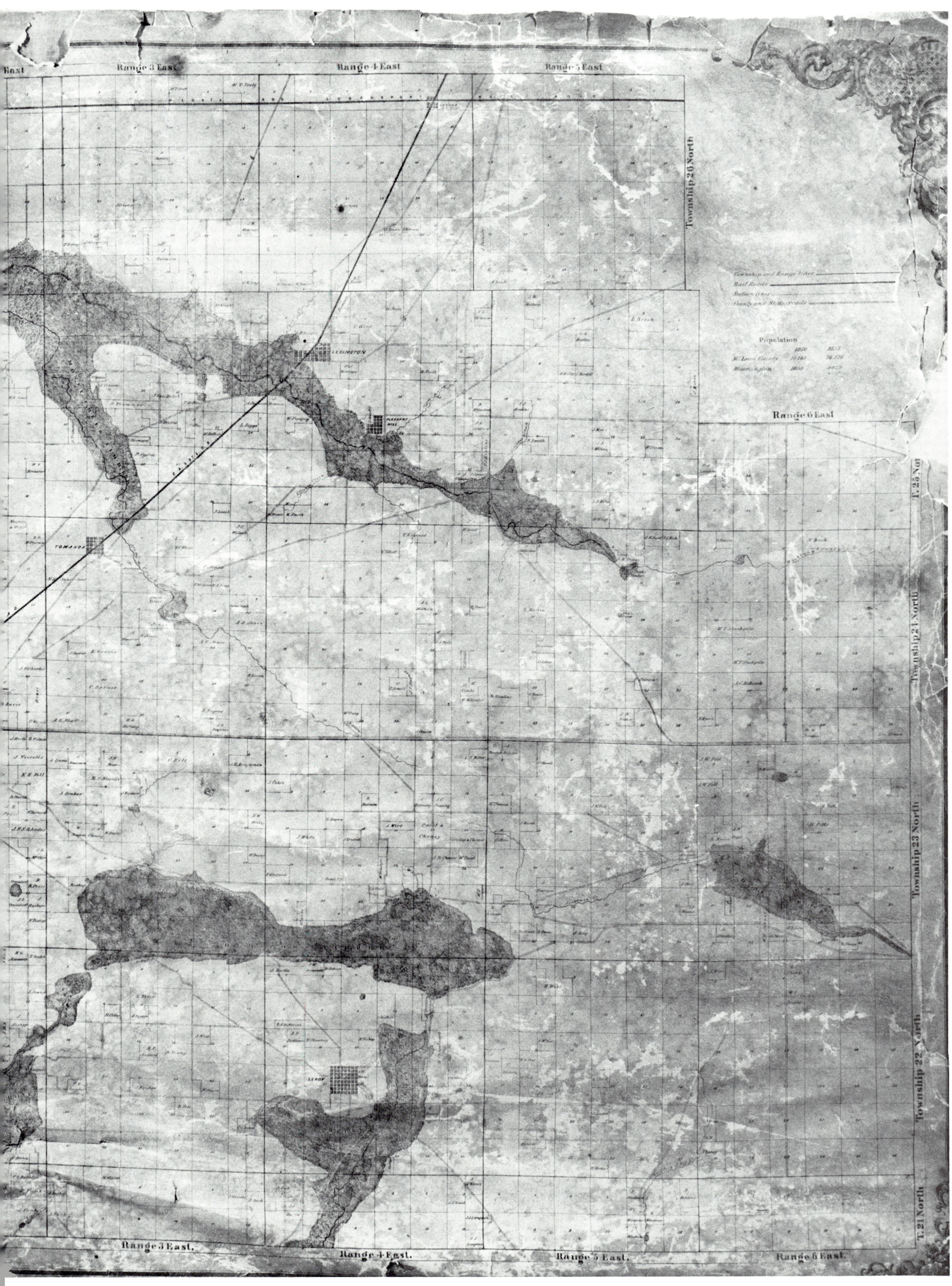
Range 3 East
Range 4 East
Range 5 East
Township 26 North
Township and Range lines
Rail Roads
Section lines
County and State roads
Population
1850
McLean County
Bloomington
Range 6 East
T. 25 Nor
LEXINGTON
TOWANDA
Township 24 North
Township 23 North
LEROY
Township 22 North
T. 21 North
Range 3 East.
Range 4 East.
Range 5 East.
Range 6 East.

Log cabin of Isaac Funk, built in 1830

With no way to get crops to market in those pre-railroad days, the rich soil did little good beyond yield feed for hogs and cattle. Isaac Funk and others would drive the livestock overland to markets in Galena or Chicago or Ohio.

It wasn't easy. Funk would chop footholds in the ice one winter to keep the porkers moving across Livingston County. And he would hang on to the mane of his swimming horse one summer in Missouri in order to cross the swollen rivers on a buying trip.

But Funk bought and sold livestock and land, grew corn, and became a millionaire. He was an Illinois state senator when he died in 1865 and he had worked his way up from a primative shanty to the beautiful family homestead that once sat near Funk's Grove. Ike Funk slept in it only twice before his death.

His wife, Cassandra, shared the burdens of pioneer life. She died only four hours after her husband.

". . . Thousands of hogs are raised without any expense, except a few breeders to start with . . . One of our Illinois frontier men . . . in 1829 . . . drove forty-two fat hogs to market, which he sold for one-hundred and thirty-five dollars. The amount of corn given to the whole . . . did not exceed one bushel. They lived on the range, and grew fat on mast; the fruit of oak, hickory, etc. . ."

— **Peck's Gazetteer**
1834

Split rail corn cribs

". . . Maize is a staple production. No farmer can live without it, and hundreds raise little else. This is chiefly owing to the ease with which it is cultivated. Its average yield is fifty bushels to the acre. I have oftentimes seen it produce seventy-five bushels to the acre, and in a few instances, exceed one hundred . . ."

— **Peck's Gazetteer**
1834

". . . Funk's Grove settlement is 12 miles southwest from Bloomington. The grove is roundish in form, contains about eight square miles, and lies on the main branch of Sugar Creek. It has an excellent soil, fine water, and is monopolized by a family connection of the name of Funk, from Ohio, who raise large numbers of cattle . . ."

— **Illinois in 1837**

Isaac and Cassandra Funk

HUNTING

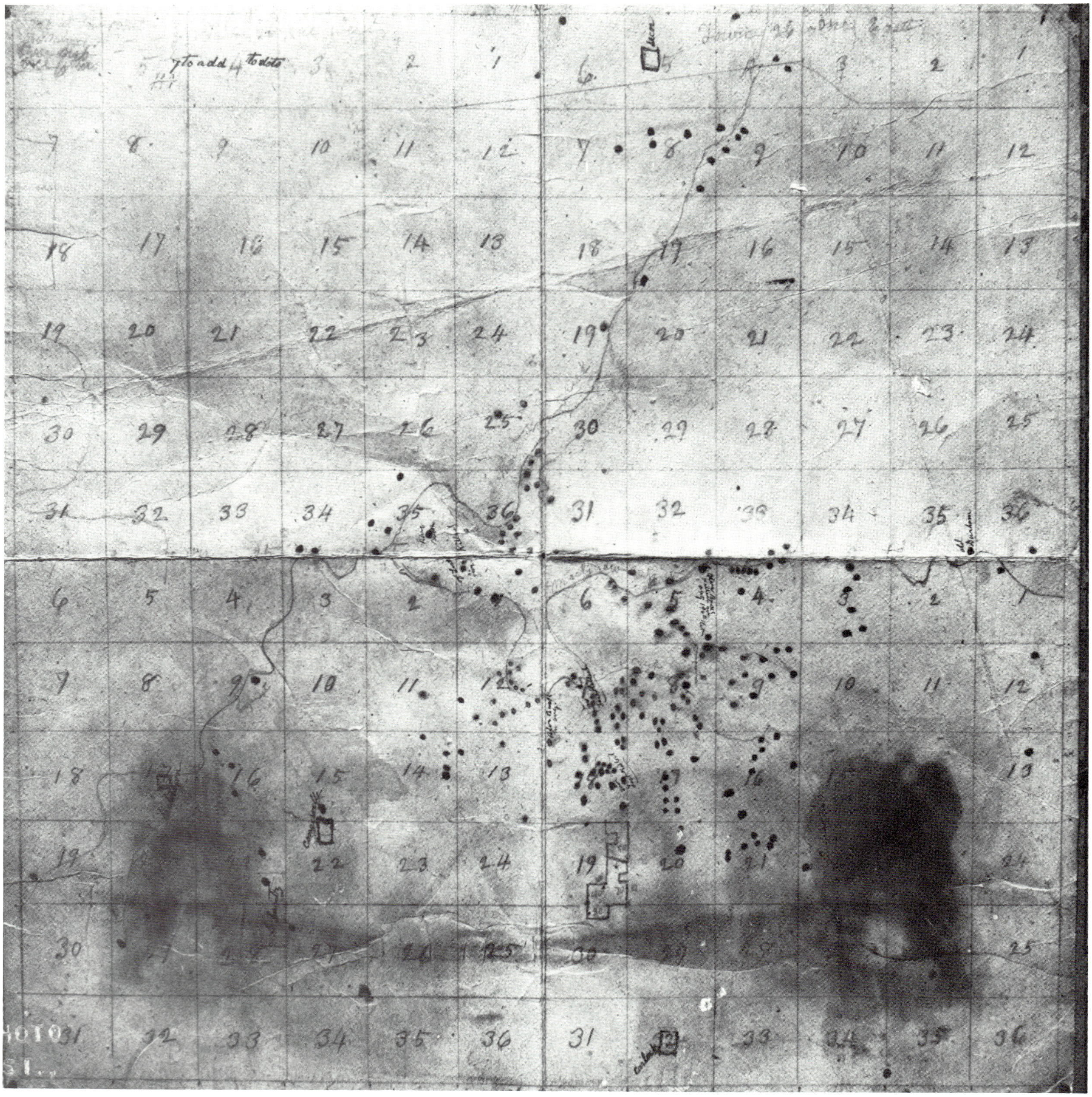

Map made by Winton Carlock showing where he killed deer 1832-62

The Carlock boys were typical of the early hunters in McLean County. They would catch 20 or 30 prairie chickens at a time in a trap, but they also hunted deer, wild turkeys and squirrels.

Hunting honey was not as exciting, but bee trees were found in abundance in the groves.

Every family had its rifle and fleet horses and a good dog, and some had packs of wolf-hounds. Wolves were great lovers of poultry and young pigs, and quite brazen about approaching the settlements to carry away their prey. The wolf chase was usually a spirited one.

In a ring hunt, other "varmints" were hunted without guns, with a group of "beaters" driving the victims inward toward the center of a large circle where they would be killed with clubs.

". . . Hunters seem to be subject to queer freaks of fortune, which they always express by the word 'luck,' and Mr. Messer's was occasionally hard luck. He was once walking in the snow towards a deer, near Wolf Creek, and he pulled off his boots and walked through the snow in his stocking feet, in order to move silently. He killed a deer and hung it on a bush, and that was good luck; but his boots became so frozen that he could not put them on, and that was his hard luck. He saw more deer and had a fine opportunity to kill them, and this was his good luck; but the stopper had fallen out of his powder horn, spilling all of his powder, and that was his hard luck. He killed no more and was obliged to walk home through the snow in his stocking feet . . ."

— Prof. E. Duis
The Good Old Times in McLean County
1874

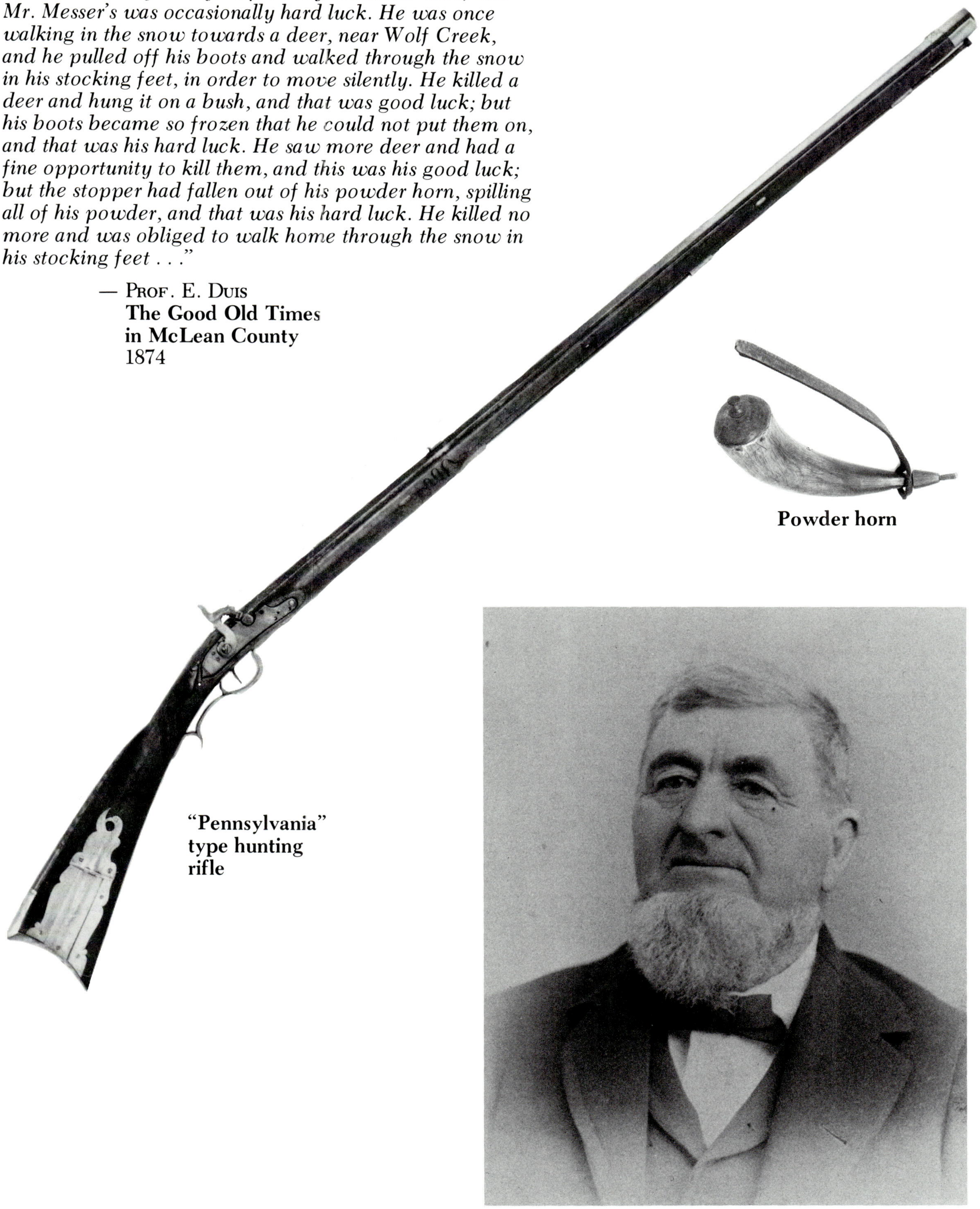

"Pennsylvania" type hunting rifle

Powder horn

Winton Carlock

FARMING

Yoked oxen, G.P. Davis Farm, ca. 1895

For the first 20 years of McLean County's life, people lived in the groves and grew only enough crops to feed themselves and their livestock. The trees of the groves furnished shelter. On the prairie the farmer would hack a hole with his axe, drop in some seeds by hand, and tap some dirt on top with the heel of his boot.

The first plows were made of wood with iron plowshares and pulled by oxen or horses—each row would be plowed three times. The work in the prairie was difficult—breaking the tough prairie-grass sod took 8-12 oxen. And the rich soil stuck to the blades of the plows.

Ox shoe

"The Carey Plow" used by Thomas Orendorff

". . . The first plows used by the settlers were made of wood, the next of iron and the last of steel. The first plow which Mr. Orendorff used was called the Barshear. This was a plow having a piece of iron for a shear, which ran flat on the ground and had a bar attached which extended from the point several feet back, and held the plow steady. The mould board was made of wood, and the plow worked very well. Many hundreds of thousands of acres have been ploughed with the Barshear . . ."

— Prof. E. Duis
The Good Old Times in McLean County
1874

HARVESTING

At harvest time, the reaping hook and cradle scythe were used to cut the grain. It was then threshed with wooden flails and cleaned by tossing it into the air with a fork so the wind would blow away the chaff. The straw was raked and fed to the livestock.

Harvest time was a social time, with the huskers working in the fields and the women setting a liberal table.

". . . The first wheat we cut was with a sickle or reaper, cut by hand . . . we would cut a row and then put our clipper on our shoulders and bind the bundles . . .I remember Hardy and I was ruled out once, they didn't want a half-hand in the field and a whole hand at the table . . .We could make a full hand at the table all right . . ."

— John Stubblefield
1899

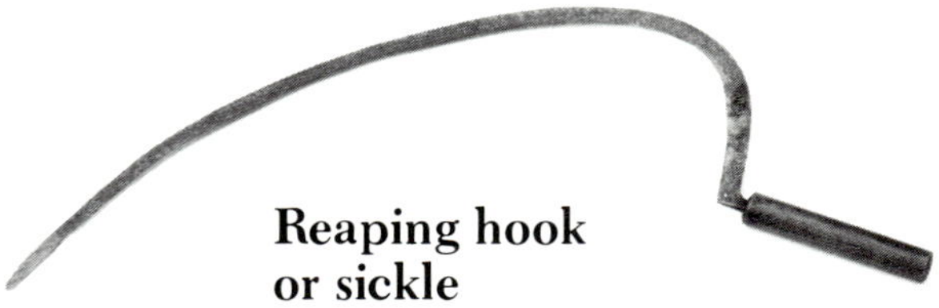

Reaping hook or sickle

Wooden pitchfork

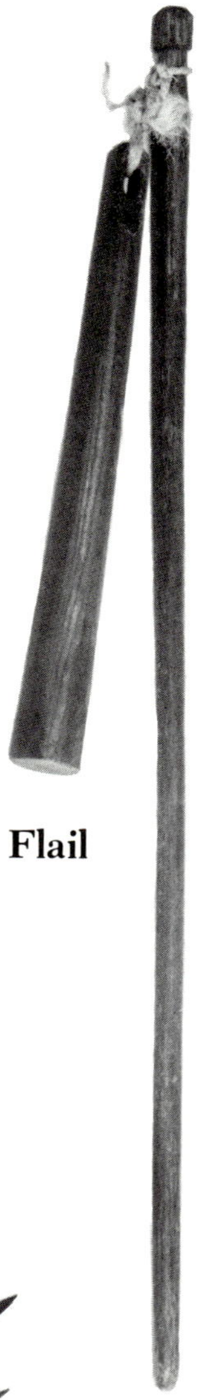

Flail

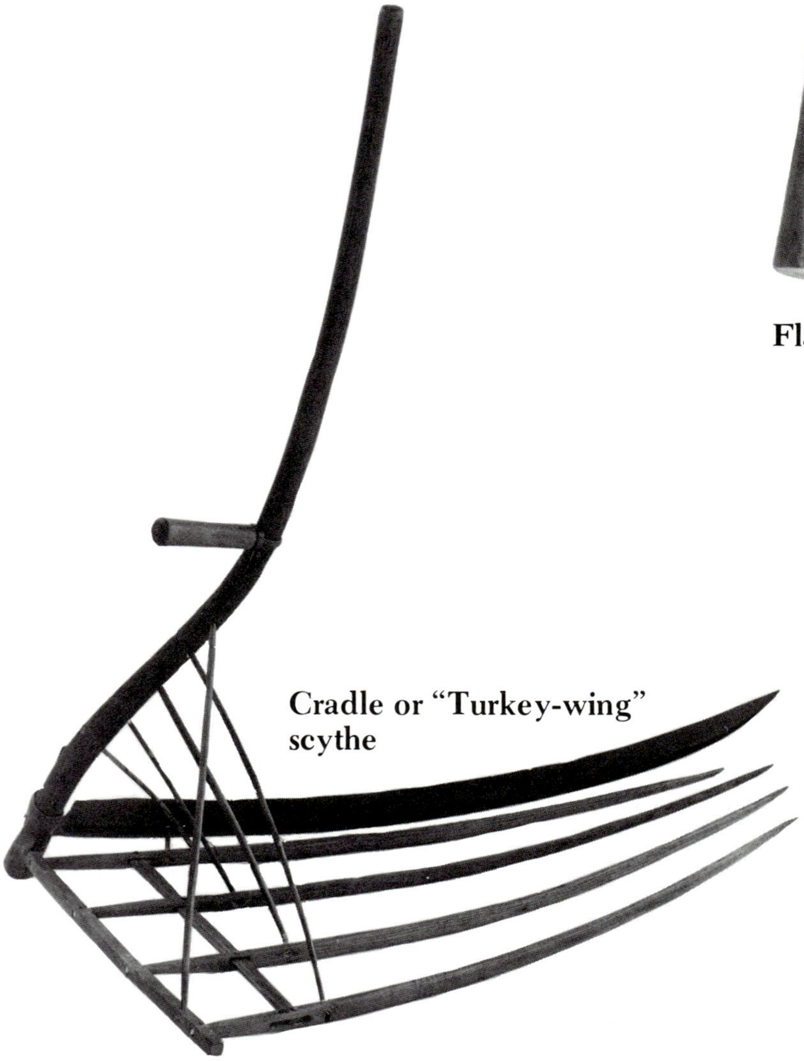

Cradle or "Turkey-wing" scythe

PIONEER COOKING

Few went away from the table hungry—particularly during the summer when peas, beans, squash, pumpkins and other vegetables were available. The first settlers ate little fruit—it took too long for the newly-planted fruit trees to reach maturity—but they did manage to gather berries in the groves, and the women baked some great pies.

Pork was the meat staple during the early years, then beef. But the beef was never broiled. It was fried, boiled or baked.

Copper tea kettle

"Dutch" oven

Rolling pin for maple sugar

Iron pot

". . . They had what they called an 'oven' with a lid to it, it would hold about six gallons; it had three legs to it . . . and they baked bread with it, corn loaves . . . It was about six inches deep and about a foot and a half across . . . It was made out of cast iron . . . Then they had what we called a skillet, the handle to it was about a foot long and had a lid to it . . . Then they had a pot that would hold perhaps four or five gallons . . . It was made of cast iron and was hung on an iron; they boiled cabbage or anything they wanted in it . . . We didn't have any coffee, but we had some tea that we raised in the garden called 'sage' tea . . . The sugar we had was maple sugar, that we made . . . Salt we had to go to Danville for . . . Our first bread was made out of corn . . ."

— John & George Stubblefield
1899

Rug loom, ca. 1863, made by the Hon. Sylvester Peasley, Downs, Illinois

CLOTHING

". . . The first year we came here I wore buckskin for pants. As to how long they wore those pants, they wore them out . . . It must have been four or five years before we got new ones . . . The first jeans I ever wore—that was in '30—Mother spun and wove the materials to make them; the jeans were made of cotton for woof, and they spun the wool on a wheel; the color of them was butter nut; the wool was spun on a big wheel and the flax on a small wheel . . . The flax they got by raising it, and spread it out and let the stalk decay—rot—and they gathered it up in bundles and brake it on what they called a flax-brake; there was three pieces on the bottom part and two on top and they lifted up and struck down and brake the flax; and the women would take the coarse tow out and gather the fine stuff and spin it into thread . . . the women made the men's clothes as well as their own . . ."

—John Stubblefield
1899

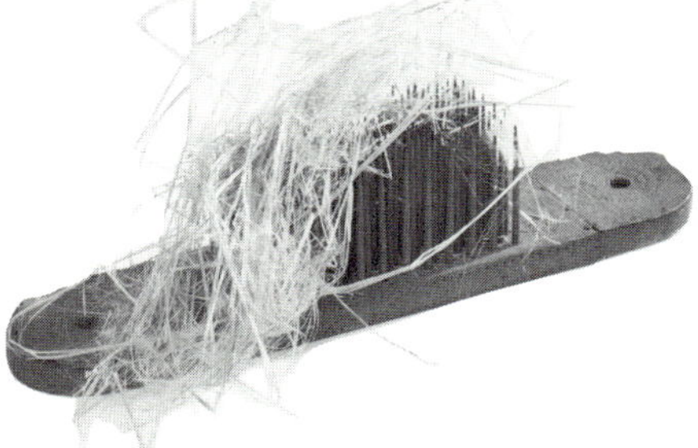

Flax hackel

Spinning wheel for flax

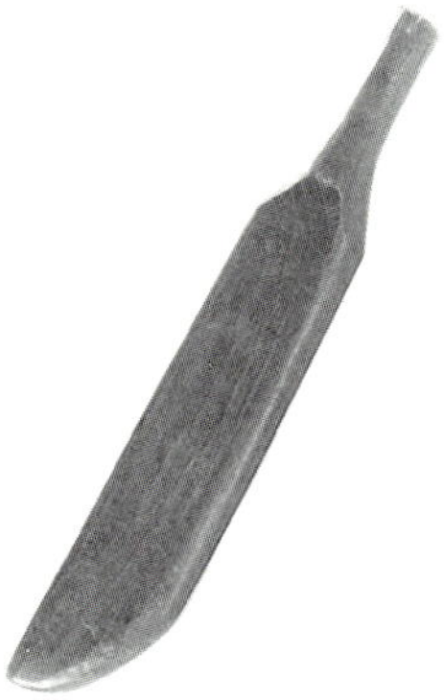

Scutching knife

Yarn reel

Spinning wheel for wool.

Wool cards

THE WEATHER STRIKES BACK

Isolation in winter and swimming across flooded streams in summer were a way of life. But dry weather was a problem, too. That's when the prairie fires raged between the groves.

McLean became a county December 25, 1830, but the snow was so deep it took James Latta and Thomas Orendorff several weeks to return from Vandalia with the news. Thirty-six inches of snow piled up and one family, stranded in their cabin for weeks, discovered they were observing the Sabbath on Saturdays, one day early.

The sudden freeze six years later dropped the mercury 60 degrees in mere seconds. Hiram Buckles dashed for home, but in those few seconds, his overcoat billowed out and froze solid. He was obliged to take off his coat to get through the front door.

Survivors of those memorable winters called themselves "Snowbirds," and they gathered annually in later years to relive the memories.

Mortar used for "pounding corn" by Gardner Randolph and John Moore during the "Deep Snow" Winter

". . . The great hurricane, which swept through Blooming Grove came on the 19th of June, 1827 . . .The hurricane unroofed the houses of William Evans and William Walker, although they were not in its immediate track. It passed through the timber and piled up the trees in some places 20 ft high. Nothing in the forest could stand before it . . . The width of the hurricane was about a half a mile and its length no one knows . . . It passed through . . . at about twilight . . ."

— E. Duis
The Good Old Times in McLean County

". . . The winter of 1830 and '31 was the . . . winter of the deep snow. The weather during the fall had been very dry, and continued mild until late in the winter. But at last the snow came during the latter part of December . . . The settlers were blockaded in their cabins and could do very little except pound their corn, cut their wood, and keep their fires blazing. A great deal of stock was frozen to death . . . The deer and wild turkeys . . . were almost exterminated. The wolves . . . had a pleasant time of it. They . . . caught all the deer they wished, and were bold and impudent . . ."

— Ibid.

". . . The month of December, 1836, was marked by a sudden change in the weather . . . The weather had been mild for some time, and rain had been falling, changing the snow to slush, when suddenly a cold wind storm came and lowered the temperature instantly from about 40 degrees above zero to 20 degrees below. The face of the country was changed from water to ice immediately and . . . appeared like a picture of the polar regions . . . It came from the west to the Mississippi . . . It continued eastward and reached Leroy at 3 o'clock P.M. . . . It moved at the rate of 30 m.p.h. . . ."

— Ibid.

A NEW COUNTY

AN ACT CREATING M'LEAN COUNTY. In Force Dec. 25, 1830.

Sec. 1. *Be it enacted by the People of the State of Illinois, represented in the General Assembly*, That all that tract of country lying within the following boundaries, to wit: Beginning at the south-west corner of township numbered twenty-one north, of range numbered one, west of the third principal meridian; thence north between ranges numbered one and two, west of said meridian, to the north-west corner of township numbered twenty-eight north; thence east, between townships numbered twenty-eight and twenty-nine, to the north-east corner of township numbered twenty-eight, of range numbered six, east of the third principal meridian; thence south, between ranges numbered six and seven, east of said meridian, to the south-east corner of township numbered twenty-one north, of range numbered six, east of said meridian; thence west to the place of beginning; shall constitute a new county, to be called McLean. Boundaries.

— **Laws of Illinois, 1830.**

When the first white settlers, the Hendrix and Dawson families, arrived at Keg Grove in 1822, the present McLean County was a part of Fayette County.

Mrs. William Orendorff renamed the small settlement Blooming Grove in 1824, and as the Indian population diminished, white families arrived in increasing numbers.

Lobbying for a closer county seat resulted in the formation of Tazewell County in 1827, with the Orendorff Voting Precinct providing a polling place for the residents of what was to be a new county.

James Allin arrived in 1829 and entered with the government a quarter section of land at the north edge of the grove. He opened a general store there in 1830 and made contacts in Vandalia to pave the way for the petition carried there Christmas day by Latta and Orendorff.

The new county was quickly approved, and named after the late U.S. Senator, John McLean. The county seat was to be named Bloomington and it was left to the locals to place it. Allin was ready with the donation of land for a courthouse and surrounding lots for the county to auction the following day.

Bloomington was a paper town first, and Allin made sure it grew up around his store at the edge of Blooming Grove—at what is now Grove and East streets.

James Allin's cabin

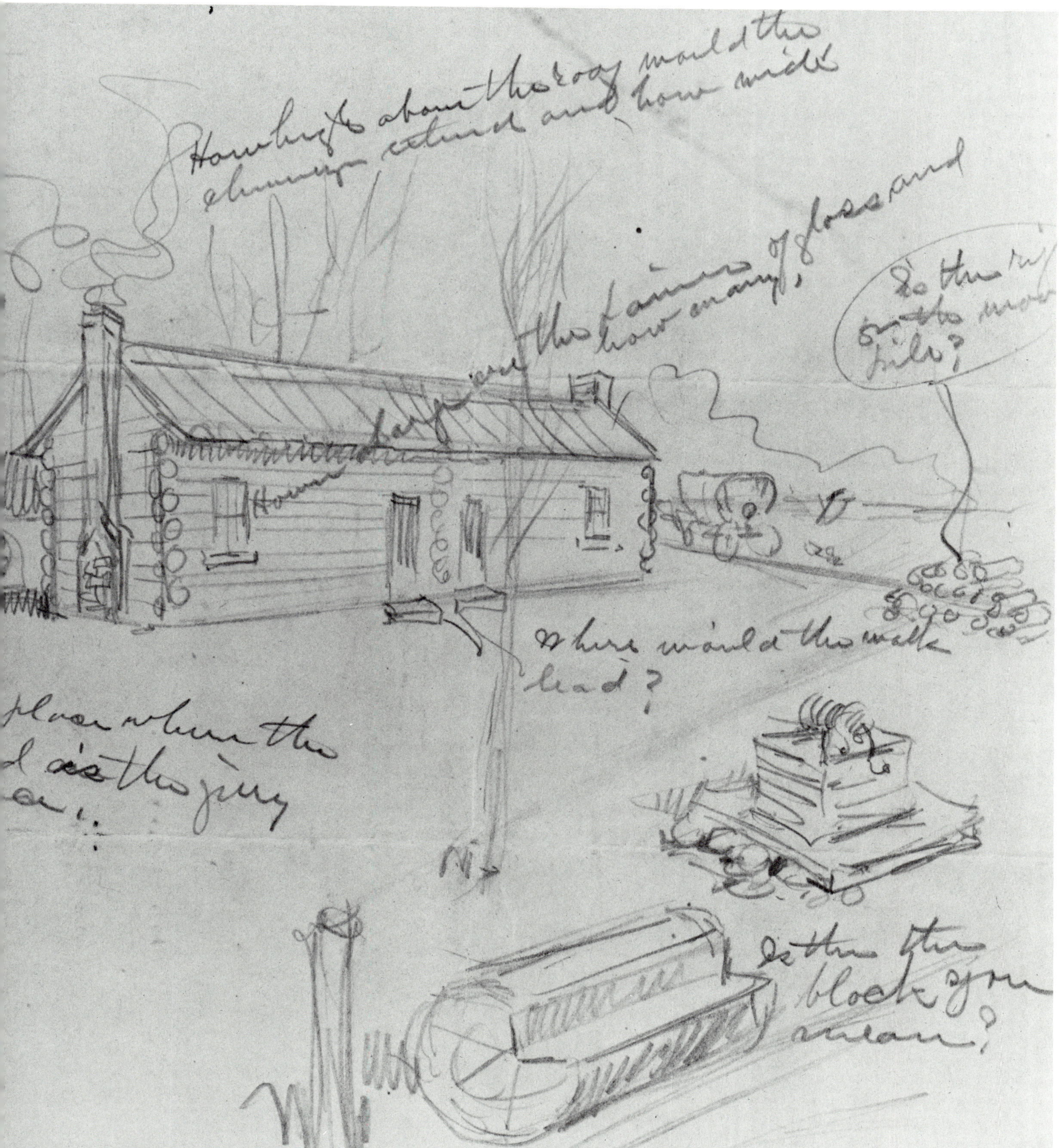

Sketch by R. Sidney Smith, 1900

THE FIRST COUNTY BUILDINGS

Allin's store-house was the site of the first court term in September of the county's first year. Mrs. Allin was "sick abed in the same room," but the Circuit Court went about its business anyway, and received a report from the Grand Jury, meeting in the yard outside, that "it had no business to report."

Asahel Gridley built the first court house on the Bloomington Square and charged McLean County $339.25 for it. Meanwhile William Dimmitt was putting up the first jail on the north side of the same block and charging the county only $331. Those accused or convicted of the more serious crimes were housed downstairs; the petty thieves and poor debtors upstairs.

The first courthouse, 1832

The first jail, 1832

"INJINS AT EVERY JUMP!"

The final Indian danger was from a Sauk chief, Black Hawk, and his followers, waging war against the whites in northern counties.

Three companies of militia sent from McLean County failed to acquit themselves with much honor in their only engagement with the Indians, riding home ahead of a cloud of dust after the battle of Stillman's Run.

The upper part of the county was the northern frontier of Illinois and people were nervous enough to put up four blockhouses for sleeping. General Joseph Bartholomew built one of them at Clarksville and journeyed to Livingston County to receive assurances of peace from the Kickapoos there.

General Joseph Bartholomew

"*. . . When the Indian fears were running high in the spring of 1832, 2 unnamed men as they were returning from Bloomington spotted blood on the ground near the present site of Normal. Unaware that it was the spot where Isaac Funk had bled his horse they concluded the savages had come to McLean County. They whipped their horses into a fury across the prairie and spotted rossin weeds waving in the wind which they concluded were Indians. One called 'Wait for me, Isaac' to which his companion is said to have replied only, 'Whip the pony, Matt.' When they reached Cheney's Grove he was 'laughed out of his fright.'*"

— E. Duis
The Good Old Times in McLean County
1874

Blockhouse erected in Money Creek Township, 1832

HERE TO STAY

Most of the whites arriving in McLean County had little money, but great determination to make good homes. Life was keyed to daylight—to the out-of-doors. People often went to bed at 6 p.m. in the winter due to lack of light and in order to keep warm.

They settled in near the edge of the groves. And the first thing the pioneer did was build a crude shelter for himself and his team of horses, using the trees he had cut down in carving his niche. Neighbors would appear from near and far to lift the heavy logs and enjoy a free meal.

There were no roads at first—only Indian trails across the open prairie—and no bridges. Doctors would swim swollen streams to reach their patients and pioneers often rode a hundred miles across the prairie to grind flour or sharpen a plow.

Mills went into operation, and the settlers had an alternative to their wooden mortars for grinding their corn and wheat.

Moore's Mill on Sugar Creek, west of McLean. Built in 1840

"... WE ARE PREPARING TO BUILD A HOUSE ... WE HAVE HITHERTO LIVED IN A CABBIN ..."

— William Brown, 1830

By the 1830s log houses were giving way to frame houses, and steam "jennies" were being brought from the East to saw the fine building timber available in the groves.

Near Randolph, Samuel Stewart was burning the local clay to make brick for the first brick house in McLean County.

A few roads and bridges were appearing. And there was talk of the coming of the railroads.

John Dunham House

S.P. Cox House (Note construction technique where clapboards have been removed)

Samuel Stewart House, built 1834

RELIGION

Rev. James Stringfield preached a sermon in the home of John Hendrix in 1823, and organized religion was here to stay.

Preachers, such as William Stoddard Crissey, traveled large circuits. Perhaps the most colorful was two-fisted Peter Cartwright of Sangamon County, the Methodists' presiding elder of the Bloomington district and one of the founders of Illinois Wesleyan University.

Camp meetings in the groves attracted people for several weeks at a time. They would live in their covered wagons, arriving just after harvest in September to rejuvenate their social—as well as their spiritual—selves. New family members born the following June and July were destined to be known as "camp meeting babies."

Bloomington Methodist Church, built in 1839

". . . but, thank God you can't whip me; but don't you attempt to strike me, for if you do, and the devil gets out of you into me, I shall give you the worst whipping you ever got in all your life . . ."

— **Autobiography of Peter Cartwright**
1856

EDUCATION

Delilah Mullin opened the first classes for small children in the home of John Dawson in Blooming Grove. That was in 1825, and for the next 20 years, the schools in McLean County were private—or subscription—institutions. Some, in fact, were complete academies, providing room and board along with education.

Then, there were the "loud" schools scattered about the county. Shelton Smith attended a "loud" school in Mackinaw Timber in 1836 and reported his "first teacher was an Irishman who made the scholars study at the top of their voices."

One section of land in each township was given to the schools—and sale or rental of the farmland provided some revenue to pay the teachers. But the state legislature approved taxation to support public schools in 1855 and the era of Illinois public education had begun.

Delilah Mullin Evans
First school teacher
in McLean County

The Academy, corner Mill and Madison Streets, Bloomington, built 1834

Seminary, Hudson, Illinois, built 1836

". . . And now to give you a history of our management of matters and things I describe the schoolhouse which answers for a schoolhouse, meeting house and dwelling house. It contains 2 school rooms on the basement story with a hall or space running through between them of 6 feet wide. The upper story is a meeting house. It is built very much like the school house in West Granby excepting the stairs go up inside of the building. Under the stairs is a small room partitioned about 8 or 9 feet square running back under the stairs. This we make use of for a buttery. I have put up a partition across the space. One end we use for a bedroom. We have an old fashioned cookingstove in the schoolroom where we do our cooking. For furniture we have of Mr. Foster in part pay for J's board a bedstead and bedding. This he furnished together with the privilege of living in the school house and pays me 87½ cents a week for my wife's board. Don't you think he is a very liberal man? Boarding is worth in this town only from \$2 to \$5 per week. We have bought a set of common winsor chairs second hand not new by a good deal at the moderate price of \$10. We have a table of my own make. Don't you think it is a nice one? Mrs. Foster has been kind enough to lend us three knives and forks and three teaspoons. We have bought some necessary articles of crockery. Also a dutch oven or bake kettle, and a tea kettle, tea pot, 3 twelve quart pails, 6 six quart pails, 2 tin pans, 11 tin dippers, and a frying pan. Don't you think we are well provided for? For provisions I bought a hog that weighed 155 lbs. when dressed, 250 lbs. of flour, 2 bushels of cornmeal, 2 venison hams, 5 or 6 bushels of potatoes, etc, etc. I made sugar—probably 150 lbs—did not weigh it. Our stock consists of a horse, 1 cow and calf, 6 hogs, 2 hens, and 3 chickens. The hens were a present of one of our neighbors. We have plenty of beans, peas, cucumbers, squashes, and new potatoes. Just come over some afternoon and make us a visit and see how we live in the "Sucker State.". . ."

— Samuel J. Hayes, teacher at the Bloomington Academy
1837

WITNESSES

James Allin

". . . We have no knews to tel you except Indien matters and that I suppose you air in poscession of Sum of our citizens air very much alarmed and is moving of on account of the Indiens . . ."

— James Allin
Bloomington, May 23, 1832

William Evans

William Evans was born in 1775. He settled at the present site of Bloomington in 1824, and died in 1868.

"A man always takes his neighbors wherever he goes."

— William Evans

Katherine & Jonathan Cheney

". . . During that winter (1825) Mrs. Cheney remained alone with her family, and saw, during the whole time, 4 white people, 2 men and 2 women . . ."

John Hougham

". . . A heap of people spell it Huffam . . ."

Dr. Cyrenius Wakefield & son Oscar

". . . We . . . prepared to supply the demand for medicines which were sought for within a radius of fifty miles . . ."

Jane Brittin Hendrix

". . . The rough puncheon floor was scrubbed with soap and sand until it shone almost like a mirror . . ."

SILENT WITNESSES

Miss Jennie Briggs
Daguerreotype taken in Peoria, Illinois, 1844

Milton Bozarth, 1832-1900
Daguerreotype taken 1852

R. W. Dibble
Clerk, Bloomington, Illinois

Mr. and Mrs. Archer Martin
Veteran of the War of 1812

The first settlement, Blooming Grove, gave way to the county seat, Bloomington, built on its northern boundary. The edge of the grove became Grove Street.

Farms pushed from the other three sides, and, like all of McLean County's magnificent groves, Blooming Grove shrank.

Today there are Crestwicke Country Club golf fairways where the trees of Blooming Grove stood, and a mile to the north of the first tee lie the remains of the first white settlers.

Blooming Grove Cemetery

3. The Yankees and Their Towns

There were fortunes made—and lost—during McLean County's first decade, as it became clear there was money to be made by starting-up a town. Land was abundant, credit was cheap and Illinois was promising massive internal improvements, canals and railroads. An explosion of townsite speculation was under way.

LeRoy was laid out in 1835, followed the next year by Lexington, Concord (later to become Danvers), Hudson, Clarksville, and Lytleville.

South Center Street, Bloomington, ca. 1857

WILSON ALLIN'S WIND MILL
THIRD JAIL
BAPTIST CHURCH
N
W
E
S
NORTH
ST.
B. HAINES
ICE
HATFIELD
DR. HENRY
OFFICE
W. ALLIN
B.C. HAINES
J. GLYMPSE
WM. THOMAS
JEFFERSON
SECOND JAIL
1ST. LOG JAIL
DR. ANDERSON.
OFFICE.
BILLINGS
ELLSWORTH
WM. THOMAS
JAMES ALLIN
I. WILLIAMS
COURT HOUSE
McCLUN
WASHINGTON
LEWIS BUNN
McCULLOM
HAINES. COPPER SHOP.
HATFIELD TAVERN
MERRIOTT LYON
BROKAW'S SHOP
HOTEL BARN
TAVERN
I. WALTON
STAGE BARN
PORK HOUSE
WATCH SHOP
ADOLPH
GEN. COVEL.
JOHN STEELE
E. ROCKHOLD
J. STEELE
BLIAN'S SHOP
FELL'S SHOP
BIG TAVERN.
JESSE FELL
ROBT. FELL
DR. HAINES
FRONT
T. FELL
EVANS
COLMAR'S FURNITURE
ROBT. GUTHRIE
HENRY BAY
E. PROVOST
GEN. MACOM.
VESSY
McKISSON
McKISSON'S SHOP
HAYDEN
LARRISON
BAKER
J. ALLIN
ALLIN WITHERS
FIRST CHRISTIAN CHURCH
WM. COX
POST OFFICE
GREENMAN
TIN SHOP
McELHINEY
LARRICK
DR. BAKER
GATES
OAK
LEE
WEST
MADISON
CENTER
MAIN
EAST
GROVE
HARDY
T. EWINS
TEMPERANCE TAVERN.
HAWKS + POWERS
OIL MILL
HAWK'S
SOLOMON DODGE
HOBB'S SCHOOL FOR BOYS
JAMES ALLIN
A. GRIDLEY
CARDING MACHINE SHOP
SHINGLE MILL
INDIAN FAMILY LIVED HERE.
T. FELL
OFFICE
OLIVE
ROWEN
J. HOBSON
WARRINER
DAVE DIXON.
BEEMAN
HANEY.
DICK EDWARDS
1ST. M.E. CHURCH-1836
DR. COLBURN
GIRL'S SEMINARY
HAYES
HAYES
KENTUCKEY
ALLEY
HARDY
PAT. O'CONNOR
SETH BAKER
HAGGARD
OIL MILL
STAGE ROUTE.
ALBERT
WATER
ALLEY
SAW MILL
SPRINGFIELD
FLOUR + SAW MILL

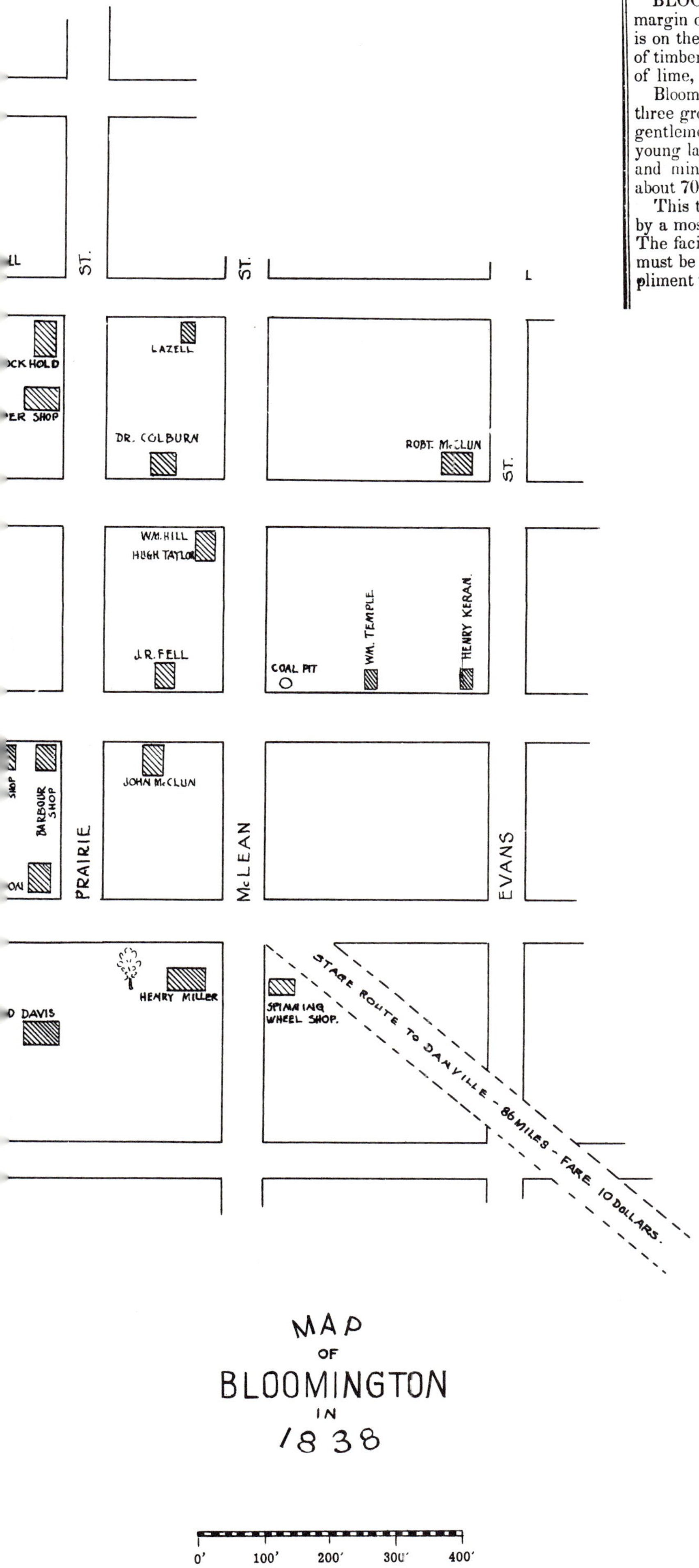

From A Map Drawn From Memory By C. E. Fell.

Redrawn By Fred Muhl With Corrections By Wayne Townley

AND PRINCIPAL TOWNS OF ILLINOIS. 117

BLOOMINGTON, the seat of justice for M'Lean county, is situated on the margin of a fine prairie, in the midst of a beautiful and fertile district. The town is on the north side of Blooming Grove, which comprises a large and valuable tract of timber, of all the varieties of the country desirable for building, consisting chiefly of lime, maple, ash, oak, and black and white walnut.

Bloomington has eight or ten stores, which do a general and extensive business, three groceries, two taverns, two lawyers, three physicians, an academy for young gentlemen, which is highly commended, and an institution for the education of young ladies; also two steam-mills, a Presbyterian and a Methodist meeting-house and ministers, a number of various mechanics, and an intelligent population of about 700.

This town is a point on the great central rail-road, &c.; and, surrounded as it is by a most desirable farming country, must increase in importance with its age. The facilities for building furnished by the steam saw-mills situated in the town, must be felt in the rapid growth of the place. It can scarcely be considered a compliment to say of Bloomington, that it is among the most beautiful towns in Illinois.

—Illinois in 1837
S. AUGUSTUS MITCHELL

Nearly half the new towns didn't make it. By 1837, credit had dried up, loans were being called in and the State of Illinois was hopelessly in debt.

Two of the most prominent speculators, Jesse Fell and Asahel Gridley, declared bankruptcy, as did so many others. But each would be back within another 20 years, laying out towns and arranging to have railroads routed through them.

In the meantime, both Fell and Gridley invested their time and energy in their county seat—Bloomington.

THE PROMOTERS

Bloomington Obs
AND McLEAN COUNTY ADVOCATE
BLOOMINGTON, ILLINOIS, JANUARY 13, 1838.

Jesse W. Fell

". . . it was a time of unrest, the age of iron and steel and steam was coming in, breaking up the old physical monotony of life. The daily paper was just beginning to assert true. Channing was preaching a new gospel in Boston. Garrison and Phillips were just being heard from. From the Brook Farm Community and many another came strange new ideas. Peoples' minds were in a ferment . . ."

—David McFarland
on Mt. Hope Colony,
ca. 1900

First Printing Press in McLean County, 1837.

Fell was an attorney and Gridley operated a general store. Gridley lived in Bloomington's first house, the one that housed James Allin when he founded the town. And Allin, Fell and Gridley made an investment in 1836 that spread Bloomington's story and kept it on the map.

Gridley, making a buying trip, secured a press and pair of editors in Philadelphia. And the first newspapers were delivered from a small room in the courthouse January 14, 1837.

The enterprise, the interest and the ideas of the outside world were suddenly brought much closer.

McLean County Courthouse, 1836-1868

"But no Yankee was ever satisfied with his condition. More, more riches, knowledge, power or whatever may be his ideal. The great hunger of the Anglo-Saxon is land, land, more land. But the stoney, sandy soil of Rhode Island and Providence Plantation could hardly satisfy this race hunger. The more a man had of it the poorer he was . . ."

—David McFarland,
Mount Hope Colony

General Asahel Gridley

James Allin/ Asahel Gridley House.

LAND COLONISTS

While the town site speculators were establishing their villages on the edges of McLean County's timberland, organizers were forming two colony experiments.

The Mount Hope Company was formed in Rhode Island and each of the shareholders received 320 acres of McLean County land. Horatio Pettit, meanwhile, spearheaded a group in Jacksonville which entered more than 23 sections of land near Havens Grove. Each member of the Hudson Colony paid $235 for one share—and the share entitled him to 160 acres of prairie land, 20 acres of timberland, 4 lots in the proposed village—Hudson—one outlot and a share in the profits. The colony took hold and the names of some of its original members—Burtis, Gildersleeve—continue to appear on Hudson mailboxes today.

Horatio Pettit

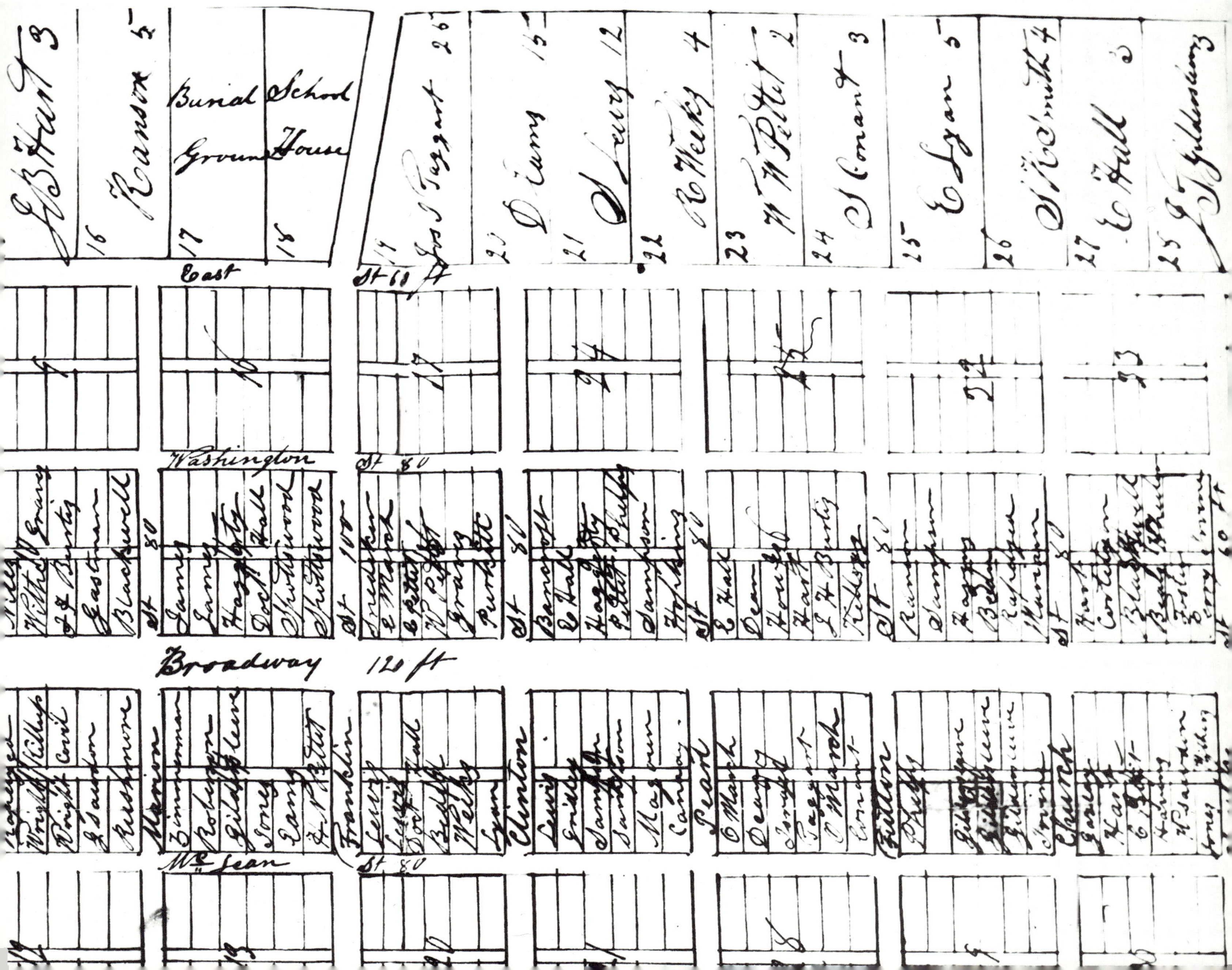

Original plat, Hudson Colony (Detail)

BUILDERS

Panorama of Van Schoick Brickyard, ca. 1860.

The pamphlets circulated out East brought the people in great numbers to sample the riches of the West. What the advertising pieces didn't point out was the lack of living accomodations.

But arrive the Easterners did, by steamboat, horse, ox team and foot—sleeping in wagons and tents or crowding into hastily-built shanties.

There was no transportation system for the importation of building materials so the people made do with local bricks and lumber. The towns were built beside the groves, many of which soon had their own sawmills.

And the brickyards—like Van Schoick's at today's Forest Park in Bloomington—sprang up on the edge of the groves. The clay was better there, and timber was available to fire the bricks for the new homes, stores and schools.

". . . Mr. William Van Schoick . . . while in Richmond (Ind.) . . . did the largest day's work in the molding of sand brick that has ever been known, the number being 14,369, time, 13 hours; upon the completion of it, he was forced upon a scaffold and carried upon the shoulders of his men and the students from the brickyard up through the streets of the city. In 1858, when he came to this city, he began the manufacture of brick, giving employment to from 40 to 100 men. He contracted for and completed the building of the Wesleyan College. . ."

—**History of McLean County**
Wm. LeBaron, 1879

EDUCATORS

Before he became state treasurer, James Miller was one of several citizens offering land in 1852 for Wesleyan's first building. The offer wasn't accepted—the land instead became Miller Park. But Miller served on the first Wesleyan board, along with town founder James Allin, farmer Isaac Funk, evangelist Peter Cartwright and attorney Kersey Fell.

Fell's brother, Jesse, was meanwhile coaxing cash and land from Bloomington's elite to win the state's first university for his new town.

The McLean County offer was better than Peoria's and the rival group's leader, Charles Hovey, was hired as the Normal School's first president.

North Hall, Illinois Wesleyan University

James Miller

". . . we urge it upon parents, to send us their sons . . . better forego their help upon your farms, and in your shops, and hire the necessary labor . . . and bear the expense of their education, than when you leave the world, leave them uneducated and unqualified to manage your estates, or accomplish your incomplete plans and purposes of life. Better that you should spend the half of your estates in giving them a good education, that they may the more advantageously manage the other when you are gone, than now to double those estates by their unremitted labors . . . and die and leave them in a condition to scatter to the four winds all of your possessions, in a much shorter time perhaps than you employed in collecting them . . ."

— **Illinois Wesleyan Circular 1851**

". . . but how can good teachers be had at home? In the same way that they may be had elsewhere—make them. Establish, at the 'state's charge,' a school or schools, specially to train up TEACHERS, and fit them for the duties which they are to assume. Let us have a NORMAL SCHOOL . . ."

— CHAS. E. HOVEY
1856

Charles Hovey

Old Main, Illinois State Normal University

MANUFACTURERS

Brokaw Plow Factory, North Main at Market.

Before the railroads, it was cheaper to manufacture virtually all the county's needs at home. Abe Brokaw was turning out the quality plows needed to break the prairie sod while Flagg and Ewing were employing 150 men to manufacture reapers and threshing machines.

Within years, McLean County manufacturing extended to clothing, furniture, patent medicines, cigars and, according to Dr. E. Duis in 1874, "as the city contains many school girls, it has been necessary to start a chewing gum manufactory."

Abram Brokaw

WILLIAM POULEY,
TIN AND SHEET IRON MANUFACTORY,
DEALER IN
STOVES AND HARDWARE,
LEXINGTON, ILLINOIS.

THOMAS J. COX,
EAGLE FLOURING MILLS,
WEST END OF JEFFERSON ST.,
BLOOMINGTON, ILL.,

NEAR THE STATION OF THE
St. Louis, Alton & Chicago R. R.
EXTRA FAMILY FLOUR,
WHOLESALE AND RETAIL,
Constantly on hand and Warranted to give satisfaction.

J. W. Evans Planing Mill, 511 North Center Street

MUTUAL AID

When Bloomington was incorporated as a city in 1850, fewer than 2,000 people lived within its borders. But the population tripled in the next five years and the need for community services became evident—particularly the need for a fire company.

Though there was no organized group to fight it, the destructive fire south of the courthouse in 1855 proved only a temporary setback. New buildings rose from the ashes almost immediately—among them the so-called "Phoenix Block" facing the courthouse. Four of the newly built buildings on that block stand today, as do several other re-built stores facing Front Street.

Fr m our Extra of Wednesday Morning last.

GREAT FIRE!

ONE ENTIRE SQUARE DESTROYED!

LOSS OF LIFE!

Two Printing Offices, Business and Dwelling Houses, Stores and Shops, of all kinds, Offices, &c., &c., &c., in Ruins!

LOSS OVER $150,000!

At about 9 o'clock last night, a destructive fire broke out in the Livery Stable in this city attached to the Morgan House, situated on the east side of Centre street, betwen Washington and Front streets, in the block south of the public square, and spread north and south entirely destroying all the buildings on the whole block, except the buildings of the McLean County Bank and the building of Messrs. Dietrich and Bradner, occupied by them for a Hardware store.

It has seldom ever been our duty to record a calamity from the ravages of fire so unfortunate in all its effects on a whole community; and we tender to the sufferers all our sympathies in their several losses, and assured that they will receive the unreserved favors of a generous and enlightened community.

It is to be greatly regretted that the city was so badly supplied with water and was without an engine, hooks, or fire company, or any of the means of successfully and in an organized manner extinguishing the flames.

Dry goods, furniture, groceries &c., are scattered all over the Public Square, and along the streets, in heaps, and are in such a confused condition, that the owners scarcely recognize them. There were from four to five thousand persons on the ground, during the continuance of the fire; which raged the greater part of the night. Disorder and noise prevailed nearly all the while. There were many persons, arrested by the "police gang," in the act, of stealing goods, and we understand that about twenty-five or thirty were committed to jail.

Great gratitude and credit are due to those persons of manly and noble souls who bravely contended with the raging elements, and risked their health, and even their lives, to avert the sad calamity with which we have been visited. We regret to say upon the other hand, that hundreds are the subjects of just censure who tamely witnessed the massive destruction of buildings and property without turning a hand or making an effort to stop the tide of devastation.

Standing around the street, wrapped up in their elegant cloaks and fine shawls, regaling themselves with the flavor of their delicious Havana cigars—while they discussed the grandeur and the magnificence of the conflagration.

Bloomington Fire Company, ca. 1860.

THE RAILROAD ARRIVES

Citizens had talked about the coming of the railroads for 15 years, but it all happened at once. State Senator Asahel Gridley influenced the arrival through McLean County of the Illinois Central in 1852, and what became the Alton line arrived a few months later. Shortly after that, the Toledo, Peoria and Western was built across northern McLean County.

By 1855, Jesse Fell secured the Alton shops, employing 150 men "out west of Bloomington," and he laid out a new town at the junction of the two railroads two miles north of Bloomington. Matthew Scott made a fortune founding Chenoa at another rail crossing.

Within five years after the rails arrived, Towanda, McLean, Heyworth and Gridley were born by the roadbed.

Building the Illinois Central R.R.

ABOLITIONISTS

Rails brought new ideas to town. As recently as 1844, the men who controlled the McLean County Court, mostly Southerners, had declared the Bloomington courthouse could not be used by abolitionists.

But now those who opposed slavery were insisting on being heard.

Former Mayor William Wallace, tired of hearing slavery defended from the pulpit of his church, helped form the Second Presbyterian Church in 1855.

A year later, a coalition of abolitionists and other factions from around Illinois gathered in Major's Hall. The editors among them were sympathetic to the abolition of slavery. Notable was the Bloomington Pantagraph, gaining national attention with its so-called "Black Republicanism" views. The newspapermen discreetly refrained from printing the volatile things Lincoln said, and historians have since labeled it his "lost speech."

William Wallace

Second Presbyterian Church, Bloomington

4. The War

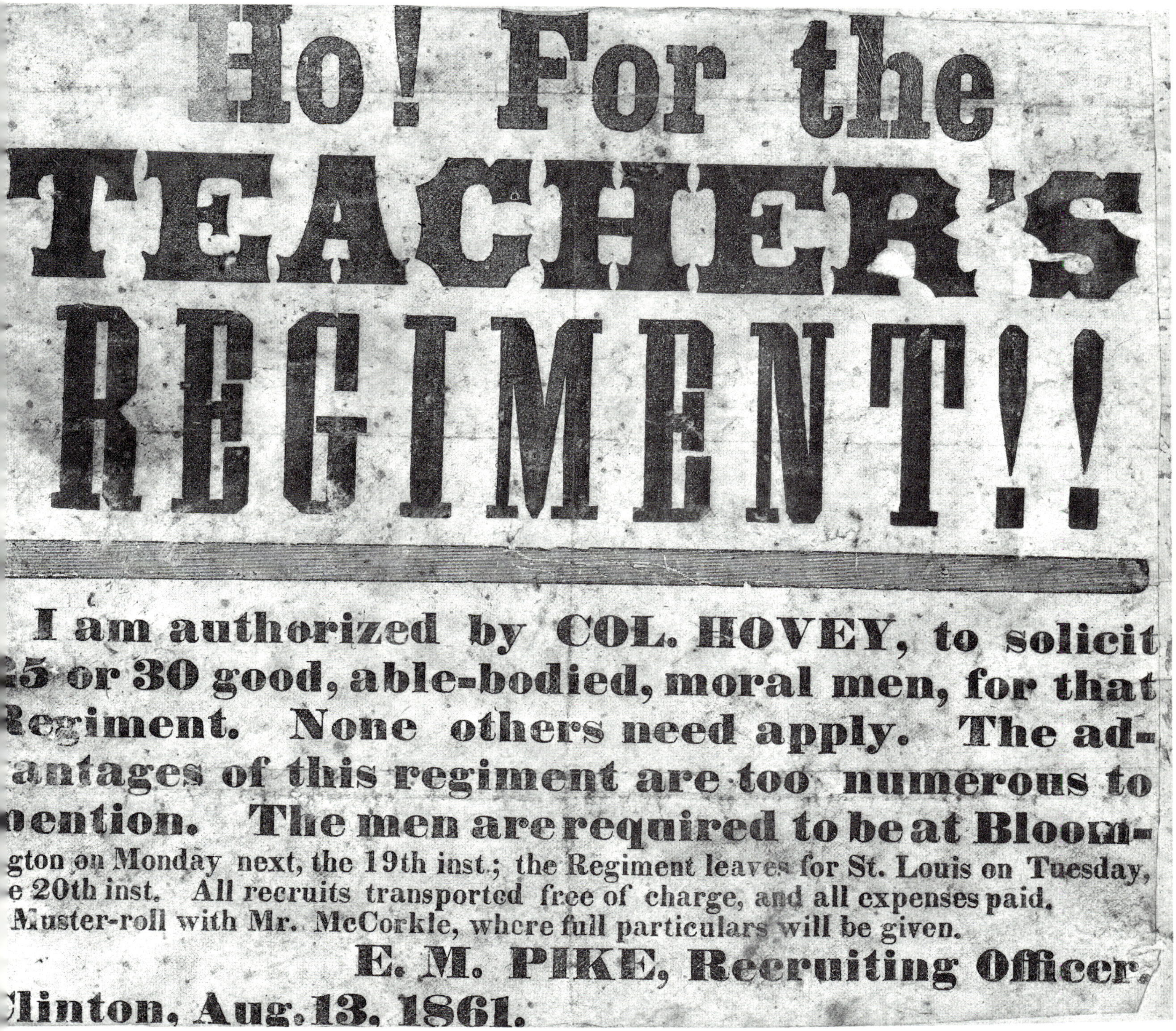
Ho! For the
TEACHER'S
REGIMENT!!

I am authorized by COL. HOVEY, to solicit
25 or 30 good, able-bodied, moral men, for that
Regiment. None others need apply. The ad-
antages of this regiment are too numerous to
nention. The men are required to be at Bloom-
gton on Monday next, the 19th inst.; the Regiment leaves for St. Louis on Tuesday,
e 20th inst. All recruits transported free of charge, and all expenses paid.
Muster-roll with Mr. McCorkle, where full particulars will be given.
E. M. PIKE, Recruiting Officer.
linton, Aug. 13, 1861.

Fewer than 30,000 people lived in McLean County when the Civil War broke out in April, 1861.

The first company of army volunteers was boarding the train at the West Chestnut Street station within a week. 4,000 McLean County men wore Union uniforms. This was more than half the county's able-bodied men.

Bloomington, McLean Co., Ill., August 6th, 1858.

To Messrs. Dr H. Noble. Jesse Funk. George Crookshank. Ira Munson, Covington Veatch William Fulton and David Noble

"THE LINCOLN REPUBLICAN CLUB" FOR M'LEAN COUNTY

Has invited the Hon. ABRAM LINCOLN, and he has consented to address the people of the County, at Bloomington, on the 4th day of September next, at 3 o'clock in the afternoon.

It is certainly proper, and I know it will meet with your hearty approval, that the Republicans in McLean should give Mr. Lincoln on that day, a reception worthy of his distinguished abilities and energetic services, and worthy of the immortal cause he so honestly and boldly advocates.

We have taken the liberty to appoint you a committee in the Town of Randolph to notify the people within your jurisdiction, of this MASS MEETING OF THE PEOPLE, to meet Mr. Lincoln at Bloomington, on the said 4th day of September, and to arrange all things so as to insure a general TURN OUT on that day, of every Republican within your reach. COME UP ALL, AND COME LIKE AN ARMY, with the shout of "UNION AND LIBERTY" on your lips, and THESE, with the other glorious principles of Republicanism, proudly displayed on your banners.

The CENTRAL COMMITTEE for the County, request me to notify you that you are also appointed by them a committee to attend to the getting up of a primary meeting of the Republicans in your Township, to elect four delegates to attend a COUNTY REPUBLICAN CONVENTION, to be held at Bloomington, on MONDAY, the 6th day of September next, at 1 o'clock in the afternoon. The Townships, and not the old Precincts, will be represented in the approaching convention.

The undersigned would respectfully suggest that your committee meet at Heyworth, on the second Saturday in this month, to-wit, on the 14th day of August, at 1 o'clock in the afternoon, to confer together on the best manner of proceeding to carry out the matters entrusted to your care.

The place and time for your meeting to elect delegates to the County Convention, will be determined by you at this conference.

The Central Committee will be under great obligations to you, if you can, within the next two months, say by the first of October, make out for the said Committee, a list of all the voters in your Township—of all parties,—and specify as far as can be ascertained, how each will vote.

Gentlemen, let us WORK this fall energetically together, and a most triumphant victory is sure.

Very Respectfully,

W. C. HOBBS,

PRESIDENT OF THE LINCOLN REPUBLICAN CLUB FOR McLEAN COUNTY.

THE LOST SPEECH

Major's Hall, site of the "Lost Speech", Southwest corner of Front and East Streets

". . . Liberty and Union,
Now and Forever,
One and Inseparable!"

— Abraham Lincoln
Bloomington, 1856

Lincoln's speech in Bloomington in 1856 propelled him toward the White House, and his election four years later made war inevitable. The Springfield attorney's Bloomington colleagues Jesse Fell, Leonard Swett and Judge David Davis were the key figures in his bids for higher office during those four years — securing for Lincoln the Republican Presidential nomination in Chicago in 1860. Before the war was over, Lincoln would appoint Davis to the United States Supreme Court, appoint Fell a paymaster of the Union Army, and summon Swett to Washington for political consultation on several occasions.

"RALLY 'ROUND THE FLAG . . ."

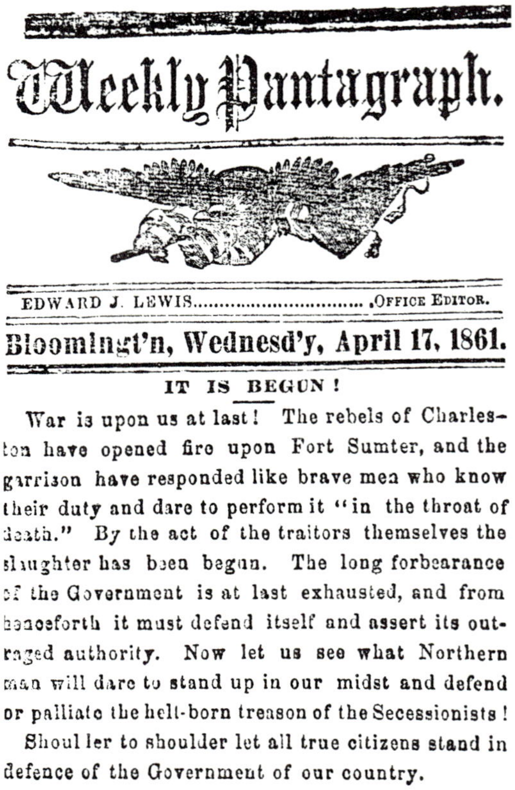

Weekly Pantagraph.

EDWARD J. LEWIS.............................. OFFICE EDITOR.

Bloomingt'n, Wednesd'y, April 17, 1861.

IT IS BEGUN!

War is upon us at last! The rebels of Charleston have opened fire upon Fort Sumter, and the garrison have responded like brave men who know their duty and dare to perform it "in the throat of death." By the act of the traitors themselves the slaughter has been begun. The long forbearance of the Government is at last exhausted, and from henceforth it must defend itself and assert its outraged authority. Now let us see what Northern man will dare to stand up in our midst and defend or palliate the hell-born treason of the Secessionists!

Shoulder to shoulder let all true citizens stand in defence of the Government of our country.

". . . Oh that God would rule all this strife and bring order out of confusion . . ."

— Diary of Sarah Withers
April 16, 1861

Henry Clay Carico, 1st Illinois Cavalry

The recruiting was enthusiastic and emotional. President Hovey of Illinois State Normal University became Colonel Hovey and raised a regiment of educators and students — the 33rd Illinois volunteers, the "Teachers' Regiment."

When Lincoln appealed for more soldiers in 1862, more than 1,200 men in McLean County volunteered in less than ten days. It was enough for an entire regiment, with two companies left over. Attorney William Orme led the 94th Illinois Infantry — the McLean County Regiment — through six states, and it wasn't defeated or repulsed in nine different encounters with the Rebels.

Orme was promoted to the rank of general, as were five other McLean County men before the war was over.

TO THE PEOPLE OF

McLEAN COUNTY!

The President has called for

300,000 MORE TROOPS!

Illinois must send her full quota! The Governor has already called for nine regiments! Time is everything! and enlistments must be speedily made! We suggest that the People of this County come together in Mass Meeting at Bloomington, on

Saturday, July 26, at 2 O'Clock P. M.!

TO DEVISE THE BEST MEANS OF PROMOTING VOLUNTARY ENLISTMENTS.

Something must be done towards paying additional bounties to Volunteers, and making adequate provision for their Families. Shall it be by private subscription, or by appropriations made by the Supervisors' Court? Let us, then, have a Mass Meeting at Bloomington, Saturday, July 26th, at 2 O'clock P. M., to determine.

J H Wickizer	Thos P Rogers	J Leaming	W J Ballard
Jas S Ewing	Z L Hoover	A Gridley	C W Holder
John E McClun	W H Hanna	L Ferre	A J Merriman
John Niccolls	C P Merriman	D Harwood	O M Coleman
W H Marmon	C R Parke	H W Gunnell	J W Maxwell
H A Snowden	A Wetherbee	John L Routt	J N Larrimore
R Thompson	M S Davidson	O Rugg	E L Nason
D M Funk	J Tavenner	J M Scott	B F Hains
R Park	H Spencer	David Davis	Wm W Orme
M W Packard	H P Merriman	Hudson Burr	J H Robinson
Leonard Swett	O Barnard	J W Fell	G W Stipp
L W Capen	R W Dibble	C E Dalton	G W Monroe
R O'Connor	E D Benjamin	A T Briscoe	W A Elder
J M Major	S Pennington	B W Lewis	J Middleton
J Dietrich	W H Temple	T Pardee	J Magoun.

Bloomington Times.

BLOOMINGTON, ILL., SATURDAY, AUG. 16 1862.

"Resolved, that . . . there . . . be appointed a committee to wait upon the editors of said paper and request them to desist from further publication in this city."

— **Bloomington Times**
Sept. 7, 1861

McLean County troops engaged in their first skirmish before they left the courthouse square. As Orme administered the oath to the new soldiers, a crowd fetched the Snow brothers, publishers of the southern-sympathizing *Bloomington Times* newspaper and forced them to take the Union oath.

When the brothers Snow renounced

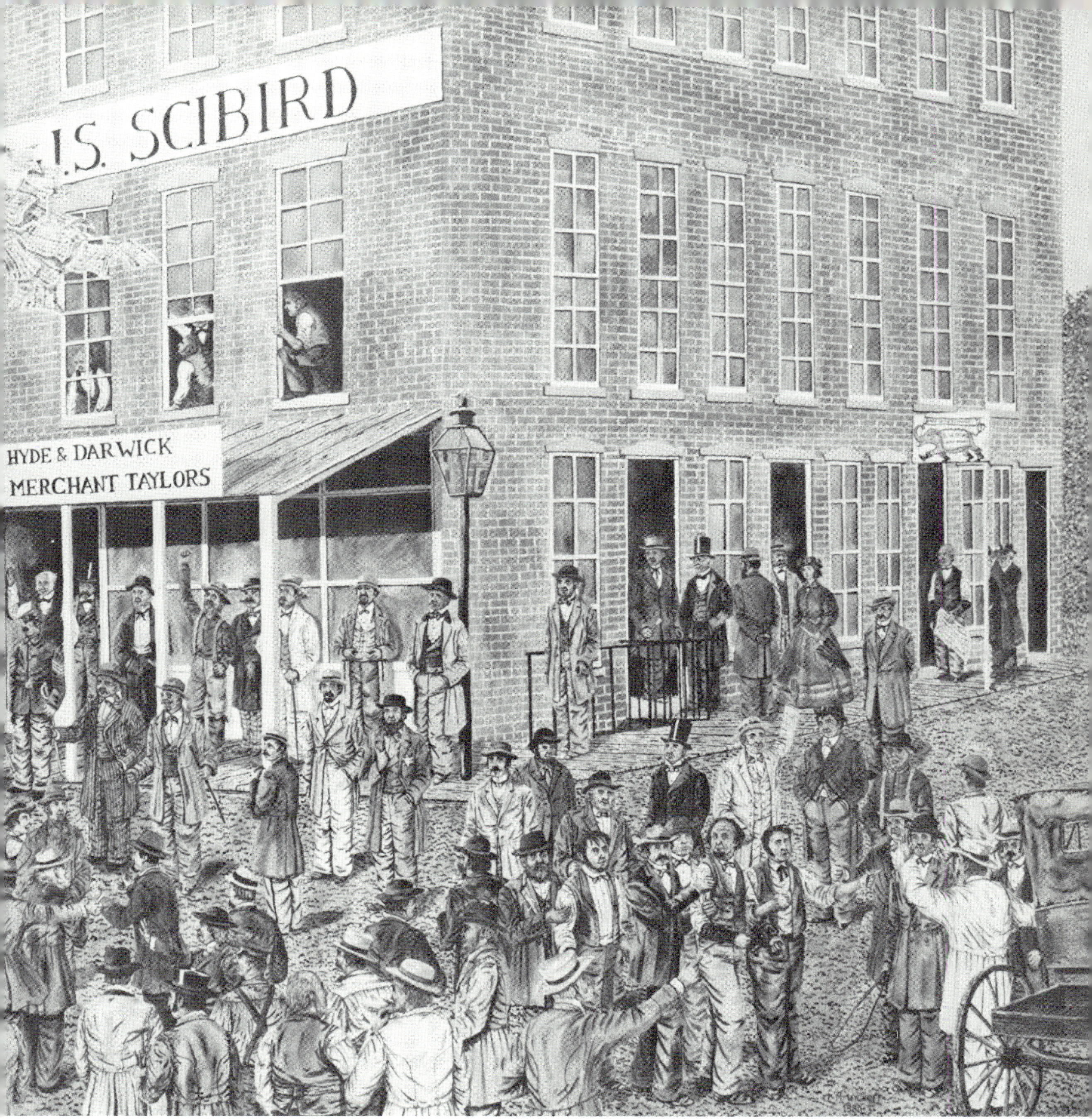

The sacking of the Times, August 20, 1862

the oath as soon as they'd taken it, the soldiers became a mob and emptied the *Times* Center Street office, burning and smashing the equipment. The Snows were ushered out of Bloomington.

Isaac Funk was 64, too old to enlist, but he was charged with instigating the mob. So was Robert Dickerson. Charges against Funk were dropped and McLean County people elected him to the Illinois Senate less than a year later.

Dickerson later told a jury that he indeed led the sacking of the *Bloomington Times*, but argued "no man has a right to publish a Confederate newspaper in Central Illinois." The McLean County jury agreed.

John McNulta, ca. 1863.

McLEAN COUNTY GOES TO WAR

". . . I do not think that the general commanding has yet fixed upon any plan of operations for this army but that we will be governed entirely by circumstances . . ."

— John McNulta
Feb. 23, 1863

Joseph & George Fifer

" 'I'll take the one on the right,' said my comrade, 'and you take the one on the left.' He fired, and the one on the right sat rigid an instant, his arms upthrown, then tumbled off his horse.

"I was a dead shot — my Virginia father had seen to that — and the one on the left wasn't sixty yards away. I raised my gun."

Then, in a hushed tone, like praying:
" 'But, before God, Bennett, I couldn't pull that trigger.' "

— Reminiscence of Pvt. Joe Fifer
to James O'Donnell Bennett
1936

Colonel Harvey Hogg

". . . Don't use your pistols but give them the cold steel. The sabre is the weapon for the Cavalry to rely upon."

— Harvey Hogg

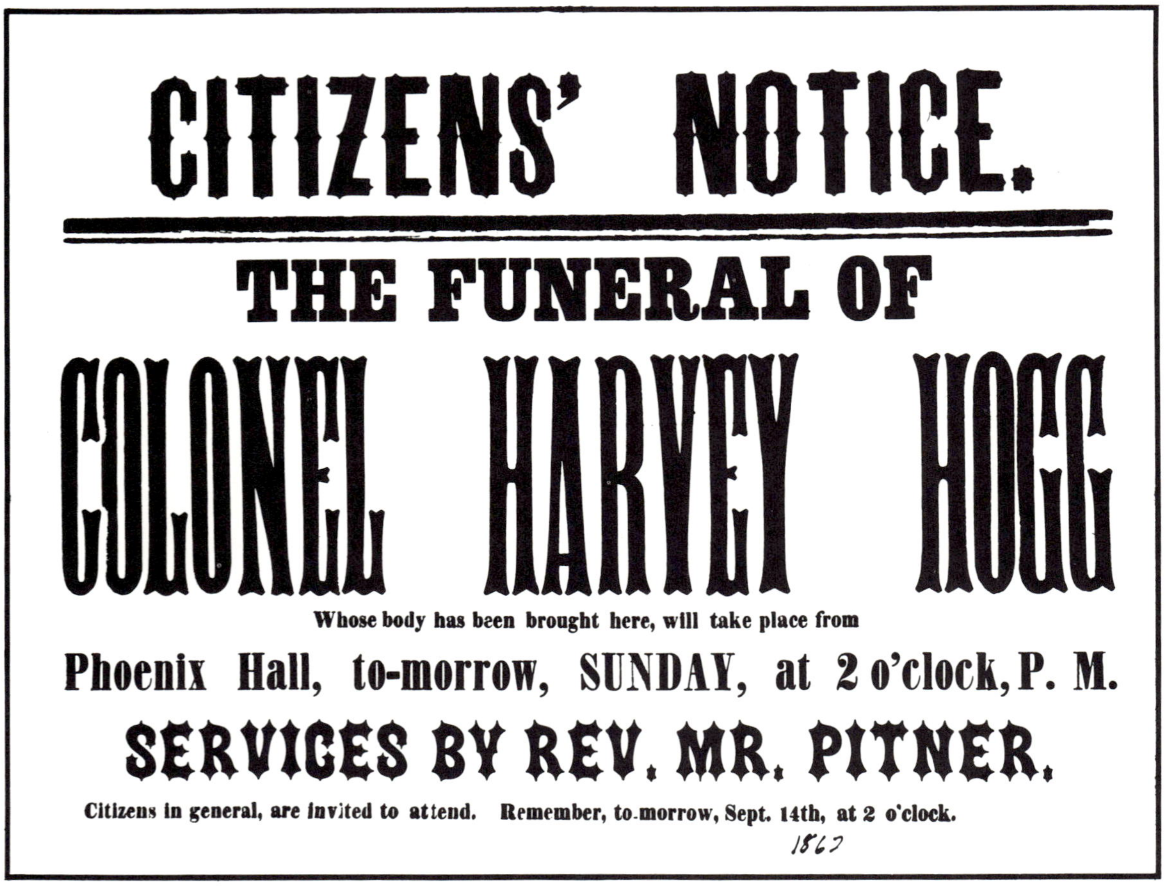

CITIZENS' NOTICE.

THE FUNERAL OF

COLONEL HARVEY HOGG

Whose body has been brought here, will take place from

Phoenix Hall, to-morrow, SUNDAY, at 2 o'clock, P. M.

SERVICES BY REV. MR. PITNER.

Citizens in general, are invited to attend. Remember, to-morrow, Sept. 14th, at 2 o'clock.

1862

Many idealists died early. Harvey Hogg had freed his inherited slaves when he left Tennessee for Bloomington before the war to become an attorney and a legislator.

He was cut down in 1862, leading a Union Cavalry charge on his hometown, Bolivar, Tennessee.

William McCullough was born in Kentucky, became a Blackhawk War hero, then McLean County sheriff and circuit clerk. He was 50, had only one arm and sight in only one eye, when he was allowed to enlist in the Illinois Cavalry by the intervention of President Lincoln.

Reins in his teeth, sword in his only hand, he was rallying his troops when the Confederates caught him.

Colonel William McCullough

". . . Dec. 5, 1862. Just in the dusk of the evening . . . the Rebels came up on both sides and demanded his surrender. A very emphatic refusal was the reply, to which the enemy responded with a volley of musketry, killing Col. McCullough instantly."

— War Record of McLean County, 1899

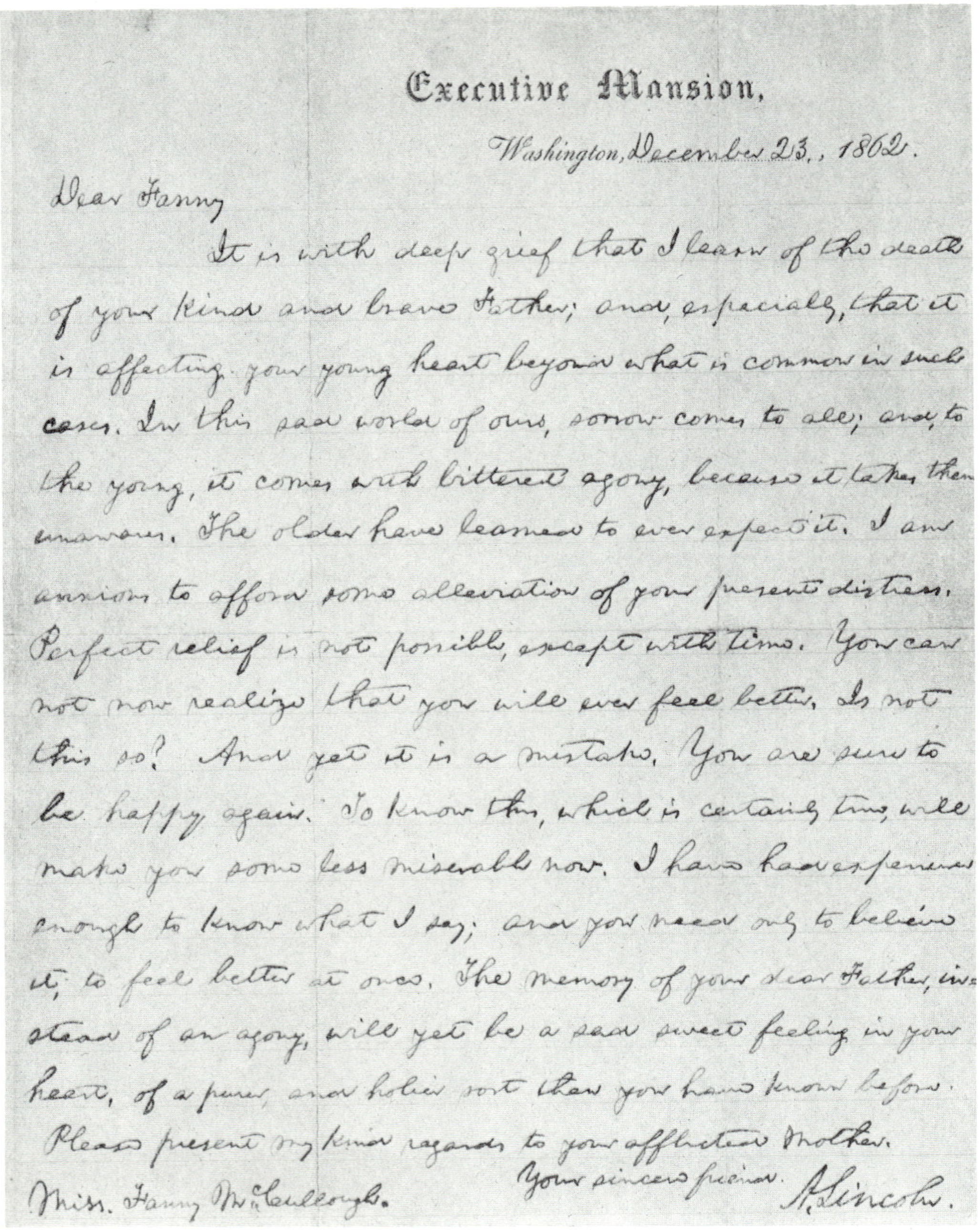

Executive Mansion,

Washington, December 23., 1862.

Dear Fanny

It is with deep grief that I learn of the death of your kind and brave Father; and, especially, that it is affecting your young heart beyond what is common in such cases. In this sad world of ours, sorrow comes to all; and, to the young, it comes with bitterest agony, because it takes them unawares. The older have learned to ever expect it. I am anxious to afford some alleviation of your present distress. Perfect relief is not possible, except with time. You can not now realize that you will ever feel better. Is not this so? And yet it is a mistake. You are sure to be happy again. To know this, which is certainly true, will make you some less miserable now. I have had experience enough to know what I say; and you need only to believe it, to feel better at once. The memory of your dear Father, instead of an agony, will yet be a sad sweet feeling in your heart, of a purer and holier sort than you have known before.

Please present my kind regards to your afflicted Mother.

Your sincere friend.
A. Lincoln.

Miss. Fanny McCullough.

Dear Fanny

It is with deep grief that I learn of the death of your kind and brave Father; and, especially, that it is affecting your young heart beyond what is common in such cases. In this sad world of ours, sorrow comes to all; and, to the young, it comes with bittered agony, because it takes them unawares. The older have learned to ever expect it. I am anxious to afford some alleviation of your present distress. Perfect relief is not possible, except with time. You can not now realize that you will ever feel better. Is not this so? And yet it is a mistake. You are sure to be happy again. To know this, which is certainly true, will make you some less miserable now. I have had experience enough to know what I say; and you need only to believe it, to feel better at once. The memory of your dear Father, instead of an agony, will yet be a sad sweet feeling in your heart, of a purer and holier sort than you have known before. Please present my kind regards to your afflicted mother.

— Your sincere friend.
A. LINCOLN

Fanny McCullough

Left to right: 1. unknown. 2. Captain Hudson Burr. 3. Mrs. Burr. 4. Mrs. John McNulta. 5. unknown. 6. Mrs. Orme. 7. General Wm. Orme. 8. General John McNulta.

William W. Orme

". . . I feel well & in good spirits, and am glad of the opportunity to take part in the grand struggle for opening the Mississippi & ending the Rebellion — I shall try to bear myself so that whatever may be my fate you and our dear little ones shall only have reason to be proud of me . . ."

— William Orme
June 3, 1863

Quarters of Lieutenant R.N. Evans, 20th Illinois Infantry

We tend to think of soldiering during the Civil War as constant action — but it was not.

The enthusiasm of enlistment day at the McLean County Courthouse often gave way to boredom.

The county's two most active regiments — the 94th and the 33rd — both fought well, but spent much more time waiting, marching and longing for home.

"I remember drum major William C. Rolls with something of amusement . . . I recall him best, as all of you will, with a pet alligator in his arms . . ."

— History of the 33rd Regt.

THE EQUIPMENT

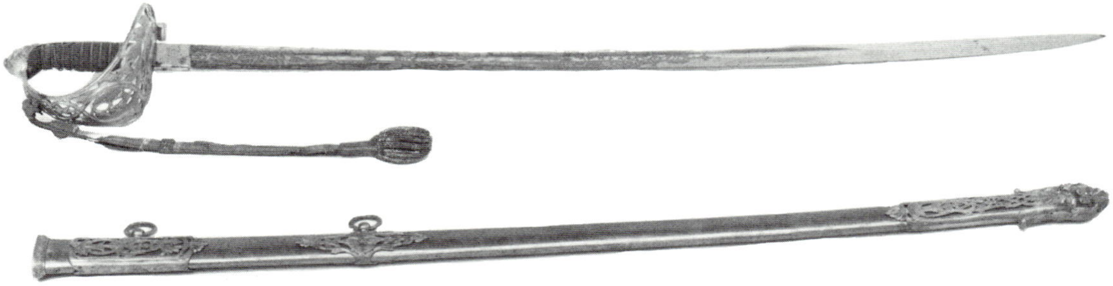

Dress sword

Springfield rifled musket

Enlisted man's buckle

Remington revolver

Field desk

Binoculars and case

Bayonet

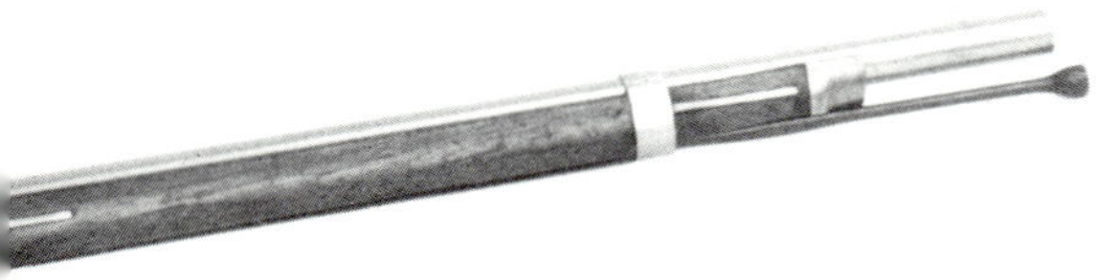

Sergeant's cap

Officer's uniform

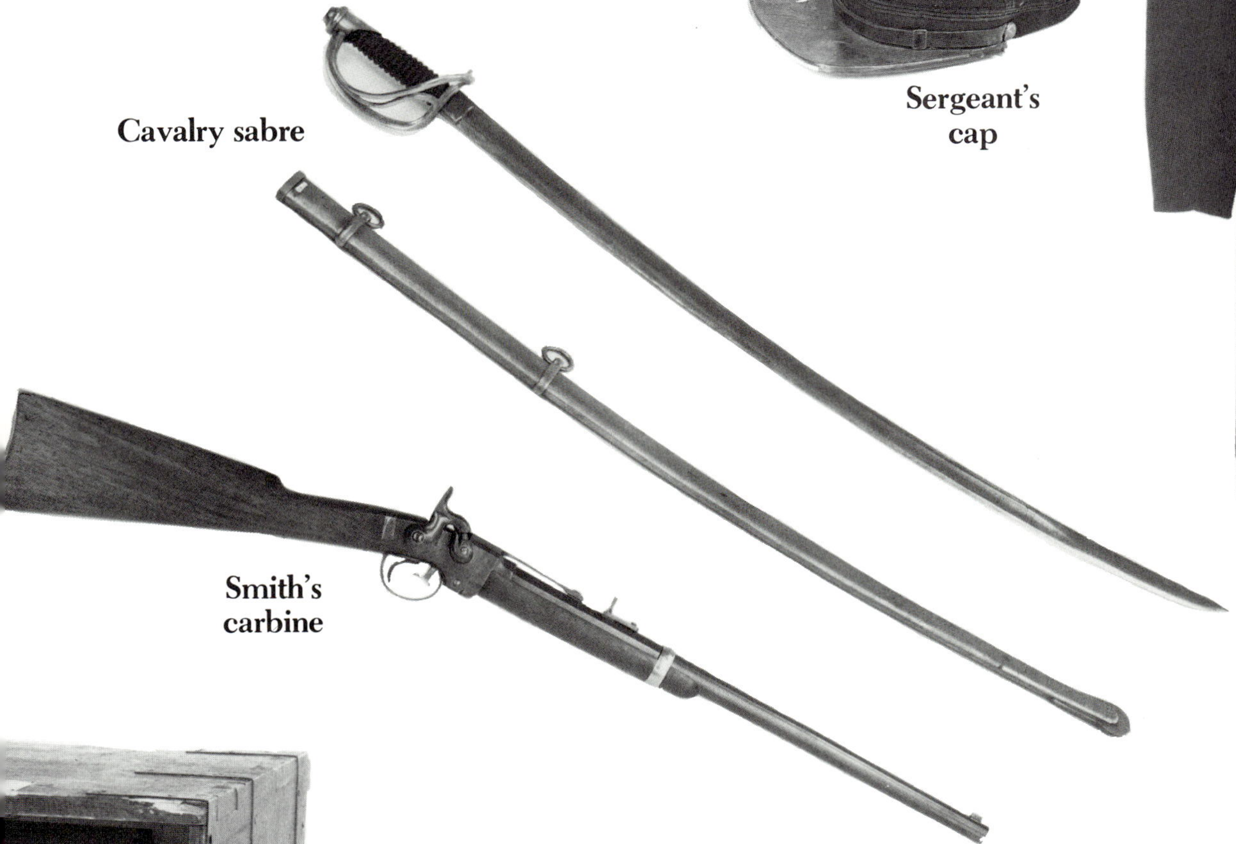

Cavalry sabre

Smith's carbine

Mess gear

Cartridge box

WITH THE 33RD ILLINOIS VOLUNTEERS

"*. . . A squad of Cavalry went early this morning and captured a mule and some bacon belonging to a Rebel captain . . .*"

— May 6, 1862

"Saddling Up"

"*. . . Fair in morn. Fired and cleaned revolver. . Boys fishing this morning, and caught a fine lot of fish . . .*"

— April 29, 1862

"Fish for Dinner"

DRAWINGS BY COL. JULIAN E. BRYANT

QUOTATIONS FROM DIARY OF CAPT. E. J. LEWIS

"Recitations as usual this evening. Much excitement on the subject of volunteering on the gunboats, and volunteers offering freely."

— Feb. 3, 1862

"Union Gunboat on the Mississippi"

". . . Order received to prepare for a 4 days expedition per boat, and company held in readiness. Quite a fleet of gun-boats & rams, and some transports with troops passed down in morning . . . Order received at 10 P.M. to go on board the boat, but countermanded in a few minutes . . ."

— August 16, 1862

"Flotilla of Union Troop Transports"

". . . Crossed Ten Mile Creek . . . a fine stream. Wagons, especially pressed ox wagons, stuck repeatedly . . . causing great delay of the rear guard."

— No date

"Union Troops Fording a River"

"Rainy. No drill. Playing cards and chess, reading and so forth. Sutler Milner under arrest today for selling liquor. Paid Capt. Moore for my sword today."

— April 11, 1862

"Union Officers Off Duty"

SOLDIERS' LETTERS

— Wm. H. Horine and G.W. Houser
94th Illinois Infantry

Camp Benton, Mo. Sept. 1, 1862
". . . I have been doing first rate since I've here, have plenty of swill and slop to eat and drink . . . the barracks is about 4 miles northwest of St. Louis . . . When they are all out on drill, I tell you what it looks like a young army, that's what . . ."

Mill Springs, Mo. Sept. 23, 1862
". . . Of all the countries that anybody ever saw this is the d...dest. For 2 days or more we wouldn't see the first house or any other live thing at all. I ain't seen the first bird since we left St. Louis. I ain't hardly seen a woman and what I did see were all Secesh. I didn't appreciate them much on that account. I would like to come across some good looking Union galls. I think I could do them justice plentifully . . ."

Springfield, Mo. Oct. 14, 1862
". . . If you have any counterfeit money, broken banks or anything of that kind just send them along. Here is the place to pass all such furniture. The Secesh brings wagon loads of things, pies, canes, cider, apples, peaches, chickens, turkeys, milk . . . and they will take anything that looks like money . . . Send that ten dollars that I used to carry, on the State of Ohio, and I'll work it . . ."

Huntsville, Ark. Jan. 8, 1863
". . . I also begin to like soldering pretty well too, indeed I would like it verry well, if it was that we did not get into such a scrape as we did on the 7th of last month with the mean low life outrageous rediculous scandulous ignominous heaven defying helldeserving gray backed black backed blue backed redbacked yellowbacked greasy backed rebels. I tell you Wood they would just as leaf shoot a fellow as not and they don't care where they shoot him either, they just bang away anyhow. . ."

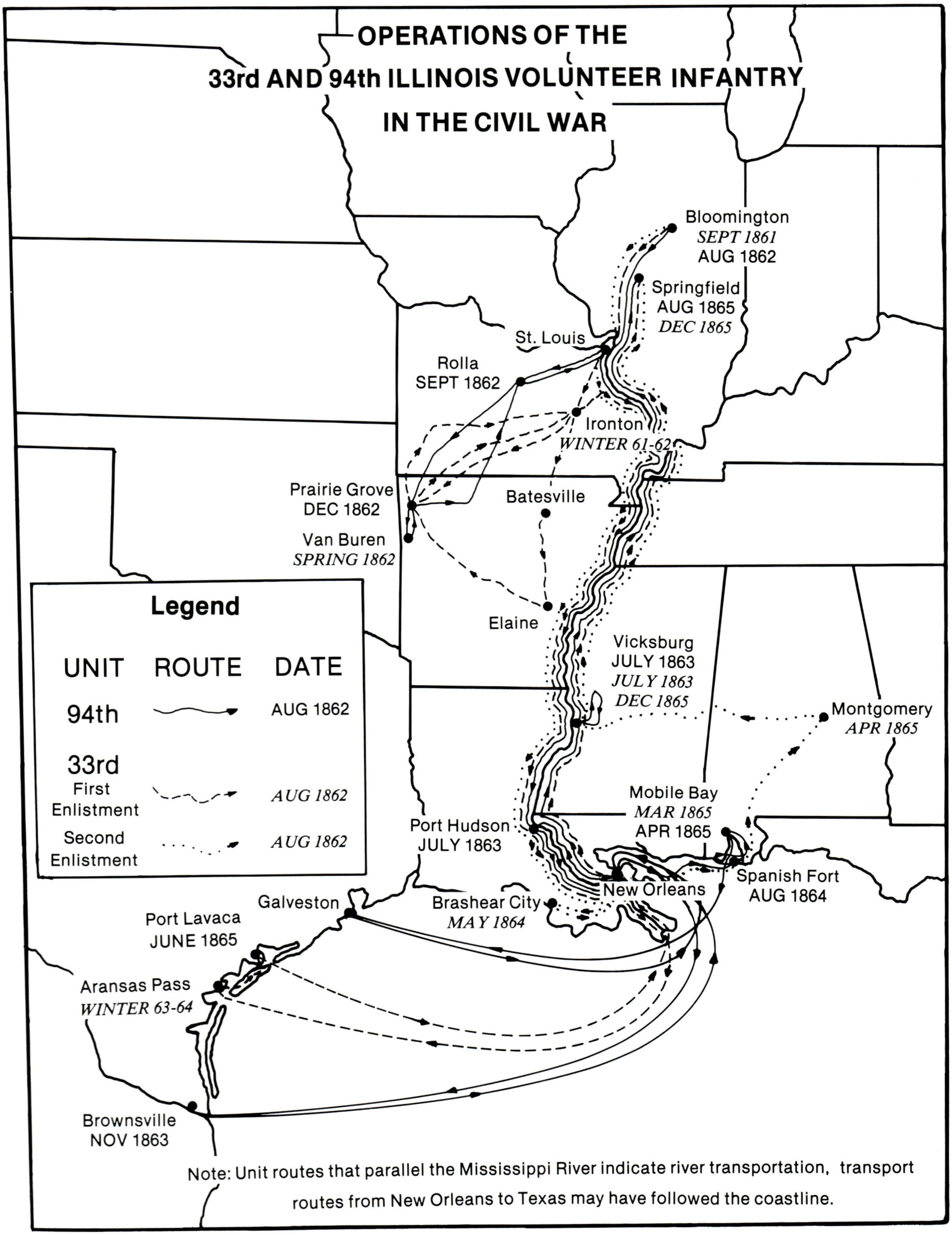
OPERATIONS OF THE
33rd AND 94th ILLINOIS VOLUNTEER INFANTRY
IN THE CIVIL WAR
Bloomington
SEPT 1861
AUG 1862
Springfield
AUG 1865
DEC 1865
St. Louis
Rolla
SEPT 1862
Ironton
WINTER 61-62
Prairie Grove
DEC 1862
Batesville
Van Buren
SPRING 1862
Elaine
Vicksburg
JULY 1863
JULY 1863
DEC 1865
Montgomery
APR 1865
Mobile Bay
MAR 1865
APR 1865
Port Hudson
JULY 1863
Spanish Fort
AUG 1864
New Orleans
Brashear City
MAY 1864
Galveston
Port Lavaca
JUNE 1865
Aransas Pass
WINTER 63-64
Brownsville
NOV 1863
Legend
UNIT
ROUTE
DATE
94th
AUG 1862
33rd
First Enlistment
AUG 1862
Second Enlistment
AUG 1862
Note: Unit routes that parallel the Mississippi River indicate river transportation, transport routes from New Orleans to Texas may have followed the coastline.

THE CAMPAIGNS

McLean County units were involved in the Union's strategy of splitting the Confederate forces along the Mississippi Valley. They closed from the north, joining General Grant's Army of the Frontier.

The 94th fought at Prairie Grove, Arkansas, in 1862, and at Vicksburg in 1863; raided plantations; occupied Brownsville, Texas; and engaged in the Mobile Bay expedition in 1865.

The 33rd was engaged in minor skirmishing until Vicksburg, participating in that battle. The regiment then moved through Texas, served as an occupation force in Louisiana, and joined the 94th and others in a siege of Spanish Fort at Mobile, Alabama.

Skirmishing on the advance to Vicksburg

Camp, 57th Illinois Infantry, Fort Williams

21st Illinois leaving Ironton, Missouri

THE NORMAL PICKET.

We cannot at the same time extend to Rebels the rights of peace and enforce against them the penalties of war. Gen. Halleck.

VOL. I. IRONTON, MO., FEBRUARY 5, 1862. NO. 7.

THE NORMAL PICKET

IRONTON, MO., WEDNESDAY, FEB. 5, '62

Our Colonel.—Obeying orders. Col. C. E. Hovey of the Normal Regiment, when not on duty, wears the uniform of a private. One of his companies detailed to guard the Iron Mountain Rail Road bridges, was recently relieved, and returned to camp. While preparing the quarters, one of the privates lately recruited, seeing him assisting the boys, said to him—"See here, old fellow: you're acquainted round here:—go and get a saw for me, quick." The Colonel, who is a strict disciplinarian, *obeyed the order.*

On Sunday night, a soldier of the 21st. under confinement, got into a quarrel with "old Hall" of Arcadia, and threw a stick of stove-wood at him, cutting his head badly. The soldier was put in irons, and tied up for the night.

The Yazoo Daily Yankee.

PUBLISHED SEMI-OCCASIONALLY BY MR. MUDSILL, MR. SMALL-FISTED FARMER, MR. GREASY MECHANIC & CO.

YAZOO CITY, MISS., JULY 20, 1863.

The Yazoo Daily Yankee.

"*To Hold, Occupy and Possess.*"

FOUND.—Floating in the Mississippi river on the evening of July 13th a torpedo, which the owner is requested to call for, pay charges and take it away. For further particulars call on Capt. Walker, on the Gun Boat Dekalb.

AT AN END

Peace Oh what Joyful news is this to us pore Soldiers. No Set of men in all Gods Creation has A write to Rejoice and Even Shout over the glad tidings of Peace more than the war worne Veteran. He who has with Musket and Bayonet Waded throug Snow, Rain, Hail, and Swamp, Amidst Rivers of Blood Living on Hard tack and Sowbelly with the Heavens for our dwelling place for the Space of four Long years far from our Homes and friends in the midst of Enemys Boath Male and female. Why should we not Rejoice at Peace and A Return to our Beautiful Homes and warm Harted friends far in the North.

— James T. Ayers
Apr. 30, 1865

James T. Ayers

The mustering-out process was slow. But most of McLean County's soldiers were on their way home by August, 1865.

Seven hundred of them — nearly one out of five who served — did not come home alive.

Camp Butler, Springfield, Illinois

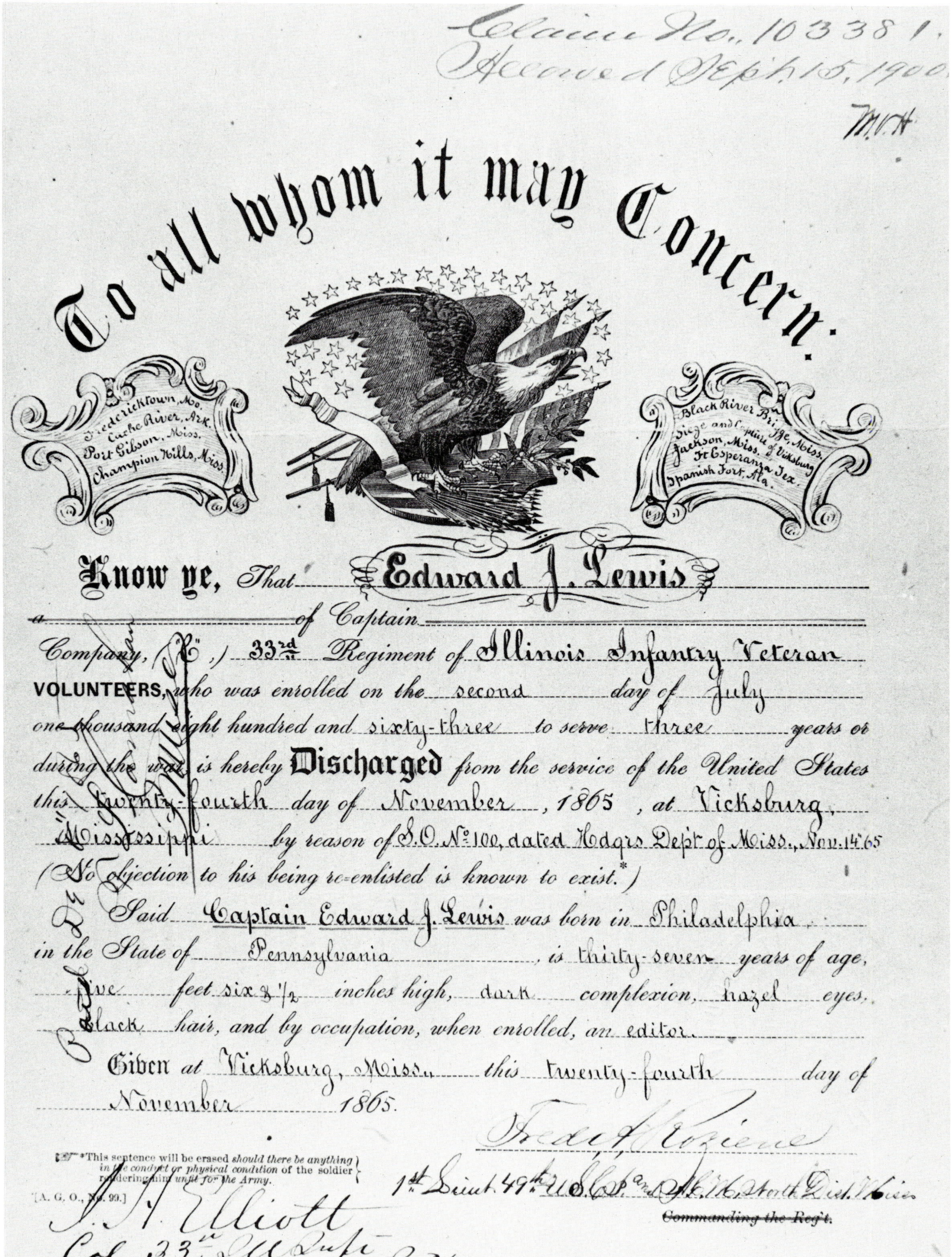

Claim No. 10338 1.
Received Sept. 15, 1900.
M.O.H.

To all whom it may Concern:

Fredericktown, Mo.
Cache River, Ark.
Port Gibson, Miss.
Champion Hills, Miss.

Black River Bridge,
Siege and Capture of Vicksburg,
Jackson, Miss.
Ft Esperanza, Tex.
Spanish Fort, Ala.

Know ye, That Edward J. Lewis ~~a~~ of Captain Company, (E) 33rd Regiment of Illinois Infantry Veteran **VOLUNTEERS,** who was enrolled on the second day of July one thousand eight hundred and sixty-three to serve three years or during the war, is hereby **Discharged** from the service of the United States this twenty-fourth day of November, 1865, at Vicksburg, Mississippi by reason of S.O. No 100, dated Hdqrs Dept of Miss., Nov. 14. 65 (No objection to his being re-enlisted is known to exist.*)

Said Captain Edward J. Lewis was born in Philadelphia in the State of Pennsylvania, is thirty-seven years of age, five feet six & 1/2 inches high, dark complexion, hazel eyes, black hair, and by occupation, when enrolled, an editor.

Given at Vicksburg, Miss. this twenty-fourth day of November 1865.

Fred A. Roziene
1st Lieut. 49th U.S.C.I. and A.A.G. Northern Dist. Miss.
~~Commanding the Reg't.~~

*This sentence will be erased *should there be anything in the conduct or physical condition* of the soldier *rendering him unfit for the Army.*

[A. G. O., No. 99.]

J. H. Elliott
Col 33rd Ill Infy

Lincoln Indignation Meeting

Lincoln's return was also not a happy one. His likeness was the first to appear in the Pantagraph, in 1864, and less than a year later it was there again — with the news the President was dead. Citizens gathered at the Courthouse Square to express their indignation.

Mourning badges

Two weeks after that, church bells rang in Bloomington and Normal at 3 a.m. Several thousand people got out of bed and gathered at the Chicago and Alton station.

Abraham Lincoln's funeral train stopped for just a moment — and then took him home to Springfield. Crowds were reported all along the line.

AFTER THE WAR . . .

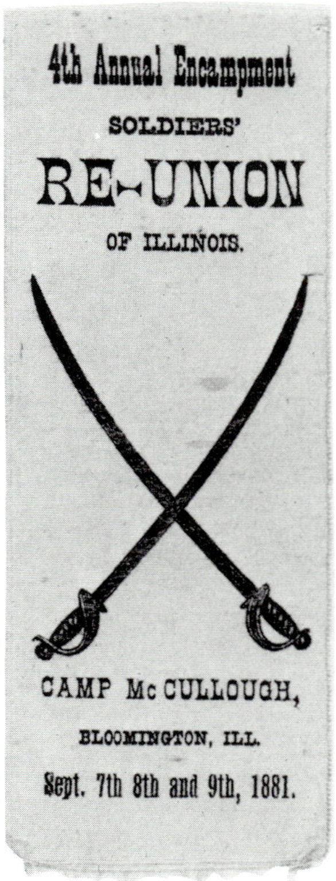

The war changed millions of lives and uprooted people.

When the veterans gathered in Bloomington 20 years later (former President Grant was himself a speaker at one of the gatherings), they had some fascinating "Whatever became of . . . ?" stories to tell.

Private Joe Fifer of Danvers became governor of Illinois. Captain John Routt of Bloomington became governor of Colorado.

Among those settling in McLean County after the war, Colonel John Sobieski, claiming he was heir to the Polish throne, became a nationally famous temperance lecturer. Major John Wesley Powell of Wesleyan put together an expedition of the first white men to explore the Grand Canyon.

Hat badge

It was nearly a century later when Bloomington author Harold Sinclair borrowed from the record of Central Illinois' Civil War involvement to write his historical novel *The Horse Soldiers*.

Sinclair was there, book in hand, when John Wayne, John Ford and others began filming the story. And when the movie opened at the Castle Theatre in 1959, Mayor Robert McGraw proclaimed it "Harold Sinclair Day."

5. Urban Growth

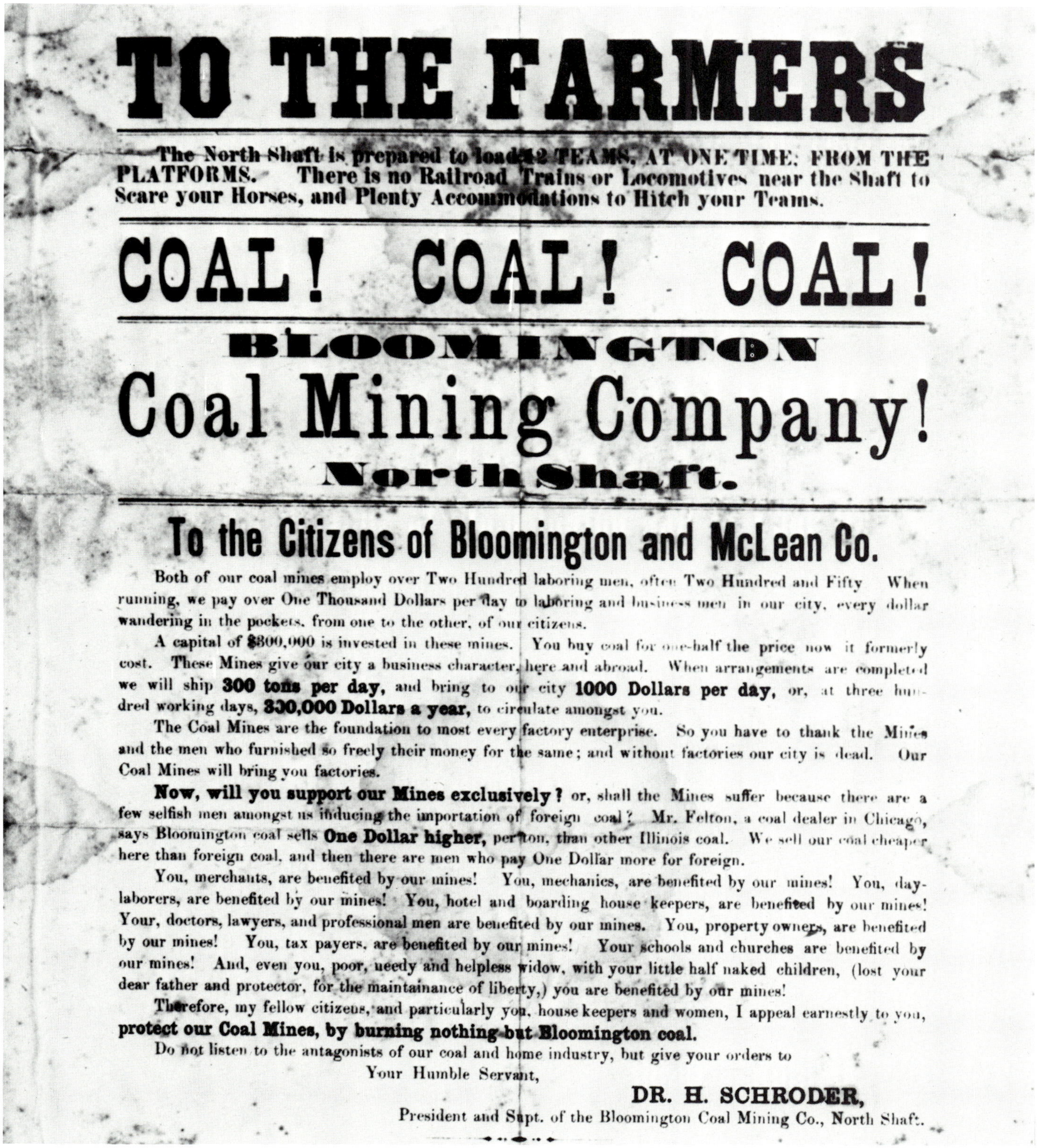

TO THE FARMERS

The North Shaft is prepared to load 12 TEAMS, AT ONE TIME; FROM THE PLATFORMS. There is no Railroad Trains or Locomotives near the Shaft to Scare your Horses, and Plenty Accommodations to Hitch your Teams.

COAL! COAL! COAL!

BLOOMINGTON
Coal Mining Company!
North Shaft.

To the Citizens of Bloomington and McLean Co.

Both of our coal mines employ over Two Hundred laboring men, often Two Hundred and Fifty When running, we pay over One Thousand Dollars per day to laboring and business men in our city, every dollar wandering in the pockets, from one to the other, of our citizens.

A capital of $800,000 is invested in these mines. You buy coal for one-half the price now it formerly cost. These Mines give our city a business character, here and abroad. When arrangements are completed we will ship **300 tons per day,** and bring to our city **1000 Dollars per day,** or, at three hundred working days, **300,000 Dollars a year,** to circulate amongst you.

The Coal Mines are the foundation to most every factory enterprise. So you have to thank the Mines and the men who furnished so freely their money for the same; and without factories our city is dead. Our Coal Mines will bring you factories.

Now, will you support our Mines exclusively? or, shall the Mines suffer because there are a few selfish men amongst us inducing the importation of foreign coal? Mr. Felton, a coal dealer in Chicago, says Bloomington coal sells **One Dollar higher,** per ton, than other Illinois coal. We sell our coal cheaper here than foreign coal, and then there are men who pay One Dollar more for foreign.

You, merchants, are benefited by our mines! You, mechanics, are benefited by our mines! You, day-laborers, are benefited by our mines! You, hotel and boarding house keepers, are benefited by our mines! Your, doctors, lawyers, and professional men are benefited by our mines. You, property owners, are benefited by our mines! You, tax payers, are benefited by our mines! Your schools and churches are benefited by our mines! And, even you, poor, needy and helpless widow, with your little half naked children, (lost your dear father and protector, for the maintainance of liberty,) you are benefited by our mines!

Therefore, my fellow citizens, and particularly you, house keepers and women, I appeal earnestly to you, **protect our Coal Mines, by burning nothing but Bloomington coal.**

Do not listen to the antagonists of our coal and home industry, but give your orders to

Your Humble Servant,

DR. H. SCHRODER,

President and Supt. of the Bloomington Coal Mining Co., North Shaft.

McLean County's boom continued when the boys returned from the war, and the availability of coal and rail transportation began to form the basis for new manufacturing opportunities.

The discovery of coal on Bloomington's west side in 1867 made cheap fuel available to the area, and more than 300 miners were soon bringing more than 500 tons of the "black gold" to the surface daily.

Nearby, the Chicago and Alton shops were the county's largest employer, turning out the first Pullman sleeper, the first commercial dining car and the first reclining chair car. The C&A engine "Major Nolton" became nationally known after it sped the Bloomington Fire Company in record time to fight the great Chicago fire of 1871.

The Alton shops were the cornerstone of the Bloomington economy, and when they burned to the ground Halloween night, 1867, citizens quickly donated $55,000, at the insistance of the railroad, to acquire more land, rebuild the shops and keep the jobs in McLean County.

The junction of the Chicago and Alton with the Illinois Central lured new east-west railroads — one of them financed by McLean County people — and Bloomington-Normal became a rail hub.

Employees, C&A Shops, ca. 1885

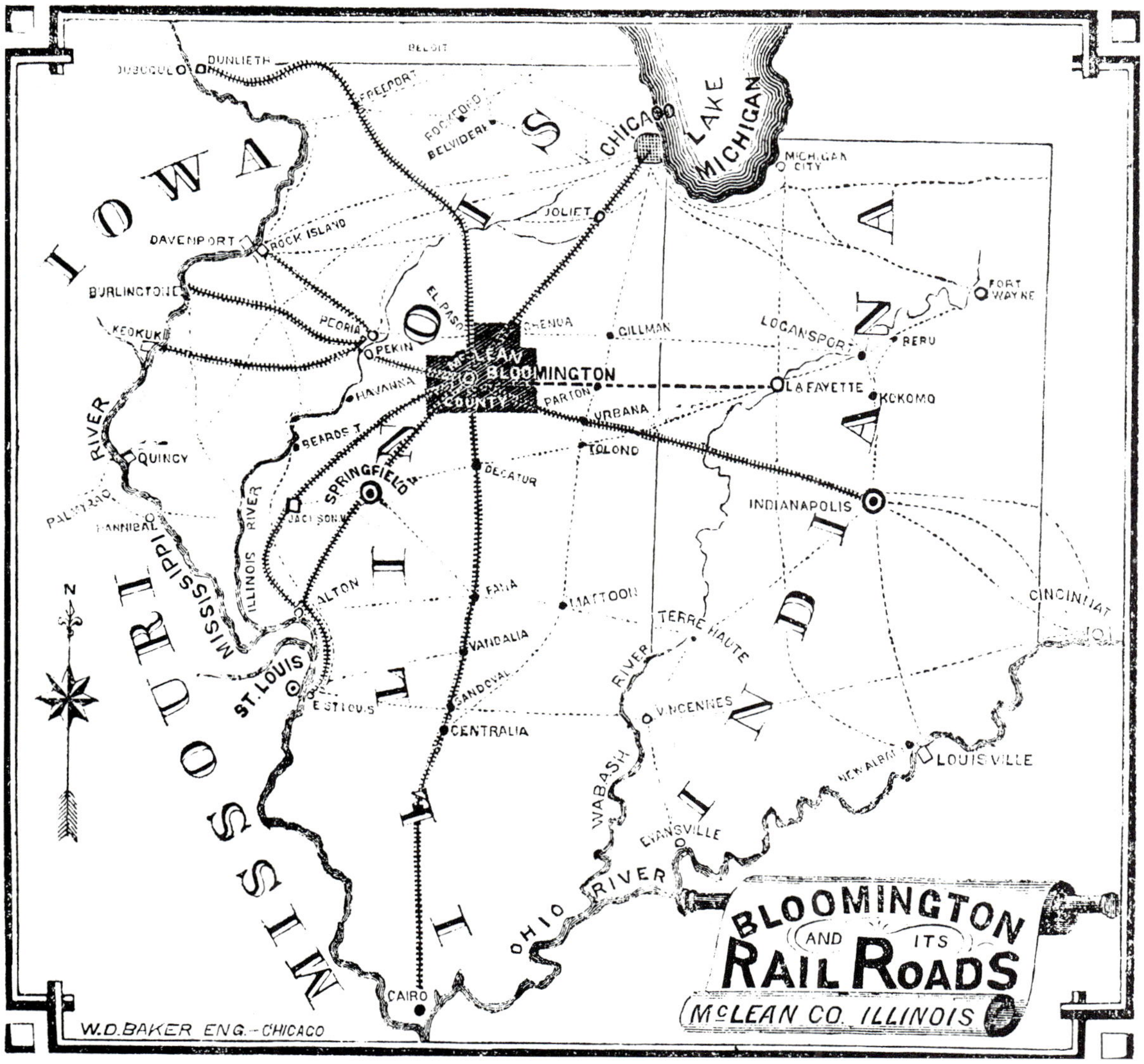

The rebuilt shops, finished in 1870, were made of Joliet stone, occupying 40 acres of Bloomington's west side. By 1881, the 1,200 workers there were turning out six to eight new railroad cars each day.

The workers were also becoming permanent citizens, buying their own homes, settling in; and their company, the Chicago and Alton, was doing its part by aiding the city in macadamizing the street from the freight depot to the courthouse square.

Car shop, 1889

"Yesterday was Chicago and Alton pay day and the city was from $60,000 to $70,000 the better off for it. This monthly influx of coin of the realm is a fine thing for the city. It is a regular periodic boom and it is expected each month by our merchants with the certainty of its stimulating business matters."

— **Daily Pantagraph**
Nov. 18, 1886

EXPANDING MARKETS

In addition to providing jobs, the railroads gave McLean County a distribution system — a way of exporting products from factory to far-away stores. Manufacturers were no longer producing for home consumption only.

Cyrenius Wakefield, in fact, sold his patent medicines to more than 8,000 druggists across the United States, including Theron Fell in Bloomington. Wakefield employed 50 people in his factory at the site of today's Bloomington Junior High School, and he advertised his products through the $1^{1/2}$ million almanacs he printed annually at his factory in four languages.

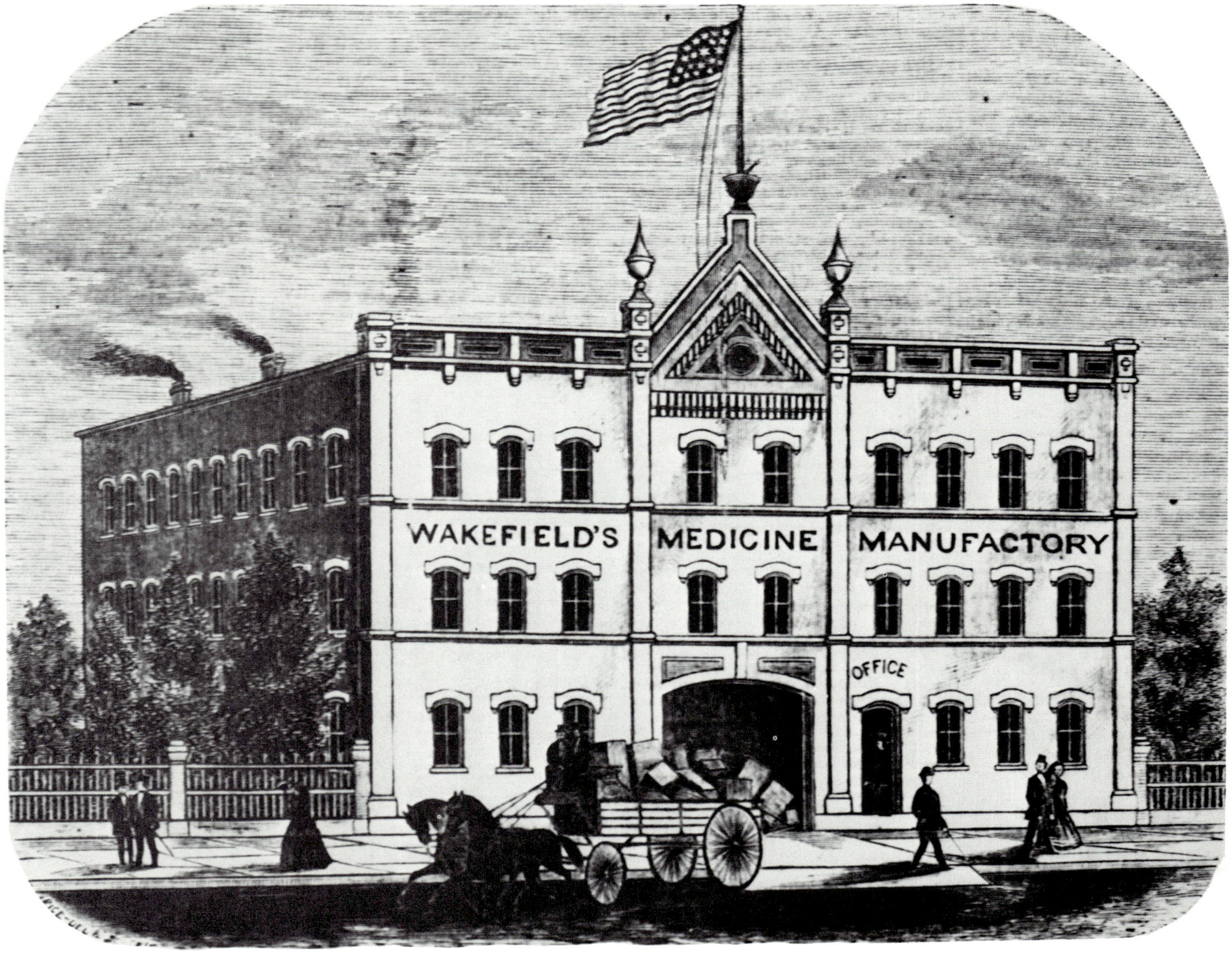

C. WAKEFIELD & CO.'S MEDICINE MANUFACTORY.

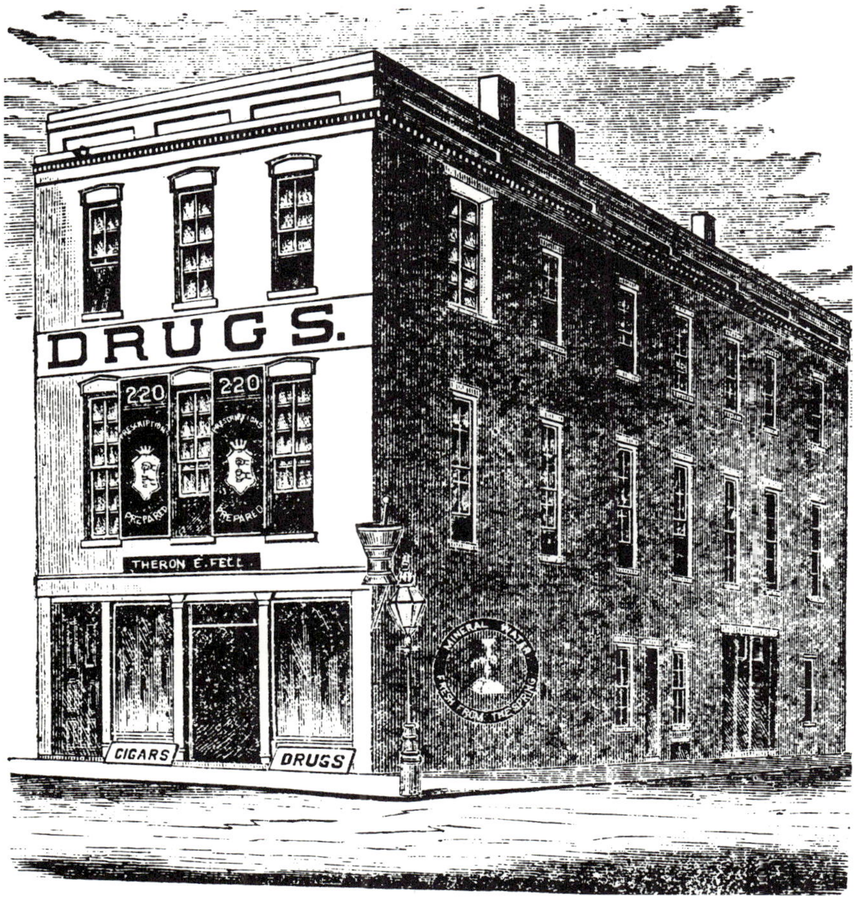

Theron Fell Drug Store
Southwest corner Center & Jefferson

Bloomington Pork Packing Company employees, ca. 1885

WM. VAN SCHOICK GEO. A. TRYNER. U. O. ANDRUS.

Bloomington, Ill., Jany 30- 1877.

M J. H. Cheney

Bought of WM. VAN SCHOICK & CO.,

PORK PACKERS,

And Curers of the

CELEBRATED BLOOMINGTON HAM.

BURR & STEELE, PRINTERS.

DIRECTIONS.---Take meat out of packages on arrival. Hang up in a dry, airy place, and when mould appears, clean off with a dry brush.

"The Porkers' Wail of Anguish — The Pork Packing Company began the season's operation on Saturday by killing between 300 and 400 hogs. Mr. Tryner states that the hogs are of better condition and quality this year than last, or indeed than for a number of years, but are perhaps not quite so plentiful. The price is 3.50 per hundred, or about 25 cents higher than the price of the opening last year. The hogs already in are all from near Bloomington, but the agents of the company are negotiating for a supply in all the adjacent counties. The company will kill about 15,000 this year — a slight increase over the work last year."

— **Daily Pantagraph**
Nov. 29, 1886

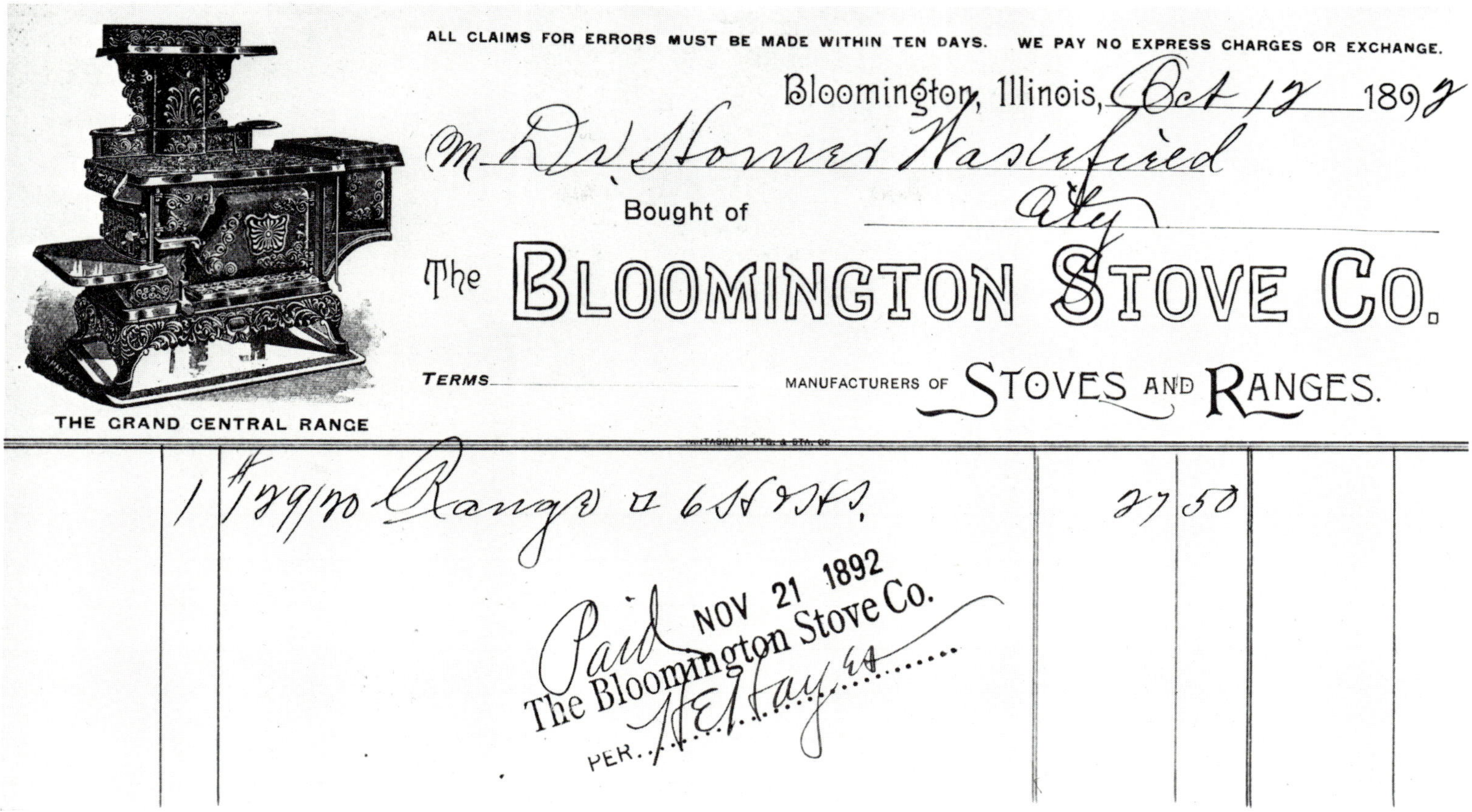
ALL CLAIMS FOR ERRORS MUST BE MADE WITHIN TEN DAYS. WE PAY NO EXPRESS CHARGES OR EXCHANGE.

Bloomington, Illinois, Oct 12 1892

M Dr. Homer Wakefield

Bought of City

The BLOOMINGTON STOVE CO.

TERMS

MANUFACTURERS OF STOVES AND RANGES.

THE GRAND CENTRAL RANGE

1	#79/20 Range & 6 H.S.H.		27 50

Paid NOV 21 1892
The Bloomington Stove Co.
PER H.E. Hayes

The exports included railroad cars and diarrhea medicine, hams and stoves and nursery stock and overalls.

The shift from a rural economy to one with a good representation of urban manufacturing came because the rails were shipping products out and bringing immigrant workers in — some unskilled workers plus a good number of skilled tradesmen from Europe.

Workmen, Higgins, Jung & Kleinau Marble Works, ca. 1885, 229 East Front

THE GERMANS

Very few of the county's early settlers were German, but by 1870, fully 13 percent of Bloomington's 17,019 people were either German-born or were children living at home with German-born parents. They came first to build the railroads, but moved into shopkeeping and skilled-labor jobs.

The Bloomington German subculture was a complete one, with numerous social and cultural events and organizations.

William Schmidt

". . . One other thing I wanted to speak of was Mr. Schmidt's red haw tree which he had trimmed in the shape of an umbrella. It grew so large that it was possible to build a table beneath it around the trunk. At Mr. Schmidt's funeral, the casket was taken out and placed on the table under this tree . . ."

— Ed. Kirkpatrick
Reminiscence, 1941

Frauleins Riebsame & Moratz as Columbia & Germania

Turner Hall, South Main St.

Turners Oskar Scholz & Robert Balke

The Turners, or Turnverein, were one such society to "develop the physical system by means of gymnastic exercise and to cultivate the intellect by literary entertainments."

The Bloomington Germans organized their own schools and churches, and built a Jewish synagogue, a building that stands to this day on North Prairie Street. Classes and services were conducted in the German language, and the city had its own German-language newspaper as early as 1868.

Moses Montefiore Temple

DR. SCHRODER

". . . My property 1848 in Germany was all confiscatet, my wifes nobel family, condemned and discartet as as rebels and so we comenced a real democratic live. I worked hard for all we had and have. My wife assisted me with all her will and power, never had in America a servant girl, we belonget to the people, no stuck up with us . . ."

— Dr. Herman Schroder
Sept. 17, 1900

Dr. Herman Schroder was probably the most colorful — and successful — of the immigrants. He married into the nobility, claimed to have built a railroad in Saxony, and escaped Prussia in 1848 by taking a soldier's rifle away and shooting him.

Dr. Schroder took Bloomington by storm, growing grapes and selling his vines around the world. He built a hotel in Bloomington, planted 200,000 mulberry trees, imported silkworms, owned a pickle factory and a sausage factory, and was president of the Bloomington Coal Company.

And he practiced the free speech he had fled Prussia to find — often to the discomfort of his wife — sending a stream of letters to the newspaper editors. Mrs. Schroder sued for separate maintenance in the 1880s, and the pair lived mostly apart for their last 15 years.

MARIE LITTA

East side of square

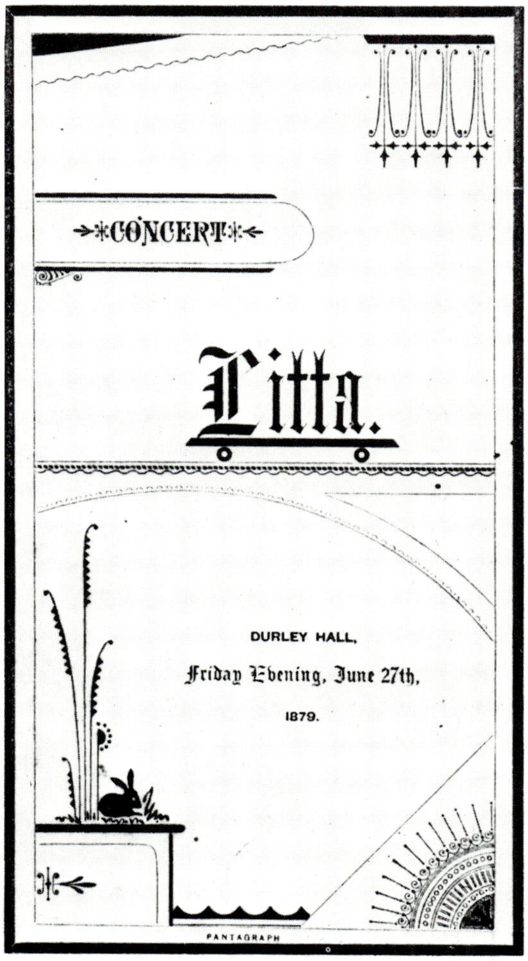

Marie von Elsner (Marie Litta)

Hugo von Elsner was one of a number of Bloomington Germans who disassociated himself with Dr. Schroder — and no record exists that the von Elsner daughter ever joined the distinguished list of performers who entertained at Schroder's Opera House.

The daughter performed at Bloomington's Durley Hall instead, and in Paris, Vienna, Chicago and across America. The European press called Marie Litta the "Queen of Song," the "American Jenny Lind."

Litta was America's biggest star — and only 27 years old — when she became ill on a concert tour and died in 1883.

THE IRISH

If the "South Hill" area, south of downtown Bloomington, was the German neighborhood, then the "Forty Acres" neighborhood west of the Alton shops belonged to the Irish. The first Irish, in fact, had come here to build the railroad.

They also came to avoid starvation in their famine-ridden homeland. The Irish were aware of political power, having suffered from the lack of it, and used the clout, filling the patronage jobs. The early police force was mostly Irish.

But respect was hard to come by. Newspaper accounts years later often omitted names, pointing out simply that "an Irishman was arrested."

First uniformed Bloomington police, 1874

Residence of William O'Neill, ca. 1910

"I love that starry banner
For this to me it means,
No Irish knee is made to bend
To haughty kings and queens.
Old Erin's sons and daughters, too,
Of freedom here may sing.
And every lass may be a queen
And every lad a king."

— Unknown

Insignia, Ancient Order of Hibernians

Interior, Holy Trinity Church
ca. 1900

Sometimes I have wondered if there was any truth in the rumor that Dr. McGovern had episcopal aspirations when he had the plans drawn up for the old Holy Trinity Church — as it was known to the present generation. Among the older priests at the turn of the century this rumor persisted. I am giving it as a rumor, and do not claim historical accuracy for it. Even if true, surely it would not be to the discredit of Dr. McGovern.

- Msgr. S. N. Moore, 1952

Dr. James J. McGovern

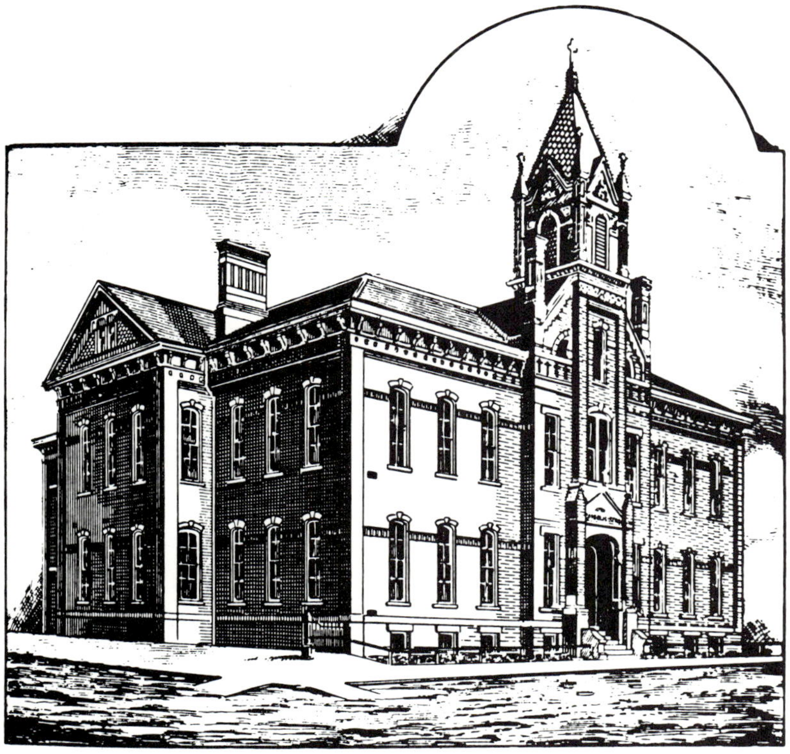

St. Mary's School

AVE MARIA.

SIXTEENTH ANNUAL

Commencement Exercises

OF

St. Mary's ✦ Parochial ✦ School

AT

Grand Opera House,

SATURDAY, JUNE 21, 1891,

AT 8 O'CLOCK P. M.

Opening Chorus - Accompanists, { L. Francis, N. Vaughn.

Essay - - - - - - - - - Heroism
Mary Crotty.

Little Boys' Drill, - Accompanists, { Annie Foley, Katie Welch.

Essay - - - - - - - Knowledge
Annie Hayden.

Duo - - - - Fantaisie from Tannhauser
Katie O'Niel and Nellie Will.

Essay - - - - - - - - - Failure
W. O'Neill.

Little Girls' Drill - Accompanist, Julia McGraw.

Essay - - - - - - - - - Sorrow
Maria Kirwin.

Vocal Trio, - - - Accompanist, Mary Ryan.
Ida Magirl, Katie Ryan and Bernardette Slattrey.

Essay - - - - - - - - - Genius
Katie O'Neill

Grand Valse de Concert { Maria Kirwin, Julia McGraw, Annie Hayden, Annie Tobin

Essay - - - - - - - - True Nobility
Mamie Neville.

The Little Troupe from the Orient - - - - - - - - Accompanist, Katie O'Niell.

Essay - - - - - - - - - Home
Mary Ryan.

Dumb Bells - - Accompanists, { Mary Costello, Mary Sullivan.

Class Song - - Accompanist, Nellie Watson.

Oration and Veledictory - - - - Power
J. Sullivan.

AWARDING DIPLOMAS.

Katie A. O'Neil.	Mamie E. Neville.
John W. Sullivan.	Mary R. Crotty.
Mary G. Ryan.	Annie A. Hayden.
Willie J. O'Neil.	Maria I. Kirwin.

Address - - - - - - - Rev. M. Weldon.

The Vesper hour - Accompanist, Mary Sweeney.

Kimball pianos kindly furnished by Mr. J. T. Adams, Main St.

While the Germans built gyms and opera houses, the Irish built churches and schools, determined to do two things denied them in Ireland —practice their Catholic religion and educate their children.

Dr. James McGovern arrived in the 1870s, shortly after a windstorm destroyed the Catholic church, and moved his flock into Phoenix Hall, opposite the courthouse. Then he began construction of the majestic Holy Trinity Church at Main and Chestnut, a building destroyed by fire during the 1930s but immediately re-built.

St. Mary's became Trinity Grade School and, in 1892, the parish was divided, establishing St. Patrick's Church and School west of the C&A Railroad. The Irish built magnificent Catholic churches at Chenoa and Merna.

Engine 143, C&A R.R. 1878

Irish life revolved around the railroad and the west side watering holes. Former Alton engineer "Stick" O'Neill emerged from one such establishment one afternoon and attempted to cross the tracks at the same place where he had previously lost his left leg when struck by a train.

It happened again, although the train wasn't moving fast this time.

The conductor, knowing O'Neill well, jumped off and yelled "Stick, Stick, are you hurt? Shall I call a doctor?"

"Hell, no," Stick barked. "Call a carpenter."

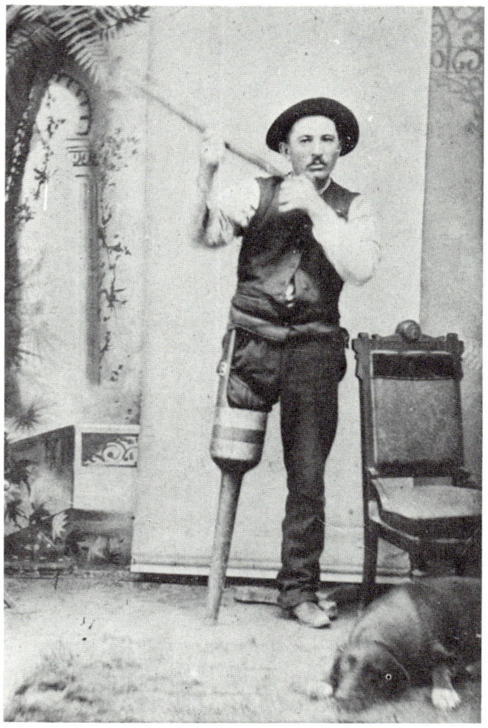

"Stick" O'Neill

John W. Trotter

John Trotter was born in Ireland and was 21 when he arrived in Bloomington. He was by trade a housepainter and by politics a Democrat.

By the 1870s, Trotter was a successful alderman, serving the Irish Second Ward, and he was a successful businessman, operating his lumber, coal and grain company in partnership with his sister.

Trotter was elected Bloomington's mayor in 1881, and re-elected twice more.

Like his sister, Georgiana, he never married.

J. W. & G. TROTTER,

Lumber & Grain Merchants,

AND DEALERS IN

Shingles, Lath,

Doors, Sash, Blinds, Produce, &c.,

1302 WEST MARKET STREET,

WEST OF C. & A. R. R. BRIDGE.

BLOOMINGTON, ILLINOIS.

228 HOLLAND'S BLOOMINGTON CITY DIRECTORY.

Georgiana Trotter

Georgiana Trotter led a remarkably active business and political life. She served as a nurse in the Union Army at Shiloh — a confidant of Dorothea Dix — and after the war became the first woman to become a naturalized United States citizen.

She was elected to the Board of Education in Bloomington, using her lumber company expertise to supervise contruction of a number of school buildings. Georgiana, who also spearheaded the drive for a public library, was labeled a "veritable steam engine of energy" in a newspaper account.

And when the Withers Library she helped build was torn down, the ornate fountain that was a tribute to Miss Trotter and her brother was left standing in the middle of Withers Park on Washington Street.

O'Neill Bros. Grocery, 1102 West Chestnut Street, ca. 1885

Retail stores became social and political centers, and few were more so than O'Neill's Grocery Store in Bloomington. West Chestnut Street was, in fact, a thriving neighborhood. The Chicago and Alton passenger depot was on Chestnut, as were many retail businesses, including the dry goods store operated by the Behr Family, west of the C&A yards.

Behr Store, 1101 West Chestnut

SERVING THE PEOPLE

Unknown Bloomington saloon, ca. 1890

Keg end

Service businesses sprang up, too, matching the population growth. A distillery occupied the west side for years, while the vineyards for Dr. Schroder's wine business occupied much of the area east of what is now Evergreen Cemetery.

The Meyer Brewery occupied today's Highland Golf Course, and the kegs of beer were stored in man-made caves there and in Forest Park.

Agitation for temperance was ever-present. Some 60 ladies, armed with hatchets, attacked and demolished the Buena Vista Saloon in Towanda one night in 1858. Colonel John Sobieski of Bloomington was less violent but equally opposed to "demon rum." He became one of the nation's most noted temperance lecturers.

The railroads allowed for the export of Bloomington manufactured goods, but they also made possible the importation of products and entertainment. P.T. Barnum's circus people spent their nights at the Ashley House, where the Illinois House stands today, while the railroadmen and the many traveling salesmen, the "drummers", checked in at the Bloomington Hotel on West Chestnut, near the Chicago and Alton depot.

Ashley House, northwest corner Jefferson & Center streets

FOR GOOD LIVERY, INQUIRE AT THE OFFICE.

GUESTS WITHOUT BAGGAGE PLEASE PAY IN ADVANCE.

ASHLEY HOUSE.

BLOOMINGTON, ILL.

All Moneys, Jewels, Coats, Valises, and other valuables, must be left at the Office, and checks received for them, otherwise the Proprietor will not be responsible for any loss.

T. ASHLEY, Proprietor.

NAME.	RESIDENCE.	Time.	Rooms.
Wednesday June 9th 1880			
Part of P. T. Barnum's Only Show Company			
R H Dockrall + Wife		13	75
Zazel + Sister		13	61

"*Dewey, Rodgers & Co. have a carload of slippers traveling in even procession about their windows; small dainty red slippers trudge along beside broad-soled, comfortable home slippers for the head of the family.*"

— **Daily Pantagraph**
Dec. 22, 1886

Interior, Rodgers Shoe Store, ca. 1895

Improved transportation opened the door for retailers to import goods from outside. The Rodgers family came over from Indiana when the east-west railroad was built into Bloomington, and began selling shoes manufactured "out east."

The early simple wagons gave way to fancier carriages, built in several Bloomington locations — one of which was the building at Front and Lumber still used by the Beich Candy Company.

Matern Carriage Factory, ca. 1870

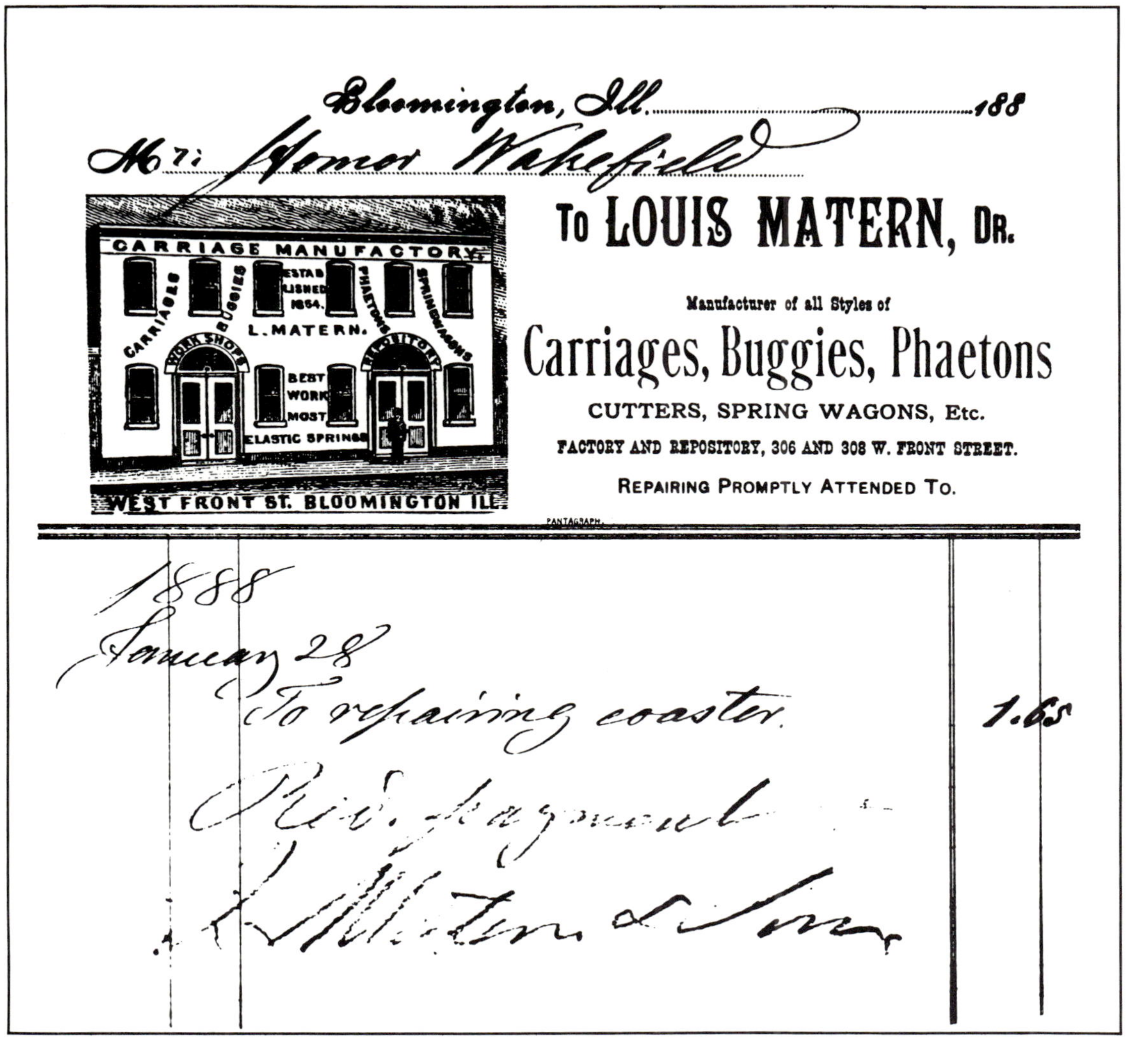

Bloomington, Ill. 188

Mr. Homer Wakefield

To **LOUIS MATERN, Dr.**

Manufacturer of all Styles of

Carriages, Buggies, Phaetons

CUTTERS, SPRING WAGONS, Etc.

FACTORY AND REPOSITORY, 306 AND 308 W. FRONT STREET.

REPAIRING PROMPTLY ATTENDED TO.

PANTAGRAPH.

1888 January 28	To repairing coaster.		1.65
	Rec'd payment		
	L. Matern & Son		

WICKIZER'S
HOME
Mrs. J. Wickizer
HOME BAKERY
602 N. MAIN ST.
BREAD, ROLLS,
CAKES & PIES
Mrs. J. Wickizer
HOME BAKERY

Wickizer's Home Bakery delivered goodies from the same building housing Susie's Cafe today at 603 North Main, using Bloomington built wagons.

Livery and horse stables dotted the commercial areas, and very few of the streets were paved.

Retail establishments occupied the lower floors of buildings, while the doctors and lawyers found office space in the upper stories.

100 Block, West Front Street

Kirkpatrick Furniture Store, North Main Street

C. W. KLEMM.
DRY GOODS & MILLINERY.
DRY GOODS & MILLINERY.
DRY GOODS.
DISEASES EYE & EAR
SURGICAL ROOMS
C. W. KLEMM.

Interior, Klemm's Dry Goods, ca. 1900

The courthouse was the magnet and Klemm's and Livingston's settled on two of its sides, there to stay for a century.

Outside, the streets were dusty. The dirt streets around the square gave way to pinewood blocks in 1870, and Napoleon Heafer laid the nation's first brick street—the block of Center Street on the west side of the courthouse—seven years later.

Dim gas lamps at each corner provided the only night-time illumination, but in the early 1880s arc lamps were hung on the courthouse dome and people rode in from the country at night to view the new electric lights.

C.W. Klemm ca. 1875

North side of square, ca. 1880

All of this urban growth required money, of course, and new banks began to meet the needs. Before 1850, there was little money to borrow in McLean County, and barter was common.

People's Bank broke ground in 1870 at Washington and Center and built the city's proudest building. The National Bank building anchored another corner of the square, and General Asahel Gridley's McLean County Bank—the oldest of them all—stood a block south of that, at Main and Front.

General Gridley's bank—built before 1855—still stands at that corner, now encapsulized in the aluminum of Mid-Illinois Title Services.

Peoples Bank, 1889

Interior, National Bank, ca. 1885

6. The Prairie Settled

Although most of McLean County's land had been claimed by the time the Civil War ended, much of the swampy prairie land was still not being cultivated.

Now, things began to happen. The railroads provided a means to haul both grain and livestock to market, new polished steel plows made easier the turning over of the sod, and ways were being found to drain the excess water off the prairie.

McLean County was ready to move to a role of feeding others — a cash-crop economy.

I.B. & W.R.R. crossing Sugar Creek E. M. Wilson, 1888

TILING

Chenoa's Matthew Scott and others dug large drainage ditches before the war, building bridges from field to field. The mole-ditcher later allowed for the burrowing of underground tunnels to help the water run off. But the coming of tile in the 1870s was what made tilling McLean County's soil practical.

They laid it by hand at first, then by special ditching machines, while steam-powered dredging machines widened the Sangamon and Mackinaw rivers and their tributaries.

The physical shape of McLean County was changing.

Tiling crew—Bellflower

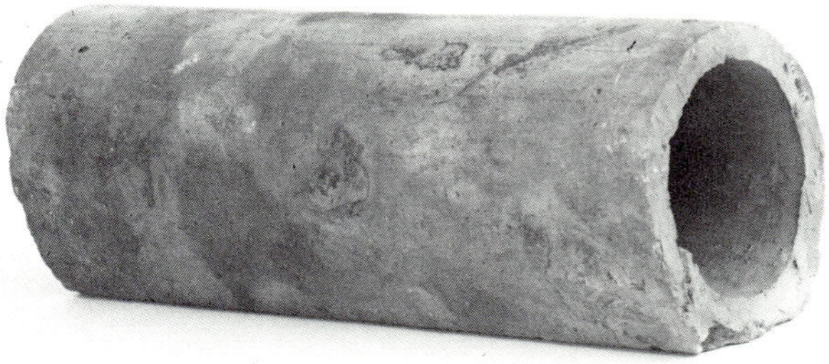

Tile section

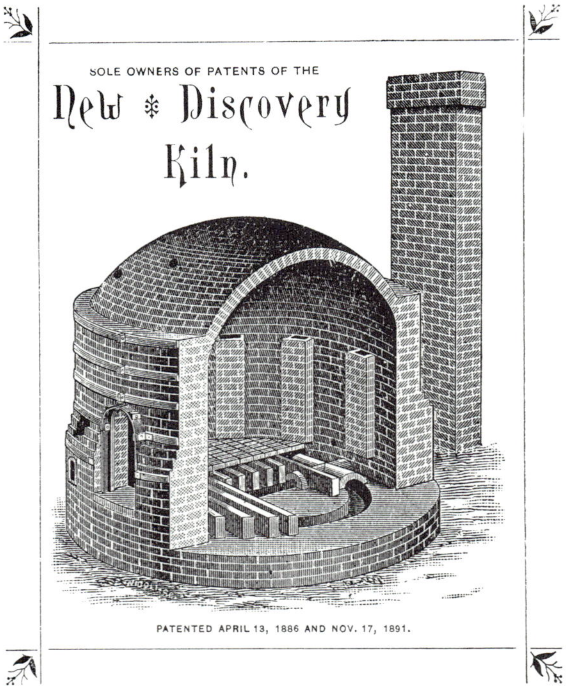

Tile ditching

Dredge boat, Old Town Township

Removing backdirt from the channel

PLOWING

". . . Mr. A.D. Benjamin is ploughing his pasture north of his house. This sod is virgin soil and the greater part of it has never been broken. Wagon tracks are plainly visible in the northern part. Traces of the old road that used to run diagonally across it before the country was fenced. Some of this pasture was plowed and fenced by an unknown person as early as 1840 but he abandoned it before he had raised anything. Furrows are still visible and the rails are lying around to this day . . ."

— Edward M. Wilson
March, 1883

Plowing near Bloomington, ca. 1915

HORSE POWER

Much of the change was being brought about by real horsepower — not the sleek horses of today, but large, strong draft horses, the most notable of which were the Percheron or Norman horses, bred and sold in Normal.

Ellis Dillon and his nephews, Isaiah and Levi, began dominating the fairs across the country right after the Civil War, and more importantly, began to impress upon farmers the enormous amount of work these beautiful Percherons could do.

Twelve-horse hitch

Percheron from the Stubblefield Stables

THE DILLON BROTHERS

This cut represents the Barn where this sale will be held.

By 1870, the Dillons were traveling to France, choosing horses from the Normandy region and shipping them home. Special trains, flying both French and American flags, would greet the ships in Boston or New York and crowds would gather.

Crowds gathered at Bloomington's Big Four station to watch them arrive, and customers followed from across the nation to pay two or three thousand dollars for a good Percheron. Selections were made from any of several Dillon barns, one of which still stands at 102 West Phoenix, Normal, across the tracks from city hall.

The beautiful frame home the Dillons bought sat on a hill east of Normal. Today, it is surrounded by more modern houses along William Drive, just north of Ash Park.

AT HOME

A family entertainment, ca. 1895

"... I enjoyed nothing more than to sit on the edge of the woodbox, toasting by the kitchen fire, while the wind blew and whistled outside ... There were no surroundings more enjoyable than those, as I pored over that book of animals, pondered over the terrible adventures of that man Cummings in Africa, or drew the blood-curdling picture of the ham-stringing of the elephant. But after all, I was pretty much of a boy ..."

— E. M. Wilson
1891

David Stephenson Farm, Danvers Township

Family farms, actually extended-family farms, dotted the McLean County landscape. Two, sometimes three, generations worked the land, shared the chores and lived on the same acreage. More often than not, they were helped by a hired man.

Fences were put up everywhere to keep the grazing livestock out of the fields, and keep the chickens out of the garden. Picket and rail fences came first, then barbed wire in the 1870s. Osage hedges often served the same purpose, but the hedge took up too much valuable land and most of it was eventually pulled out.

Wells were sunk to provide drinking water for the family and its animals. The hand pumps gradually gave way to wind mills as a means of bringing the water to the surface.

Marion's hired hand

LIVESTOCK

McLean County farmers raised and fed livestock from the start, allowing the animals to graze on the open prairie land. The county, in fact, boasted many honest-to-goodness cowboys, keeping track of huge numbers of cattle and hogs, eventually driving them overland to market.

But the railroads enabled the farmers to ship fattened livestock to far-away markets, and ensured that the stock would be fat when it got there. Area farmers began to improve the animals by breeding, and they began to spread the risk of doing business by raising several commodities — grain, hogs, cattle, sheep and perhaps some poultry.

Johnny Ramseyer and his pig "Columbia"

L. N. Kerrick's prize-winning cattle, 1904

Feeding the chickens

"Chicken thieves have been quite numerous of late. Mr. Goodrich, of near Holder, got up a few mornings ago and found that the greater part of his chickens and turkeys were gone, he also found one of his turkeys tied ready to be carried off . . . Mrs. Redman had a lot of her fine chickens stolen, among the lot was a fine rooster that had cost her $6."

— **Cooksville Weekly Advocate,** Sept. 29, 1893

HARVEST

Hand labor was still the order of the day, and a good, fast husker had everybody's respect, tossing the ears against the bounceboard to be hauled into the crib for drying and storing. The shocks were left to dry in the field — future fodder for the livestock.

The work was hard and it took large numbers of neighbors to get a crop out of the fields. When dinnertime came, the workers teamed to put away legendary quantities of food.

Husking corn

Corn shocks

Elevating corn

Threshing crew, 1887, near Carlock

Downtown Hudson

THE TOWN

"100,000 dollars was paid out at Ellsworth during the month of Jan uary by the buyers here, to farme of Blue Mound, Padua and Martir Townships, for grain and stock shipped and bought."

— **Ellsworth Chronicle** Jan. 28, 1882

Grain elevators at Gridley

'ROSPER

Southbound Illinois Central, south of Bloomington

Grain elevators sprang up alongside the railroad tracks, and villages were built around the elevators. When the farmer brought his grain to market, he picked up his mail, bought his groceries and hardware, visited the doctor and blacksmith and heard the latest news. The town had become the center of rural trade.

There were, in fact, some 49 settlements in McLean County by the 1890s, almost all of them along the railroad, all of them containing grain elevators, and spaced an average of five miles apart.

The railroad became a primary source of rural transportation, with a stop at each village. Boarding the Lake Erie and Western at Saybrook, the rider would endure stops at Arrowsmith, Ellsworth, Padua and Holder before arriving at Bloomington. Eastern McLean County residents told fellow passengers the L.E.&W. stood for "leave early and walk."

Rates charged for shipping grain were quite high early, but four cases filed in McLean County, by Reuben Benjamin, challenged arbitrary rates, reached the U.S. Supreme Court, brought about government control, and laid the groundwork for the Interstate Commerce Commission.

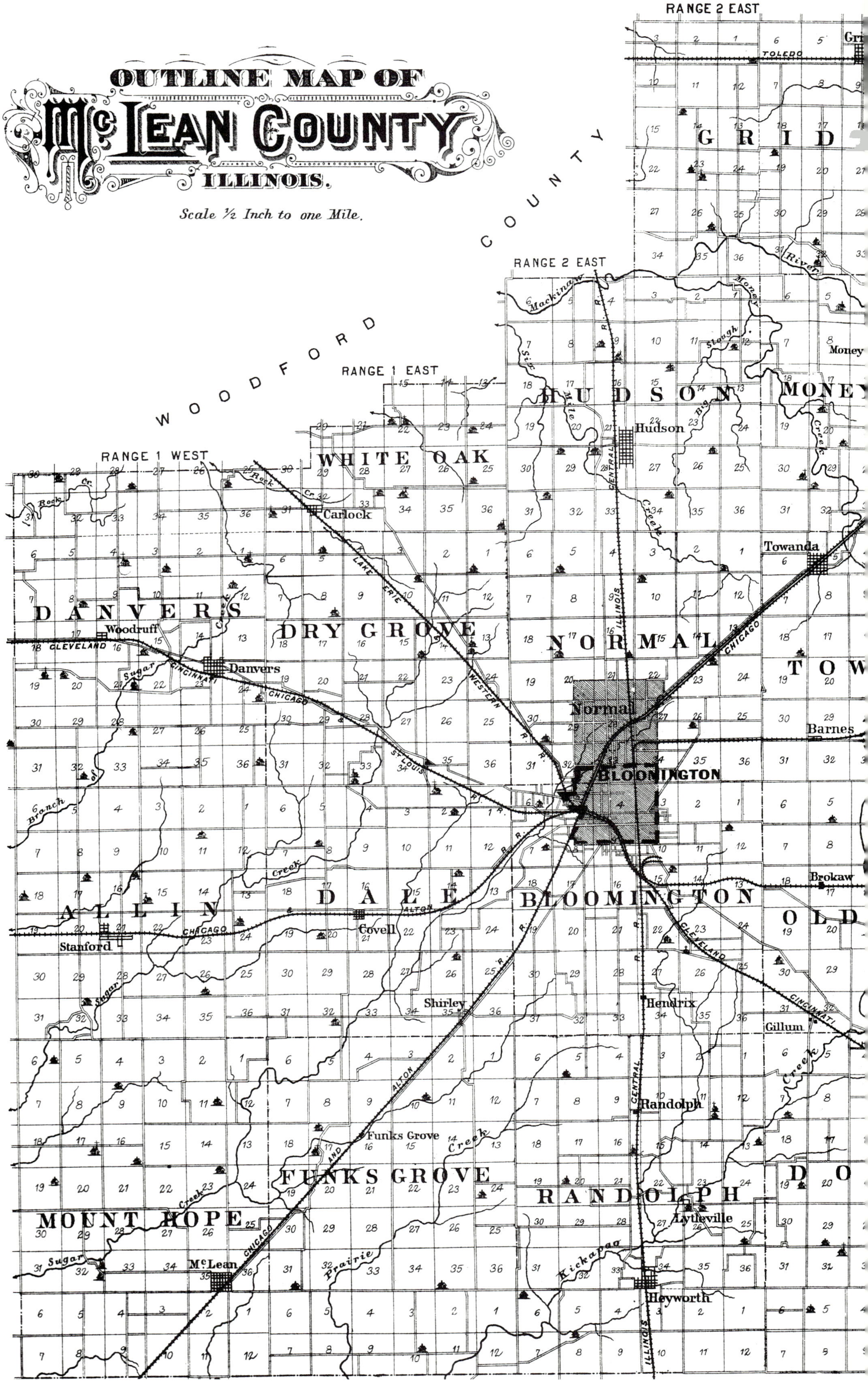
OUTLINE MAP OF
McLEAN COUNTY
ILLINOIS.
Scale ½ Inch to one Mile.
WOODFORD COUNTY
RANGE 2 EAST
RANGE 2 EAST
RANGE 1 EAST
RANGE 1 WEST
GRID
HUDSON
MONEY
WHITE OAK
DANVERS
DRY GROVE
NORMAL
TOW
ALLIN
DALE
BLOOMINGTON
OLD
FUNKS GROVE
RANDOLPH
DO
MOUNT HOPE
Hudson
Money
Carlock
Towanda
Woodruff
Danvers
Normal
Barnes
BLOOMINGTON
Brokaw
Stanford
Covell
Shirley
Hendrix
Gillum
Randolph
Funks Grove
Lytleville
McLean
Heyworth
TOLEDO
Mackinaw
Six Mile
Big Slough
Money Creek
River
Rock Cr.
Sugar
Branch
Creek
Prairie
Kickapoo
Sugar Creek
CLEVELAND
CINCINNATI
CHICAGO
LAKE ERIE
WESTERN
R.R.
ST LOUIS
ILLINOIS
CENTRAL
ALTON
AND

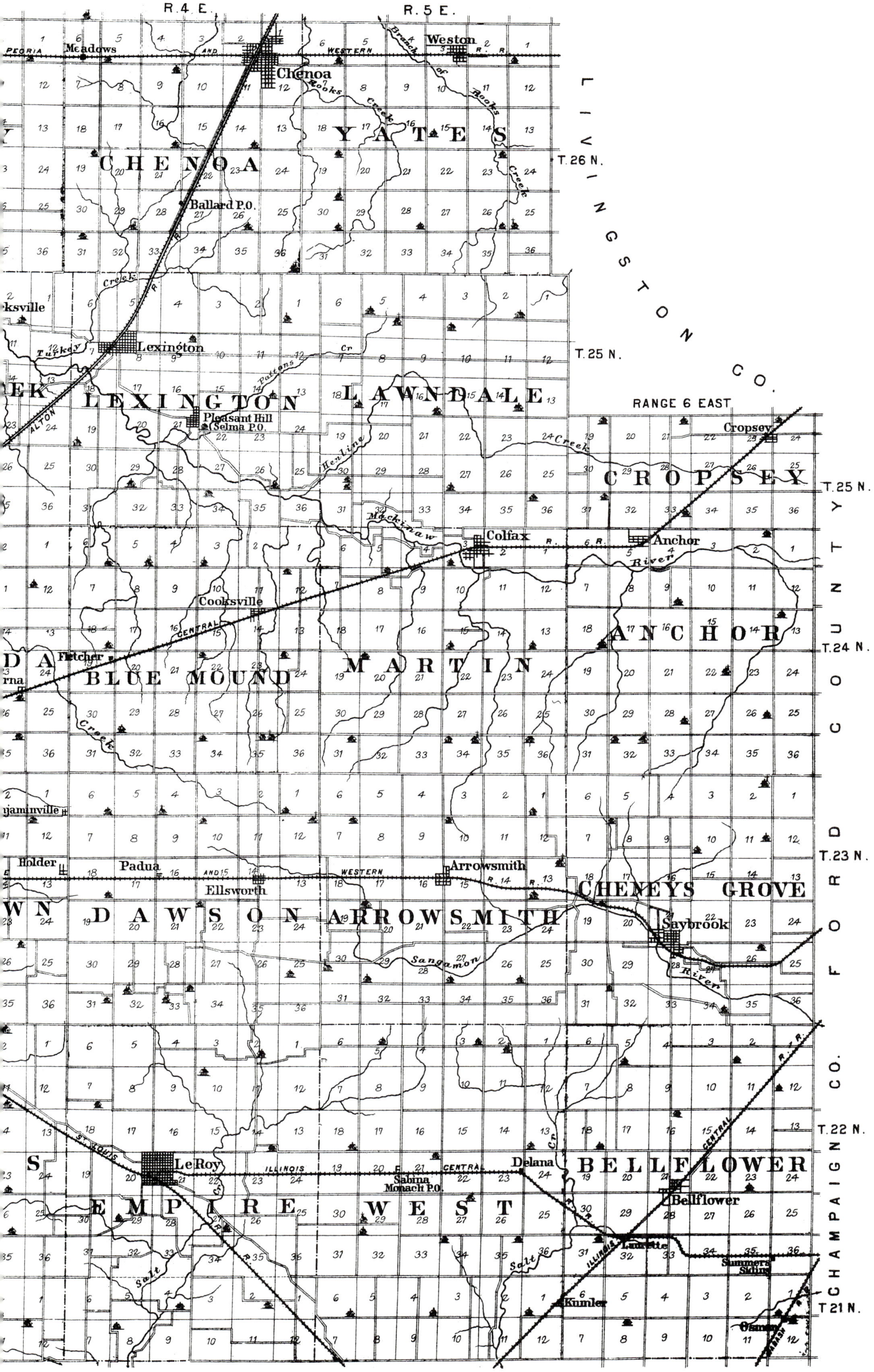
R.4 E.
R.5 E.
Meadows
Peoria and Western R.R.
Chenoa
Weston
Branch of Rooks Creek
Rooks Creek
YATES
CHENOA
T.26 N.
Ballard P.O.
LIVINGSTON CO.
Lexington
Turkey Creek
Pattens Cr
T.25 N.
LEXINGTON
LAWNDALE
RANGE 6 EAST
Pleasant Hill (Selma P.O.
Cropsey
Henline Creek
Alton
CROPSEY
T.25 N.
Mackinaw
Colfax
Anchor
River
Cooksville
Central
ANCHOR
T.24 N.
Fletcher
BLUE MOUND
MARTIN
Creek
FORD COUNTY
Holder
Padua
Western
Arrowsmith
T.23 N.
Ellsworth
CHENEYS GROVE
DAWSON
ARROWSMITH
Saybrook
Sangamon
River
St. Louis
LeRoy
Illinois Central
Delana
BELLFLOWER
T.22 N.
Sabina
Monach P.O.
EMPIRE
WEST
Bellflower
Lunette
Summers Siding
Salt
Cr.
Kumler
CHAMPAIGN CO.
T.21 N.
Wabash

Saybrook, 1870

Most of the towns were similar in appearance, with unpaved streets, mostly wooden awnings overhanging the sidewalks, giving way to brick buildings with canvas awnings by the turn of the century.

Competition between them was spirited, however, with the newspaper in one railing at the good citizens of another. Saybrook contained 1,200 residents in 1890 and was called "Tuffy" because of the rough and ready characteristics of its people. But that didn't stop the Gibson City people, across the county line, from posting a tongue-in-cheek poster.

A LeRoy insurance man used a poster in another way, sending home a free school picture with each of the children and reaping some advertising benefit.

Saybrook, 1900

SMALL POX IN SAYBROOK!

WHEREAS, it is reported that Small Pox has made its appearance in the towns of Saybrook, Belleflower and Elliott and the Island of Cuba, and that the inhabitants of the towns above mentioned are so frightened as to be bereft of reason and liable to wander off into other towns; Therefore it is hereby ordered by the Gibson Protective Committee, that a strict quarantine be enforced against all of said places, and that breastworks of the hight of 40 feet be erected on all highways leading from said towns into the village of Gibson, and that all persons attempting to enter said village of Gibson from any of said towns be immediately soaked for 48 hours in copperas water and then buried in the town park 24 feet deep.

And it is gratuitously recommended to the county of McLean, which has been continuously infected with said disease for the past six months, that all citizens of Saybrook so bereft of reason as aforesaid be immersed in a solution of asafoetida and camphor, and packed away for the inspection of future generations.

All frightened lunatics are entrusted with the enforcement of this order. By order of

THE GIBSON PROTECTIVE COMMITTEE.

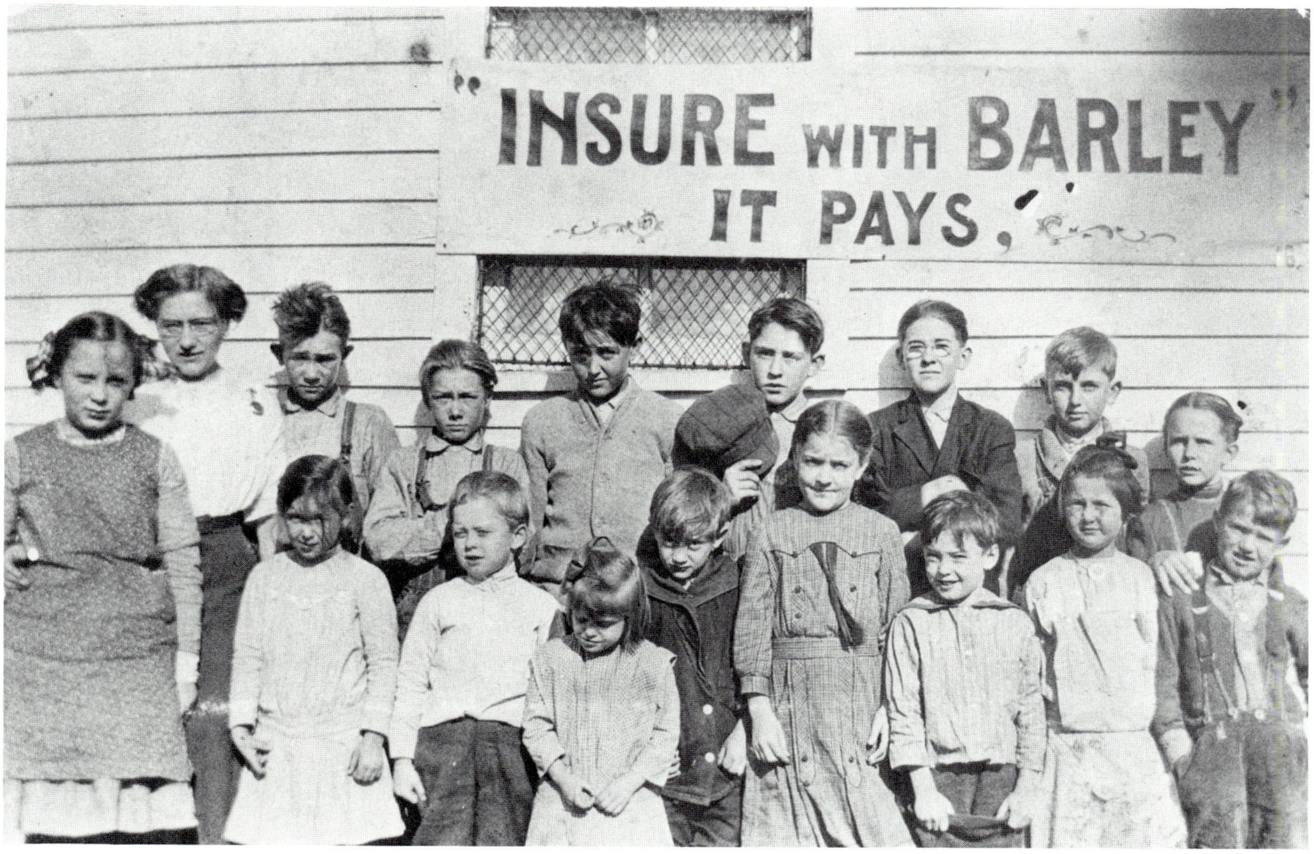

A message for the parents.
White Star School, West Township

The elevators and often post offices kept many of the smaller unincorporated villages alive — places like Kumler and Yuton, Fletcher and McNulta.

Voters had a more intimate relationship with officials — good news if the voter was on his supervisor's good side, possibly bad news otherwise. Residents were sometimes assessed several days' labor, rather than tax dollars, to maintain roads.

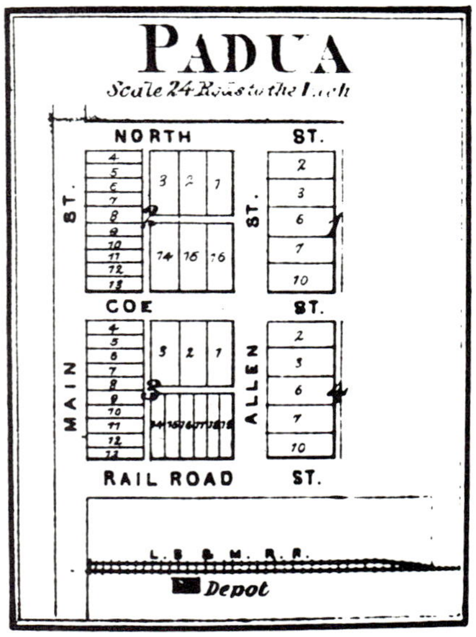

George Brown's grocery/cobbler shop/post office/library; Bentown

MT. HOPE REPUBLICAN PRIMARY ELECTION.

MARCH 14, 1896.

Township Ticket.

For Supervisor,
MARION McCORMICK.

For Town Clerk,
S. B. VANNESS.

For Highway Commissioner,
ISAAC STUBBLEFIELD.
T. R. PLACE.

For School Trustees,
SAMUEL B. KINSEY.

For Assessor,
WM. T. GIBBS.
N. L. KINSEY.

For Collector,
C. W. WHEELOCK.
W. W. HARRIS.
CHAS. M. PUMPELLY.

For Delegates to County Convention,
EDWARD STUBBLEFIELD.
JACOB FUNK.
W. J. BARNES.
W. H. WRIGHT.
S. B. VANNESS.
JAMES SNYDER.

For Alternates.
S. M. OVERAKER.

Gridley Town Hall

"At the (Colfax) town election held on Thursday . . . 81 votes were polled. Some 20 votes were not cast, as some did not wish to take part in the election. Others had not been residents of the place long enough to entitle them to a vote. With a full vote we would poll about 100 . . ."

— **Ellsworth Chronicle**
Jan. 28, 1882

"... BRINGING IN THE SHEAVES ..."

Healthy churches abounded in the towns, and they dotted the countryside too. In a day when the extended family occupied the farms, several generations of the same family would attend church together.

The church was a center for social activity with revivals and box socials and lectures all bringing neighbors together. And the church was a center for social enforcement, too. Standards of conduct were set and pressure put on the congregation to adhere to them.

PROGRAM

—OF—

WEST TOWNSHIP S. S. CONVENTION,

—TO BE HELD AT—

CENTER CHAPEL,

—ON—

SUNDAY, AUG. 14, 1892.

LEROY JOURNAL PRINT.

Christian Church, Shirley

12-1 :30P. M.—Dinner.............................

SONG.

1:30-1:45 P. M.—Business Meeting..............

1:45-2 P. M.—Childrens' Song Service..........

2-2:30 P. M.—Childrens' Meeting conducted by [illegible]......[redacted] West

SONG.

2:30-3 P. M.—Christ and the Children. Miss Lizzie Mace

3-3:30 P. M.—What is my duty to the Sunday School....................Rev. Geo. Arnold

3:30-4 P. M.—Question Drawer led by.....Rev. A. Wills

The LeRoy Orchestra will be in attendance. Bring Gospel Hymns No. 5, also bring your baskets well filled and spend the day with us.

J. T. RUTLEDGE, Sec. pro tem.

ALEX. DANIEL, Vice Pres.

Cumberland Presbyterian Church, LeRoy

A new crop

Friday, Feb. 24th, 1882.

The Regular Baptist Church of Old Town McLean Co, Ill met according to previous appointment and after reading of the Scriptures by Bro. Frink, prayer and covenant exercises; proceeded to business, Bro. G. S. Creel, Mod.

4th On motion and second appointed the treasurer to visit Mr. Riebe for the purpose of ascertaining how much the church owes him, for his services last winter and to pay the debt, from the money now in the treasury, and that a collection be taken at the next meeting to replace the amount in the treasury; also that he try to secure Mr. Riebe to make fires and keep the house in order, & learn what he will charge for his services

5th. A charge was brought against Bro. James Hagerman, for dancing and using profane language and against Sisters Julia and Mary Hagerman for dancing.

6th. On motion and second appointed Deacons Harrison and Creel to visit them and request them to attend the next meeting.

7th. On motion and second changed the meeting from Friday to Saturday.

8th. Bro. Bingham wishing to be released from the clerkship and having resigned at the January meeting -- was released from the duty of longer serving as clerk.

9th: A motion being made and seconded that Florence Ballard be appointed clerk was voted on and carried.

Omitted

1st. Reading the rules of order.

2nd Reading the minutes of the last meeting

3rd Bro Dooley reported that he had written to two parties for pulpit supply, without success. Bro. Frink reported that he had written to Bro. Asa Ballard of Bloomington, and that he had agreeded to preach for us March, 12th.

10. On motion and second adjourned till meeting in course. Closed with prayer by Bro Livingston.

G. S. Creel. Moderator

Florence Ballard Clerk.

On box social night, the young ladies outdid each other in preparing decorated boxes of food, and the fellows tried to outbid each other for the right to enjoy the feast — and, not incidentally, the company of the lady who prepared it.

Many of the churches built in the second half of the 19th century still stand. But most of the one-room schools are gone.

It was 1855 when the Illinois legislature passed the "free school law," allowing townships to elect school boards and tax landowners to build schools and hire teachers.

Methodist Church, Covell

Garfield Community School picnic

RURAL SCHOOLS

Schools began to appear, to serve each few sections of land, and the pupils walked to get to them. Teachers were often only a year older than the oldest student. They seldom boasted more than a high school education, and they attempted to instill some knowledge into children over eight grades.

All grades were not taught each year in each school. Grades two, four, six and eight might be offered one year, with grades one, three, five and seven the next. Students in three of the grades would be expected to work on their lessons while the others were reciting theirs at the front of the class.

Price School, Bloomington Township
William Brigham, Teacher

Skinner School, Hudson Township, ca. 1885

The Robin Hood Play

Towanda School

Schoolboy grafitti

Rosencrans School, West Township

Recess at a rural school

May Day, Pleasant Ridge School, Danvers Township

WORK/PLAY

Recess was the best time. Those quarter-hour breaks in the middle of the morning and afternoon provided time for a short baseball game (nobody in McLean County was playing football or basketball in those days) or hop-scotch or some races. The girls and boys almost always played separately.

The women attended "club," the men participated in barn raisings and threshing, the families attended the childrens' spelling bees — and each became a social occasion.

Barn raising

Sewing carpet rags at Mrs. J.H. Davis's

Rural road, ca. 1900

William Struebing horse sale, Saybrook, 1906

Not everybody made it. People sold out from time to time. But even the auction sale was a social event. It was a chance to exchange helpful information on farming, compare prices, complain about politicians and the weather, and renew friendships.

It took a stubborn desire just to get there during much of the year. The dirt roads became seas of mud and often were impassable for weeks at a time.

Horizons were expanding, McLean County people could ride their bicycles to Mackinaw Dells on a Sunday or take the train to a picnic in Kappa.

It was inevitable that a few would leave, seeking new opportunity. Some, like rural Hudson's Charlie Jones, wouldn't come back. Charlie would become "Buffalo" Jones, a star in Zane Grey novels. But others, like Eugene Funk, would return. Funk would travel in Europe, attend Yale, and come home to Funk's Grove to revolutionize the seed corn industry through the hybridization of corn.

Bicyclists, McLean, ca. 1895

7. The Age of Elegance

W.R. White residence, 612 North East Street, ca. 1895

Post-war prosperity was evident everywhere in McLean County in the 1880s and 1890s. Beautiful elms and sugar maple trees flanked the streets — many of which were brick by now — and large homes, displaying conspicuous consumption, competed for attention.

Apart from a usually sizeable midsection, a major measure of a man's success was a large home, servants and a wife, whose function it was to display his wealth. Objects of art abounded at Hazel Funk's girlhood home at 307 East Grove and Mary Gridley's home, "The Oaks," a block west — both typical of the period.

Parlors seemed to shout "look how cultured I am," often with a feminine touch. It is believed many of the Gridley pieces were obtained after the general's death. "Asahel Gridley would have spotted that fancy china doll in front of the fireplace, and kicked it halfway to Logan County," someone said.

700 block East Grove Street, south side, 1889

Parlor, "The Oaks", ca. 1885

Dining room, "The Oaks", ca. 1885

". . . In those days they believed in gilding the lily and our fine white walnut doors and woodwork all over the downstairs were coated with layers of stain and varnish and then 'grained' to look like the natural wood — which, of course, it did not! Often have I watched painters perform this technique of 'graining' with their brushes . . . The walls in the dining room were 'frescoed' with designs of plants native to Funk's Grove. There were branching blackberries, wild grape vines, among others. And around the frieze (every wall had friezes then) were round painted panels showing the game birds to be found in our prairies and woods and streams. There were paintings of quail and snipe, woodcock and prairie chickens . . ."

— Hazel Funk Holmes

BUILDING THE DREAMS

George H. Miller, ca. 1880

Snell residence, 1206 North Main

Just as designer jeans were to become the rage in the 1980s, designer houses were as much the thing a century before. For the first time, there was enough residential business to support a good local architect, and George Miller filled the bill.

Miller designed the county jail in 1880 — a building that stood more than a hundred years. In the following quarter-century, he planned the large Romanesque rectory still standing beside Holy Trinity Church, the Central Fire Station, now a Front Street restaurant, ISU's Cook Hall, and the Miller Park Pavilion.

"Mr. Thornton Snell has accepted the plans of architect George Miller for his handsome new home on North Main St. There will be some slight alterations on the house. Bids on the barn will be opened Friday."

— **Weekly Pantagraph**
July 5, 1889

"Mr. M.L. Popple is having plans drawn at the . . . office of Mr. George H. Miller for a $5000 residence, to be built on North Main street."

— **Weekly Pantagraph**
Sept. 25, 1885

Popple residence, 1307 North Main

Senseney residence, 312 West Virginia, Normal

"Architect Miller has drawn plans for a $6000 residence which Mr. H.M. Senseney wil erect on his home place near the woolen mill."

— **Weekly Pantagraph**
May 4, 1888

UP-TO-DATE HOMES

"In publishing "UP-TO-DATE HOMES' it was my intention to show a number of plans and views of buildings which are inexpensive in construction, and suit the majority of people who are desirous of making their home a convenient, artistic, and comfortable dwelling . . ."

— Paul O. Moratz, 1899

Interesting homes Miller designed stand today at 205 North Center in Lexington, and in Bloomington, 415 East Jefferson, the southeast corner of Grove and Clayton, the "castle" opposite Franklin Park on Prairie Street, and Miller's own home at 405 West Market.

Arthur Pillsbury and Paul Moratz were also designing rambling homes. Moratz supplemented his fee by selling many of the mass-produced fancy mouldings from his planing mill. For the first time, houses were being designed with electricity and indoor plumbing.

Daughters of Bloomington west side coal miners and other laborers provided a pool of domestic help, allowing time for the homeowners to indulge in some front porch sitting.

The front porch, in fact, served as a summertime entertainment center as neighbors strolled down the sidewalk to call on neighbors. With the sidewalk strollers and front porch sitters keeping an eye on things, cities were safer in those days before we became a backyard society.

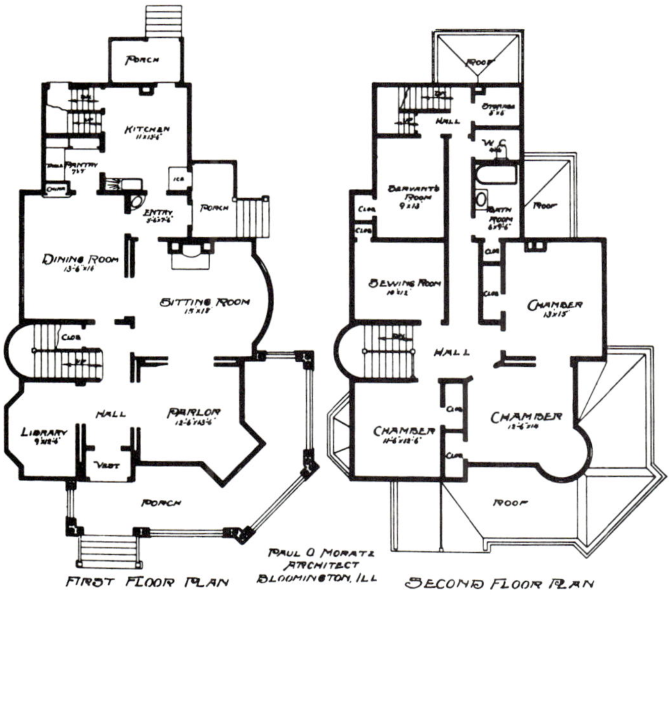

NUMBER 45 OF VOLUME XXII. BLOOMINGTON, ILLINOIS: SUNDAY, DECEM

FASHIONS

Weekend supplements like *The Sunday Eye* chronicled the doings of the east siders, but most of its pages were filled with boilerplate fashion news and filler material printed in Chicago.

McLean County people were into ornate fashions and as their incomes grew, they became more willing to sit still for more frequent style changes. Many of the best garments were produced locally.

LEISURE ACTIVITIES

For the first time, people had enough money to allow them to indulge in pleasure activities. Servants relieved wives of their household duties long enough for card parties, while their well-dressed children enjoyed new toys.

The invited crowd at Camp Bohemia, meanwhile, strummed guitars and rode high-wheelers in the '80s and "safety" bicycles in the '90s.

Athletics were polite games and the young men and women competed together.

A card game, ca. 1895

At the Sterling residence, ca. 1900

At Camp Bohemia

NEW YEAR'S DAY CALLING

When the first day of the year rolled around, young men scanned the newspaper lists of open houses being hosted by the dames and their daughters, stuffed their pockets with calling cards, donned silk hats and set out to make the rounds. The cutters jammed East Washington Street, and the jingling of bells was heard all over Bloomington.

Parties sometimes lasted for days at a time and more than one well-to-do young man prepared for future events by arranging to store dinner suits in several attics. When the canvas was placed over the carpeting and the orchestra started to play for dancing, the quick change of clothes without the long trip home was a real plus.

Northwest corner McLean & Washington, ca. 1880

PARTIES

"The Children's Party," 1901

". . . There was one party at our house that surpassed all others — The Pink Domino Ball that wound up the season's gayety for that winter . . . The invitation requested both men and women to wear long pink dominoes over their evening clothes, and pink masques. Only pink would be acceptable.

All of the furniture was moved out from the downstairs rooms, canvas was tacked over every carpet. Mother and Father as hosts remained unmasked but everyone else wore masks. There must have been two hundred pink-clad maskers and from the curving stairway, the sea of whirling pink figures, as they danced through the rooms, was a sight to remember . . . At the stroke of midnight the orchestra leader stopped the music announcing that masks could come off and that supper would be served upstairs. The cateress served shrimp salad and slices of ham, pink strawberry ice cream and cake with pink icing but the coffee was black!"

— Hazel Funk Holmes

CLUBS

In better weather, there were picnics in Funk's Grove (the 12-mile trip from Bloomington took only an hour and a half by horse and buggy), and charity cotillions. There was no United Way and there were very few fund drives for various institutions.

Leisure time allowed the blossoming of business and social clubs — the Masons and Knights of Pythias, the Grange, the Amateur Musical Club, and many more. The ladies of the Ladies' Library Association worked to secure the building of Withers Library at Washington and East streets, and the headquarters of The Bloomington Club on the library's second floor attested to the help given by that social club's 150 male members.

The ladies also yielded to the gentlemen a few blocks away. It was a girls-only tennis club when it began in the 1880s at the northwest corner of Jefferson and Madison, but men had become members by 1890.

The Margldowhe Tennis Club was named by using the first initial of each of the charter member girls. One of them, Rachel Crothers (standing, second from right), would leave the tennis court and the city and become America's most famous woman playwright.

Margldowhe Tennis Club, ca. 1890

There was time for cycling to Mackinaw Dells or out the East Grove Street Road. When they formed it in 1883, it was said the Bloomington Bicycle Club was the first such club in the United States.

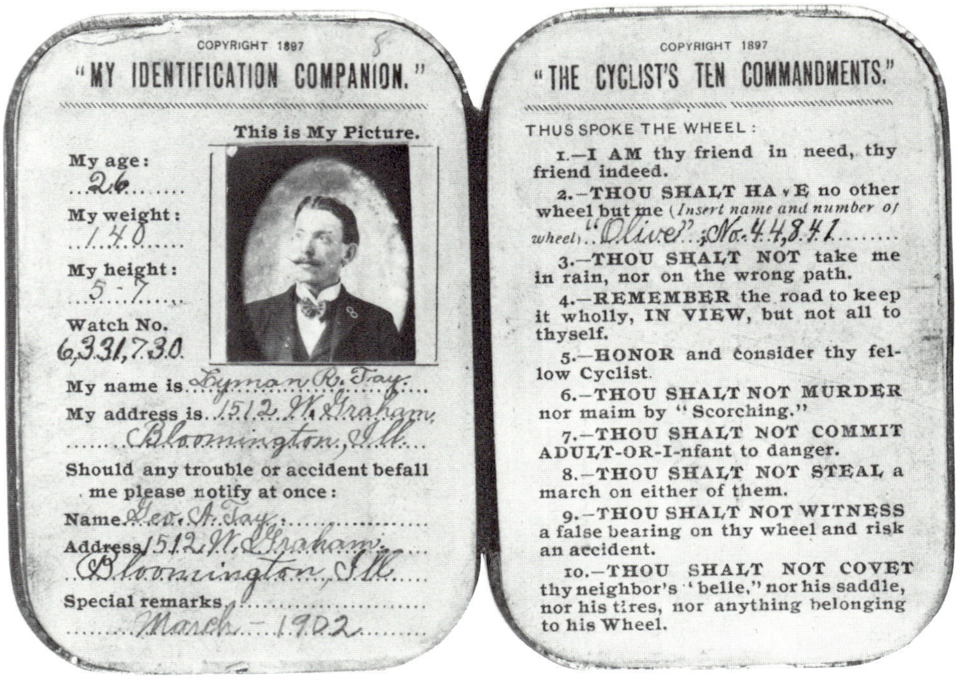
COPYRIGHT 1897

"MY IDENTIFICATION COMPANION."

This is My Picture.

My age: 26

My weight: 140

My height: 5-7

Watch No. 6,331,730.

My name is Lyman R. Tay.

My address is 1512 W. Graham, Bloomington, Ill.

Should any trouble or accident befall me please notify at once:

Name Geo. A. Tay

Address 1512 W. Graham, Bloomington, Ill.

Special remarks March - 1902

COPYRIGHT 1897

"THE CYCLIST'S TEN COMMANDMENTS."

THUS SPOKE THE WHEEL:

1.—I AM thy friend in need, thy friend indeed.

2.—THOU SHALT HAVE no other wheel but me (Insert name and number of wheel) "Olive" ; No. 44,841

3.—THOU SHALT NOT take me in rain, nor on the wrong path.

4.—REMEMBER the road to keep it wholly, IN VIEW, but not all to thyself.

5.—HONOR and consider thy fellow Cyclist.

6.—THOU SHALT NOT MURDER nor maim by "Scorching."

7.—THOU SHALT NOT COMMIT ADULT-OR-I-nfant to danger.

8.—THOU SHALT NOT STEAL a march on either of them.

9.—THOU SHALT NOT WITNESS a false bearing on thy wheel and risk an accident.

10.—THOU SHALT NOT COVET thy neighbor's "belle," nor his saddle, nor his tires, nor anything belonging to his Wheel.

Bloomington Bicycle Club, 1885

DRAMATICS

Schroder's Opera House, Phoenix Hall and Durley Hall all surrounded Bloomington's courthouse square, evidence that people now had time for dramatics. University High School's Rachel Crothers appeared in some of the plays, and within years was writing them for New York audiences. Wesleyan's Maud Light appeared in others, and within years was known as America's foremost actress.

Bloomington's society elite performed in "London Assurance" and others at the Durley, usually to benefit the public library or the girls' industrial home.

Cast of "London Assurance", ca. 1892

GRAND OPERA HOUSE

When Marie Litta returned from a triumphant European concert tour in 1877, she chose Durley Hall for her performance for the home folks. When Margaret Illington returned with much fanfare some years later, she performed at the Grand Opera House, on the north side of Market Street, near East.

But the need was evident for a hall of larger capacity. The new Coliseum was finished at Roosevelt and Front in time for a grand ball two days after Christmas, 1898. It seated 5,000.

PROGRAM
New Coliseum
BLOOMINGTON, ILL.
LEWIS J. SEYBOLD, Lessee and Manager.

CHURCHES

McLean County's churches were seating more people, too, and becoming social centers. The fire and brimstone message of the county's early preachers was still heard, but more congregations were hearing appeals to reason, to beauty and truth.

No fewer than ten churches were built within a few blocks of the courthouse — the area just east of the business district becoming a church row. St. Matthew's Episcopal, First Baptist, Christian Science, Unitarian and Second Presbyterian churches, and the Jewish synagogue competed for attention in a five-block area.

Interior, St. Matthew's Episcopal Church

econd Presbyterian Church

Church membership was high, but belonging to the "right" church was, perhaps, even more important to a number of people.

The churches were kicking up their heels a bit, becoming semi-entertainment centers. An organ concert would have been frowned upon a few years earlier.

SOUVENIR PROGRAM

Dedicatory Matinee and Concert . . .

OF THE

NEW ORGAN,

Of the First M. E. Church,

BLOOMINGTON, ILLINOIS.

BY

Frederic Archer, Concert Organist, and
Genevra Johnstone-Bishop, Soprano.

Thursday, May 30th, 4 o'clock.
Thursday Evening, May 30th, 8 o'clock.

BIG-TIME POLITICS

Political power was nothing new for McLean County, but the election of a vice president of the United States was, nevertheless, heady stuff. When Adlai Stevenson left for Washington and his term with Grover Cleveland in 1893, a whole trainload of locals went with him.

The charter train, in fact, was a hotel for the "Stevenson Escort Club" during inauguration week, parked on a side track not far from the White House. There have never again been so many Bloomington people in Washington D.C. at one time.

Cleveland and Stevenson

Stevenson party leaving for Washington

Cleve and Steve

(Tune: "When Johnny Comes Marching Home")

"Our Cleve and Steve,
We do believe,
Will win!
Will win!
In eighteen hundred and ninety-three
We'll see
Them in!
For they are right, and right makes might,
Where American people are in the fight.
And they'll show at the polls a glorious
sight
As voters come marching in."

— R.M. McS.

Stevenson Escort Club at Mount Vernon, 1893

"Clover Lawn", home of Judge Davis 1870-1886

At that, Stevenson and Cleveland failed by a thousand votes to carry McLean County against Republican Harrison. The GOP had controlled the White House, with the exception of one term, for more than three decades, and it was Bloomington's David Davis, more than any other man, who put them there.

Davis was one of Bloomington's first attorneys when he arrived in the 1830s, buying the practice of Jesse Fell. His acquaintance with Lincoln grew to a close friendship after Davis was elected judge of the 8th Circuit. The two of them often traveled together between court sessions in Bloomington, Danville, Decatur and Pekin. Lincoln was, in fact, a guest in the Davis home the night before he delivered the speech that launched the Illinois Republican Party at Major's Hall in 1856. Davis would later become executor of Lincoln's estate.

He was, with Lincoln, a strong Whig, then a devout Republican. He was the driving force behind Lincoln's presidential bid. But Davis became known as an independent during his days on the United States Supreme Court, and was a prime candidate to win the presidential nomination in 1872 when a maverick Liberal Republican group formed a third party in Cincinnati. Horace Greeley snared the nomination instead, but Davis's independence contributed to a Republican presidency four years later. When an electoral commission was set up to decide the disputed election between Rutherford B. Hayes and Samuel Tilden, Justice Davis was in line to become its fifteenth member — joining seven Republicans and seven Democrats and, in effect, casting the vote that would decide the presidency.

Davis resigned the bench to take an appointment to represent Illinois in the Senate, declining to serve on the commission and, because the justice next in line to become the commission's fifteenth member was a Republican, awarded GOP candidate Hayes the White House.

"Judge Davis is one of the most truly independent men in America. The Creator gave him not only a great deal of brains but a great deal of conscience and a great deal of self-reliance."

— **Chicago Times**
Jan. 26, 1877

David Davis

"PRIVATE JOE"

Joseph W. Fifer

If Bloomington was a seat of political influence, much of it came from "Clover Lawn," the Davis mansion built "east of town." But Franklin Square was the scene of political doings, too, with the Stevenson home opposite the park on McLean Street and Governor Fifer's home in the same block.

Joe Fifer had walked to town from rural Danvers as a youth to hear Lincoln speak on the courthouse square, and he lived to become Illinois's grand old man of Lincoln's party. Leaders beat a path to his door long after he was defeated for re-election in 1892 by John Altgeld, who ran on a ticket with Fifer's neighbor, vice-presidential candidate Stevenson.

" 'How did you get the name 'Private Joe?' I asked. He laughed, saying:

'You see, when I sought the Republican nomination for governor of Illinois in 1888 I had six candidates against me—Gen. Smith, then lieutenant governor, Gen. McNulta, Gen. Reinecker, Col. Clark E. Carr, Maj. Connelly, and Capt. Frank Wright. You see I was the only private soldier among the contenders and the cry went up, 'Why not take a private?'. . . It took like wildfire and I was nominated. Then, in the election a major general, John M. Palmer, was the Democratic candiate—and that settled it. I was elected . . .' "

— James O'Donnel Bennett
"Private Joe" Fifer

JOHN M. HAMILTON

Fifer wasn't Bloomington's first governor. John Hamilton left his home at 502 South Clayton (a house still standing, as are the Davis, Stevenson and Fifer homes) to serve in the Illinois Senate in 1876. He was only 29 years old. Hamilton was elected Senate president pro tem three years later, and lieutenant governor the year after that. When Davis retired from the United States Senate in 1883, Governor Shelby Cullom replaced him, and, at age 35, John Hamilton found himself governor of Illinois.

It wasn't a happy experience. Hamilton called out the National Guard to put down labor unrest in Southern Illinois, imposed new taxes and was turned aside by his own party at primary election time 18 months later. They called Hamilton "the blonde mistake."

John M. Hamilton

Company F, 3rd Illinois Infantry, ca. 1898

THE HAYMARKET CASE

Labor was slow to organize in Illinois, but when the 300 coal miners in Bloomington unionized in 1871, they almost immediately went on strike.

Within 15 years, strikes were commonplace. Anti-labor sentiment boiled over in Chicago's Haymarket Square in 1886 during a labor rally when someone threw a bomb and killed seven policemen. Lynch mob sentiment prevailed and four of the eight co-conspirator defendants were summarily hanged following a brief trial in Chicago. A fifth committed suicide.

In Bloomington, Chief Supreme Court Justice John M. Scott smelled vigilante justice and saved the day for the remaining three defendants two weeks after the hangings.

"Yesterday morning at 9 o'clock Judge Scott reached his office and resumed his careful examination of the brief and record in the anarchists' cases, and a little before 11 o'clock had affixed his signature to an order granting a new lease of life to the prisoners. . . . Instantly the press representatives were scaling the stairs, four steps at a time, and in less time than it takes to tell it were bowing in the presence of the Judge . . . Five minutes later the wires were hot with telegrams to the Chicago, New York, St. Louis and Philadelphia papers and the Associated Press. In fifteen minutes the anarchists were giving thanks in their cells, and yesterday afternoon the crowned heads and the socialists and anarchists of all Europe were discussing the news from Bloomington . . ."

— **Daily Leader**
November 26, 1886

McLean County Courthouse, 1868-1900

John Milton Scott

"After inspecting the foregoing manuscript of the record, the undersigned, one of the justices of the supreme court of the State, is of the opinion that there is reasonable ground for granting the writ of error applied for in the case. It is therefore ordered that a writ of error be granted in this cause, and . . . a supersedeas to each and every one of the plaintiffs in error, viz: August Spies, Michael Schwab, Samuel Fielden, Albert R. Parsons, Adolph Fischer, George Engel, Louis Lingg, and Oscar W. Neebe . . . to stay the execution of the judgment pronounced by the criminal court of Cook county . . ."

— John M. Scott
Chief Justice of the Supreme Court

Judge Scott's decision vindicated the labor movement and may have startled conservative Republicans. He, too, was a Republican, a successor to David Davis as chief judge of the old 8th Circuit—and, nearly a century later, a benefactor of the city of Bloomington, its public school system and the Morgan-Washington Home to the tune of $9 million.

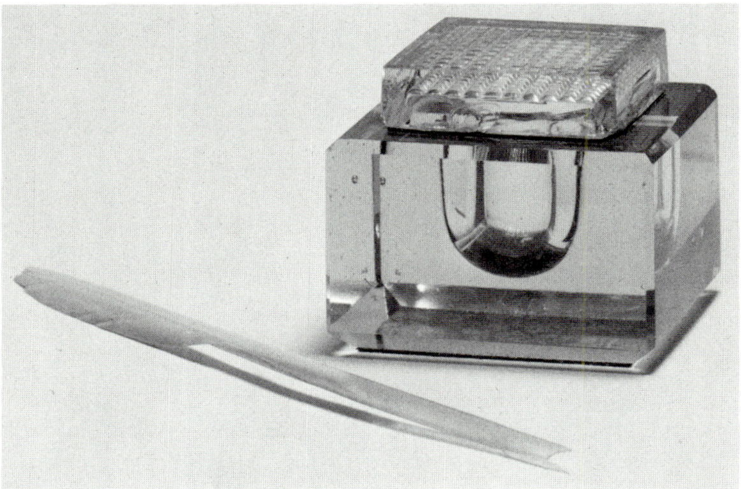

Ink well & pen of Judge Scott

It was a time when one's political party affiliation was important. On the local level, partisan exuberance took campaigning into the saloons and resulted in wild political bets, a strong patronage system and a sometimes carnival atmosphere.

Let it be said, without counting, that Bloomington's internationally-known "Baby" Bliss was the biggest vote getter McLean County had. He weighed 565 pounds and was famous from Bloomington to London, but not because of any political decision he ever made.

"Some are born great, some achieve greatness, and some have greatness thrust upon them."

— Wm. Shakespeare

Leonard "Baby" Bliss, ca. 1895

PUBLIC AWARENESS

Educators, meanwhile, were contacting Bloomington Superintendent of Schools Sarah Raymond, asking for copies of her impressive planning manual for school systems. Raymond compiled the volume, with the help of Bloomington's teachers and principals, in the 1870s, and few questioned the high quality of education available in the city during Raymond's 18 years as superintendent.

Sarah Raymond's was the highest McLean County post held by a woman up to that time, and her tenure, 1874-1892, was marked by growth. Chances of a youngster attending classes were becoming quite good as new school buildings sprang up, political ward by ward.

Sarah Raymond

No. 3 School, 1876. Southwest corner, Jackson & Mason streets

"As is the teacher so is the school." The teacher must be what he would have his pupils become. These are universally received as "school maxims, and express the general estimate of the importance of the personal character of the teacher as a factor in educational results. It is demanded of him that he be pure in thought and in life. Especially is it necessary for him to be honest. No hyprocrisy or pretense can long conceal his real character. A pronounced pretender of intellect or morals is an object of universal contempt."

— Sarah E. Raymond
Manual of Instruction, 1883

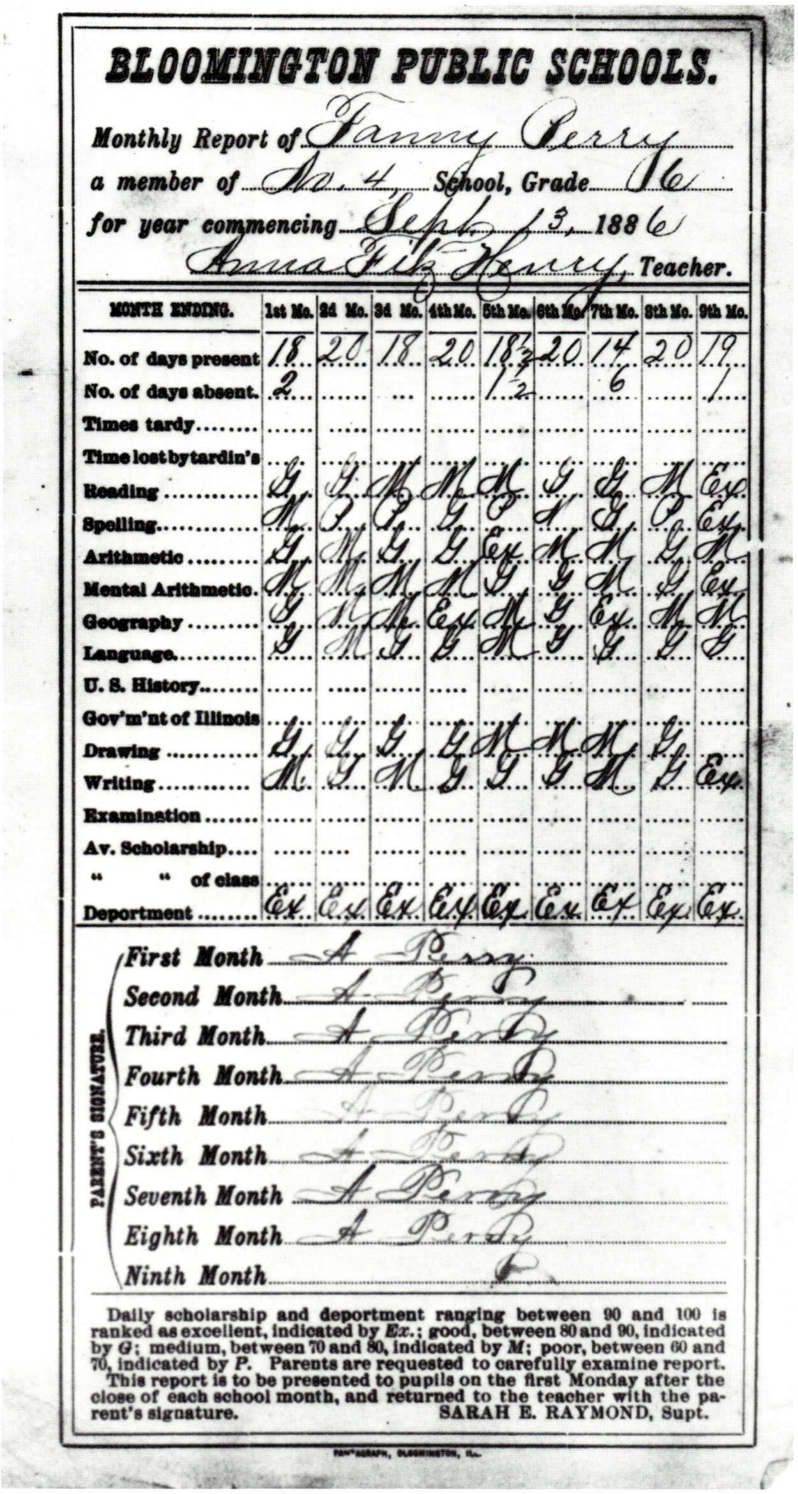

BLOOMINGTON PUBLIC SCHOOLS.

Monthly Report of Fanny Perry
a member of No. 4, *School, Grade* 6
for year commencing Sept. 13, 1886
Anna Fitz Henry, *Teacher.*

MONTH ENDING.	1st Mo.	2d Mo.	3d Mo.	4th Mo.	5th Mo.	6th Mo.	7th Mo.	8th Mo.	9th Mo.
No. of days present	18	20	18	20	18 3/4	20	14	20	19
No. of days absent.	2				1 1/2		6		1
Times tardy									
Time lost by tardin's									
Reading	G	G	M	M	M	G	G	M	Ex
Spelling	M	P	P	G	P	[illegible]	G	P	Ex
Arithmetic	G	M	G	G	Ex	M	M	G	M
Mental Arithmetic	M	M	M	M	G	G	M	G	Ex
Geography	G	M	M	Ex	M	G	Ex	M	M
Language	G	M	G	G	M	G	G	G	G
U. S. History									
Gov'm'nt of Illinois									
Drawing	G	G	G	G	M	M	M	G	
Writing	M	G	M	G	G	G	M	G	Ex
Examination									
Av. Scholarship									
" " of class									
Deportment	Ex	Ex	Ex	Ex	Ex	Ex	Ex	Ex	Ex

PARENT'S SIGNATURE.
First Month A Perry
Second Month A Perry
Third Month A Perry
Fourth Month A Perry
Fifth Month A Perry
Sixth Month A Perry
Seventh Month A Perry
Eighth Month A Perry
Ninth Month P.

Daily scholarship and deportment ranging between 90 and 100 is ranked as excellent, indicated by *Ex.*; good, between 80 and 90, indicated by *G*; medium, between 70 and 80, indicated by *M*; poor, between 60 and 70, indicated by *P*. Parents are requested to carefully examine report. This report is to be presented to pupils on the first Monday after the close of each school month, and returned to the teacher with the parent's signature. SARAH E. RAYMOND, Supt.

Natural history lesson in a Bloomington school, ca. 1890

The second high school arrived in 1897, on the north side of Monroe Street, between Gridley and Prairie.

Even then, some of the old prejudices continued to hang on. Men teachers were paid more money than women teachers and when a resolution was offered to the school board in 1892 that "equal work, no matter by whom performed, should have equal pay," it "had but one supporter and the motion died for want of a second."

HIGH SCHOOL, BLOOMINGTON, ILL.

EXCUSE FOR ABSENCE.

Date of Excuse...189

Please excuse (name)..

for .... days' absence

on ....

Cause for absence,

.... Parent.

TO THE PARENTS:—It is earnestly desired that you insist upon regular attendance as far as possible, as the *shortest* absence necessarily causes a loss to both the pupil and the school.—A. E. WHITTEN, Principal.

Bloomington High School

Market Street School, 1896

Progress was more apparent in the 1896 picture of students at the Market Street School. For several years after the Civil War, Bloomington schools were segregated by law. Black students walked long distances to attend "their" school on South Madison Street.

But black parents in Bloomington decided in 1872 to test the "separate but equal" Illinois law and sent their children to the more convenient West Side Number 5 School, whose principal was Sarah Raymond. Superintendent S.M. Etter had the children ejected and the school board attempted to solve the problem by erecting a more convenient, small school for the 2-4 black students, alongside the Number 5 School.

Judge Thomas F. Tipton heard the resultant case brought about by the black parents and declared the side-by-side schoolhouse approach a "fraud on the taxpayers." The Illinois Supreme Court agreed with him. Bloomington schools were integrated and Raymond reported in 1892 "the old prejudices of ante-bellum days soon disappeared and our young friends seemed to be very happy in their new relations."

Judge Thomas F. Tipton

JOURNALISM

Pantagraph Building, northwest corner Madison & Washington Streets

Editorial rooms, Pantagraph

By 1890, the Bloomington *Pantagraph* was already 53 years old—two years older than Chicago's oldest newspaper, *The Tribune*, and well respected throughout the Midwest. Jesse Fell had helped found the *Bloomington Observer and McLean County Advocate* in 1837. After that paper's failure in 1839, he involved himself as editor with *The Pantagraph* from 1851 to 1853, when he retired to pursue other interests. He was ready to launch a major national newspaper from Normal in 1868 when he jumped at the chance to buy his old paper back.

Fell brought in his son-in-law, W.O. Davis, to transform *The Pantagraph* from a country newspaper to a city daily, adding local news and correspondents in other towns, and installing a direct-to-the newspaper telegraph for national news.

There were several dozen papers published in McLean County, many of them in Bloomington and Normal—a newspaper for every political persuasion.

William O. Davis

Bulletin Building, southeast corner East & Washington streets

T. A. BRALEY.

There once was an editor—"Brad,"
Who thought all Republicans bad.
If a statesman "stood pat,"
He would not stick for that;
And when Teddy got beat, Brad was sad.

PUBLISHING

But if *The Pantagraph* was first Whig, then Republican, it was the *Bulletin* which provided a firm voice for the loyal opposition. The *Bulletin* absorbed the old *Pantagraph* nemesis, the *Leader*, in 1899 and the battle lines were drawn. *Bulletin* editor T.A. Braley wrote for the Democrats, the city folks, the West Siders, the afternoon readers, while *The Pantagraph* appealed to the Republicans, the East Siders, the farmers and small-town folk and the morning readers.

People were reading more—enough of them to justify local publishing of books. For the first time, books were being sent out into the world carrying a Bloomington imprint.

Composing room, Pantagraph Printing & Stationery Company

Bindery, Pantagraph Printing & Stationery Company

A PUBLIC LIBRARY

James Allin, Jesse Fell and friends bought a thousand volumes in Philadelphia and started a McLean County lending library as early as 1840, but they didn't pay enough attention to getting the loaned books returned and the project fizzled.

Later attempts required the payment of a small annual fee for the privilege of borrowing books, and some sort of citizen-run library bounced around from loaned building to loaned building until Sarah Withers came to the rescue in 1882.

Withers donated the land at Washington and East streets, George Miller designed a beautiful building and Bloomington people responded to a fund drive. The new library was occupied by 1887.

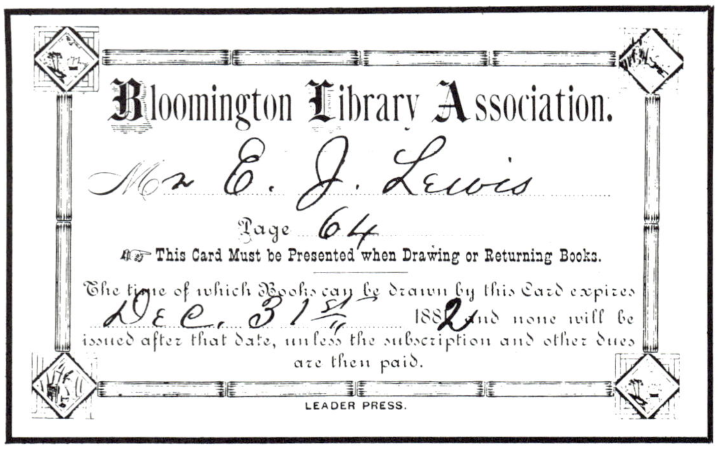

Bloomington Library Association.

Mr E. J. Lewis

Page 64

This Card Must be Presented when Drawing or Returning Books.

The time of which Books can be drawn by this Card expires Dec. 31st 1882 and none will be issued after that date, unless the subscription and other dues are then paid.

LEADER PRESS.

Withers Public Library

Librarians' picnic

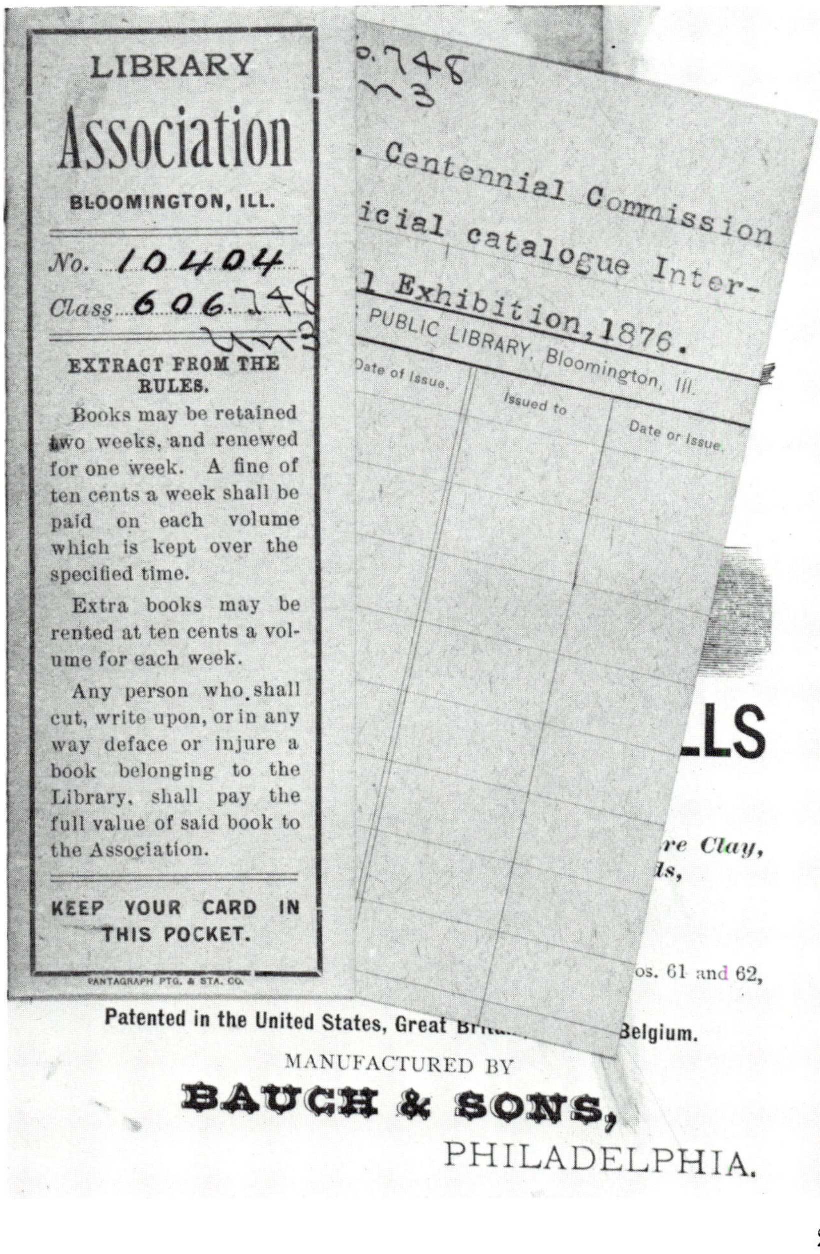

TRAVEL

Fancy Pullmans, Bloomington-built reclining-chair cars, and well-supplied dining cars made elegant travel possible. So did Bloomington's location on several good rail lines. While the first trains to McLean County 30 years earlier were combination affairs, it was becoming increasingly profitable to operate separate freight and passenger departures.

As the demand for seats increased, railroad executives decided there was no mechanical reason why longer trains couldn't be operated, and special excursion trains were soon pulling out of Bloomington, filled with bargain-rate travelers.

One such train left Bloomington August 10, 1887, for Niagara Falls, pulled by two heavy engines and crammed with 850 people in 22 coaches. A similarly-long train, also bound for Niagara Falls, left Peoria the same day, but crashed through a burned-out bridge near Chatsworth in the middle of a rainy night. The death toll was 81 and the wreck was the nation's biggest news story.

Pullman Company dining car

Union Depot on West Washington Street, 1894

Interior of Main Building, Philadelphia Exposition, 1876

Balanced Rock, Colorado Rockies

Camping in the Colorado Rockies

Destinations were not much different a century ago than they are today. There was, perhaps, a bit more interest in Philadelphia where Bloomington's schools offered an exhibit during the nation's centennial. But McLean County people, then as now, also posed for snapshots in the Rockies, on the beach at Atlantic City and on an excursion boat at Wisconsin Dells.

Riding donkeys

Atlantic City

Wisconsin Dells excursion

THE GRAND TOUR

Shortly after his cousin became vice-president, Bloomington attorney James Ewing was appointed ambassador to Belgium, and a visit to Brussels became another stop for McLean County people on the fashionable European tour.

Socialite Daisy Hill and her mother were typical of the Bloomington tourists, posing in Nuremburg, Capri and Rome. Taking "The Grand Tour" was a means of showing one's wealth, of course, but it was much more than that. It was an education, a satisfying of one's curiosity about other cultures.

At Nuremburg, Germany

"The Royal Garden Party at the Laeken Palace on Saturday afternoon brought the Brussels season to a close, and the annual exodus to Spa and the seaside has already commenced. Although terribly sunburnt, the King of the Belgians looked all the better for his holiday in Italy . . . the stables as well as the conservatories were thrown open to the 1500 guests . . . Mr. James Spencer Ewing, the American Minister, was accompanied by a very large contingent of his compatriots, including Mr. and Mrs. Potter Palmer and Mr. and Mrs. Addison Thomas, who are now doing the 'grand tour.'"

— **London World**
May 15, 1895

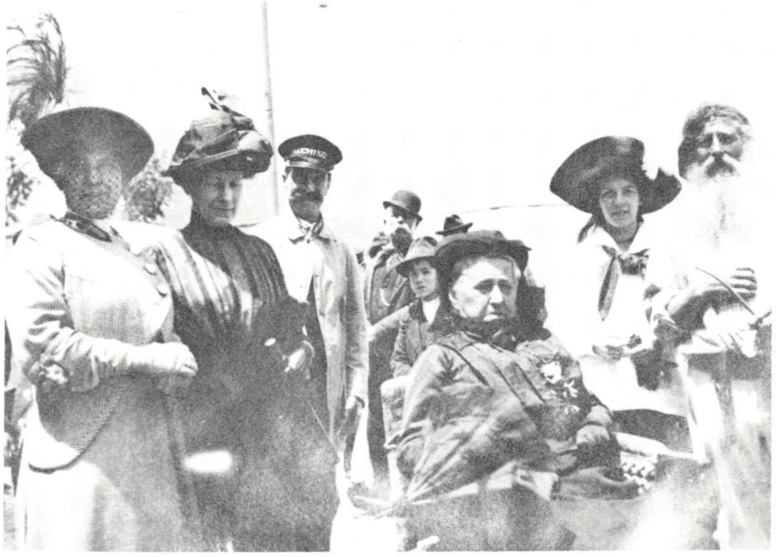

Taken at Capri, Italy

BARBER'S
HÔTEL DE L'EUROPE
PLACE VERTE, ANVERS.

Doit M

CHAMBRE N°
Avril 9?

17	3 Diners	15	00
	chambre & 3 déjeuners	20	00
18	2 Déjeuners 10 oeufs	5	50
	omnibus de port	7	
		47.	50

After an audience with the Pope

"A SPLENDID LITTLE WAR"

Times were good and Americans were feeling proud of themselves as the century drew to a close. The Spanish timing in sending the U.S. man-of-war the "Maine" to the bottom of Havana Harbor was not good. Sentiment in McLean County favored flexing American muscles and showing the Spanish a thing or two.

Three companies of soldiers quickly left the Bloomington courthouse for the popular war. But within a few months, the Cuban heat was taking its toll of American troopers, and the call went out for black soldiers, who would be "able to stand the climate better than the white troopers." McLean County offered Company G, 8th Illinois Infantry, for garrison duty at Santiago. For the first time, the Army didn't insist the black soldiers be led by a white officer.

Pvt. Lyman R. Tay

Troop B, 1st Illinois Cavalry, at Bloomington City Hall. April 27, 1898

Capt. Julius C. Witherspoon

"At this stage Gov. Tanner visited the camp and in a speech said, 'Even from the very doors of the White House I received letters asking and advising me not to officer this regiment with colored men, but I promised to do so, and I have done it. I shall never rest until I see this regiment, —my regiment,—on the soil of Cuba, battling for the right, and for its kinsmen.' "

— **History of the 8th Illinois U.S.V.**
1899

Company G, 8th Illinois Infantry

"NO MEAN CITY"

Parade, May 10, 1900, 100 East Monroe

Bloomington was 50 years old in 1900, and the attitude was evident in the outpouring of community pride. The town had made it!

Pioneers John Dawson and Abe Brokaw were coaxed to lead a giant parade that numbered more than 3,000 marchers and impressive floats, "particularly in the German-American and Irish-American sections." Celebrants gathered at Miller Park and, after dark, at the Coliseum to hear speeches of prosperity and of native sons and daughters of national prominence far out of proportion to the population.

Times were indeed good. But the hazy smoke hanging over bustling Bloomington was, perhaps, an unrecognized signal of a tragedy to visit only five weeks later.

Parade, courthouse square

". . . Fifty years ago the village became a city. In that fifty years what marvelous changes have taken place! The railroads came, the sidewalks and pavements were built; our churches have increased in size and number, and our colleges and schools, our court house and fine public buildings, our library, our water works, our fire department, our beautiful shaded streets, our literary and musical societies have all combined to more than fulfill the promise of our youth. In all this material prosperity and improvement we rejoice. But there is something more to a city than its streets and houses; something, if not so tangible, yet quite as real. It is what the French call 'L'esprit de la Ville . . .' "

— **"A Citizen of No Mean City"**
James S. Ewing, 1900

North, from courthouse dome, 1896

8. The New Century

It was a few minutes after midnight, June 19, 1900, when the flames began in the Model Laundry, near Monroe and East streets. The wind was from the northeast and firemen had little chance to keep the fire from the courthouse square.

Flames jumped across Main Street and destroyed the block north of the courthouse, leaping across Center to burn the Windsor Hotel, then south to flatten half the block west of the square. Wolf Griesheim's six-story building along the square's east side was only recently finished—Bloomington's tallest building—and it was thought fireproof. But the wooden decorative trim caught fire and the entire block east of the courthouse tumbled.

Telegraphed messages went out to firemen in Peoria and Springfield and trains rushed firefighters to Bloomington in the pre-dawn hours. Spectators by the hundreds pitched in to help save merchandise and records and attempt to blow up buildings in the fire's path. They watched while bird nests in the dome of the courthouse ignited, and the fire spread throughout the inside of the building.

Embers from the blaze carried as far west as the Chicago and Alton yards and residents as far away as Front and Allin streets sat on their roofs and hosed them down.

By 8 o'clock in the morning, the fire was under control, but more than four square blocks of the city's best property was reduced to rubble-among them the block north of the courthouse, pictured looking north on the preceding page, and looking south on this page.

View South from Monroe Street, Bloomington, June 20, 1900

Southwest corner of square

Northeast corner, Main & Washington

Looking west on Jefferson from East Street

Northwest corner, Jefferson & Center

REBUILDING

Relocation and rebuilding plans began to take shape with the dawn, and signs announcing temporary quarters appeared by noontime. Not a single business failed because of the fire, and most of the rebuilding was completed within a year.

Architect George Miller designed the new Corn Belt Bank building at Main and Jefferson (you can still see the crossed ears of corn at the top of the stone pillars). But Miller didn't get the nod to rebuild his just-finished "fireproof" Griesheim Building across the street. Arthur Pillsbury was instead chosen to design the building and told to leave out the wood trim.

Northeast corner, Jefferson & Center

Southeast corner, courthouse square, from Washington Street

Northwest corner, Main & Jefferson

PROGRESS

By necessity, downtown Bloomington took on a more modern look. Signs of technology were everywhere, automobiles and streetcars mingling with horses and buggies. Before the fire, the downtown section was crisscrossed with electrical wires, telegraph wires and telephone wires. Now, since the downtown was to be rebuilt anyway, it became practical to put the wires underground.

Because the fire happened in the middle of the building season, owners moved quickly to rebuild. The energy and optimism shown by Bloomington people was astounding, and a big jubilee celebration was planned for June 19, 1901, just twelve months after the fire. It was clear a new era had begun for the downtown section.

By that time, the County Board had opted to not repair the courthouse that had served McLean County since 1868. Instead, contracts were let for the demolition of the old building, and construction of the present courthouse was underway. It was dedicated in the summer of 1902.

But memories of that disasterous night in 1900 were retained for future generations. Stones from the razed courthouse were used to construct the bridge on Summit Street, along Miller Park's eastern edge, while the frame from the burned courthouse dome sits just east of the Miller Park Pavilion.

Intersection of Main & Washington, looking south, 1904

STREETCARS

Five cents would get you a 30-minute ride from Bloomington to nearby Normal on the street railway system as early as 1868. The cars were hauled behind a pair of small smoke-belching steam engines, whose shrill whistles quickly wore out their welcome. Mules were pulling riders over the rails within a year, and held their jobs until the system was electrified in the 1890s.

Underpasses were built at dangerous intersections with busy railroad tracks. The viaduct between Vernon and Beaufort streets in Normal is still used by an occasional auto.

Commuters from Bloomington rode across dirt streets to their homes in Normal and, in summer, rode open-sided cars to Miller Park or to Houghton Lake—now State Farm Park. On the warmest of summer evenings, the whole gang rode decorated street cars around the entire route on "trolley parties."

Viaduct under C&A tracks, Normal, ca. 1915

Northeast corner, Washington & Main, 1911

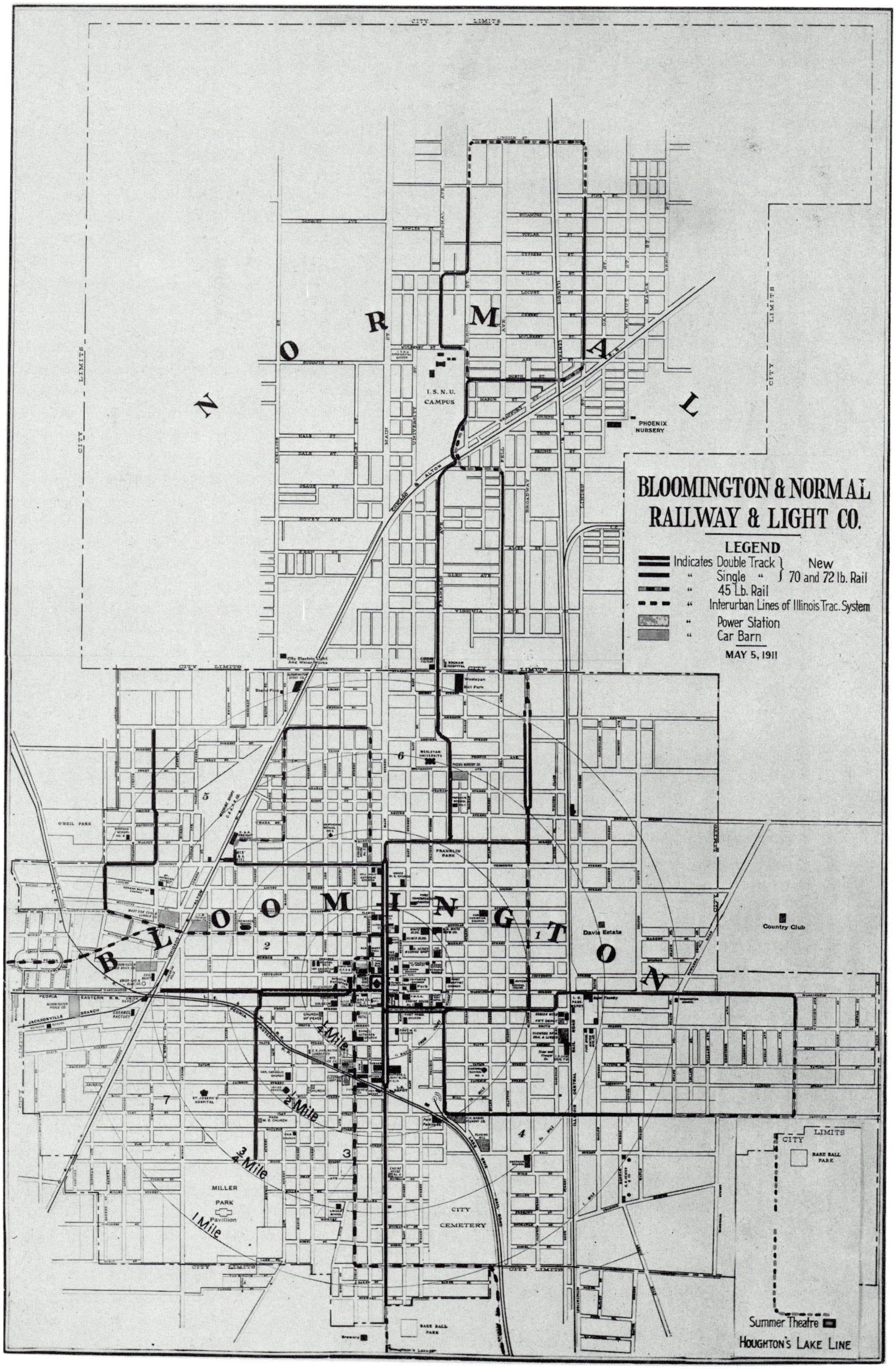
BLOOMINGTON & NORMAL
RAILWAY & LIGHT CO.
LEGEND
Indicates Double Track } New
" Single " } 70 and 72 lb. Rail
" 45 Lb. Rail
" Interurban Lines of Illinois Trac. System
" Power Station
" Car Barn
MAY 5, 1911
NORMAL
BLOOMINGTON
CITY LIMITS
I.S.N.U. CAMPUS
PHOENIX NURSERY
Davis Estate
Country Club
MILLER PARK
Pavilion
CITY CEMETERY
BASE BALL PARK
Summer Theatre
HOUGHTON'S LAKE LINE
1/4 Mile
1/2 Mile
3/4 Mile
1 Mile

Power station, South Roosevelt Street, 1911

LIGHT AND HEAT

Gas lamps lit the way from the courthouse to the depots as early as three years before the Civil War, but by 1880 Bloomingtonians were gazing up at four flickering, sputtering electric lights suspended from the courthouse dome. Officials first believed wide areas of a city could be lit by suspending the new lights high in the air—the higher the better.

A new power company, formed on the heels of the 1900 fire, built a coal-fired generator on South Roosevelt (the building is still there), and, after consolidation with the street railway company in 1906, supplied lights for the city and power for the streetcars, and piped the steam produced underground to heat most downtown buildings. The new buildings no longer needed furnaces of their own, and were rendered more fireproof.

Display room, Gray Electric Co., 215 East Front, 1911

Power station interior, 1911

TWO PHONE COMPANIES

McLean County's first commercial telephone company, the Central Union, was in operation as early as 1880, but competing companies kept things confusing for years after that. Patrons of one phone company often couldn't be connected with those of another, the only practical solution being one of each company's phones in the house or office.

The companies worked to build their subcriber lists and one warned its patrons to "bear in mind that the instruments in your office are there for your exclusive use, and the use of them by others is a violation of your contract and *must not be permitted.*"

Repair crew, 1911

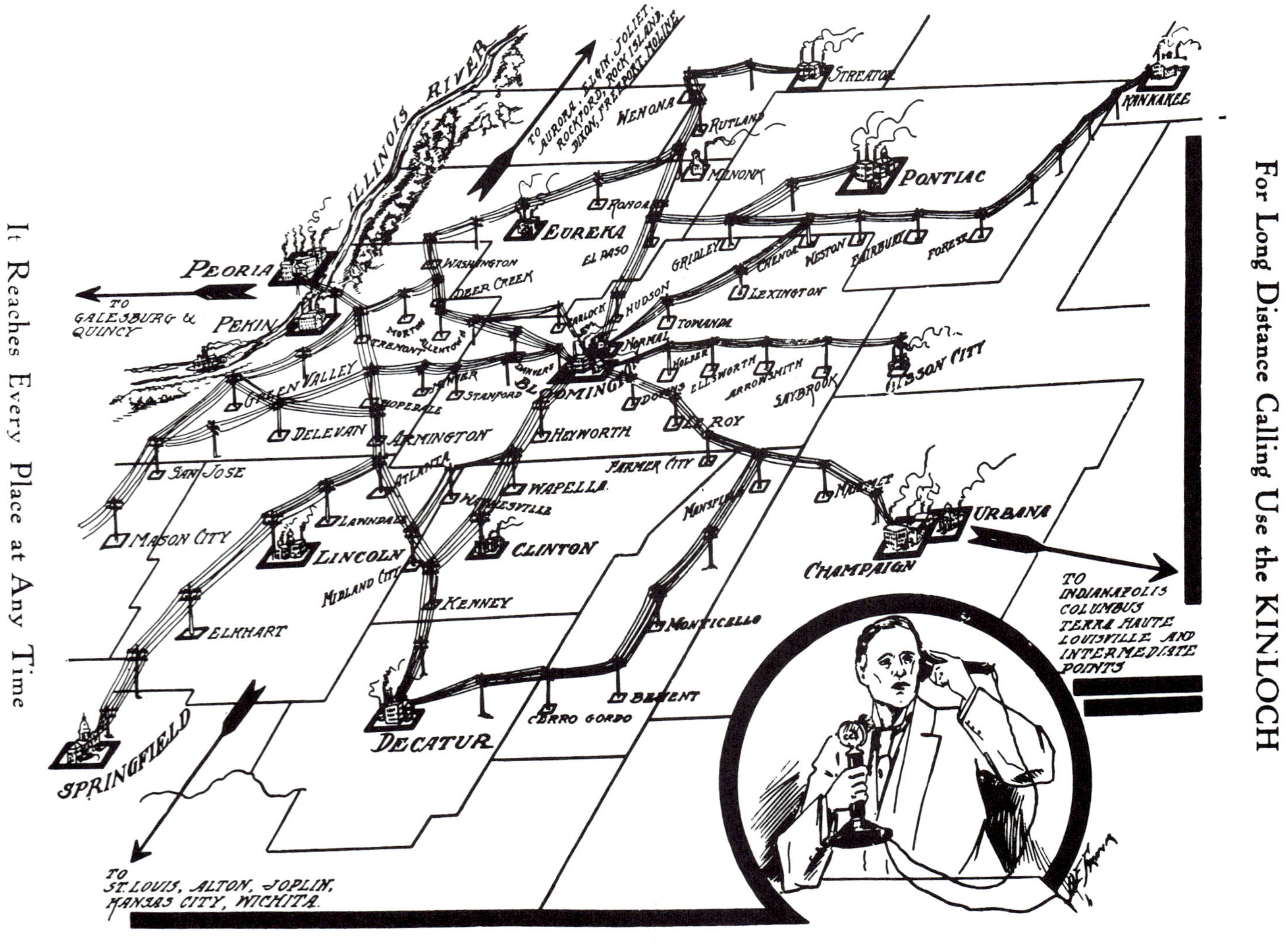

The same company allowed, however, that "any person may, with consent of subscriber, use the telephone in case of accident or fire."

"Report alarms of fire to the Central office," Union's instructions to its users read, adding: "The Central office will give all available information regarding trains. Railroad companies object to the annoyance of repeated requests for such information, but furnish it to the Central office for distribution."

"If the subscriber called for does not answer the first ring," the instructions continued, "the operator will ring a second time; if then no answer, the operator will tell calling subscriber 'they don't answer.' We have been instructed by many subscribers not to ring continuously."

"Subscribers should understand and appreciate the fact that it is no more work, and much more agreeable, for an operator to ring the number called than to say 'line is busy,' or 'they don't answer,' unless such is the fact, and subscribers who insist upon arguing the matter with the operators merely retard the service."

Do not allow Non-Subscribers to use your Telephone.

To Secure the Best Results.

The wrong way.

The right way.

Speak in your natural tone of voice.

☞ Speak INTO the transmitter, not AT it.

Always Ring Off when through talking, or your line will appear "busy."

Operators are required to be Polite; please extend them like courtesy.

DAILY WIRE TEST.

The wire of each Subscriber will be tested every morning. The Exchange **Operator will ring the Subscriber's bell, and when answered will say** "Morning **test." Subscribers are urged to promptly** co-operate in the effort to quickly locate **and remove wire and instrument trouble. If the Subscribers** wish the test to be **made at a special hour, the manager should be advised in writing, for record.**

THE INTERURBAN RAILWAY

William B. McKinley consolidated the power company, the street railway and his Illinois Traction System, and did much the same in other Illinois cities. The result was a series of power plants, 50 or more miles apart, lighting towns, running street cars and operating new electric railroads between Bloomington and Peoria, Decatur, Champaign, Danville, Springfield and St. Louis. McKinley secured his own right-of-way through the countryside, but obtained the rights to run his tracks down the middle of the dirt streets in the more expensive built-up areas of the towns. The interurban was convenient, with single cars leaving from Madison and Jefferson streets every hour or two, the "locals" making frequent stops along the way. Fares were cheaper than on the steam railroads.

But the Illinois Traction System didn't generate much freight revenue, and watched its heavy passenger load diminish as the popularity of automobile travel increased. The last interurban train left Bloomington in 1953.

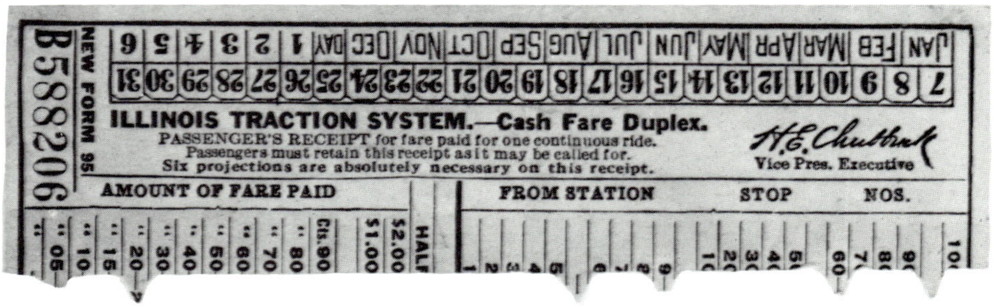
B588206
NEW FORM 95
ILLINOIS TRACTION SYSTEM.—Cash Fare Duplex.
PASSENGER'S RECEIPT for fare paid for one continuous ride.
Passengers must retain this receipt as it may be called for.
Six projections are absolutely necessary on this receipt.
H. E. Chubbuck
Vice Pres. Executive
AMOUNT OF FARE PAID
FROM STATION
STOP
NOS.

The interurban arriving at Heyworth, ca. 1910

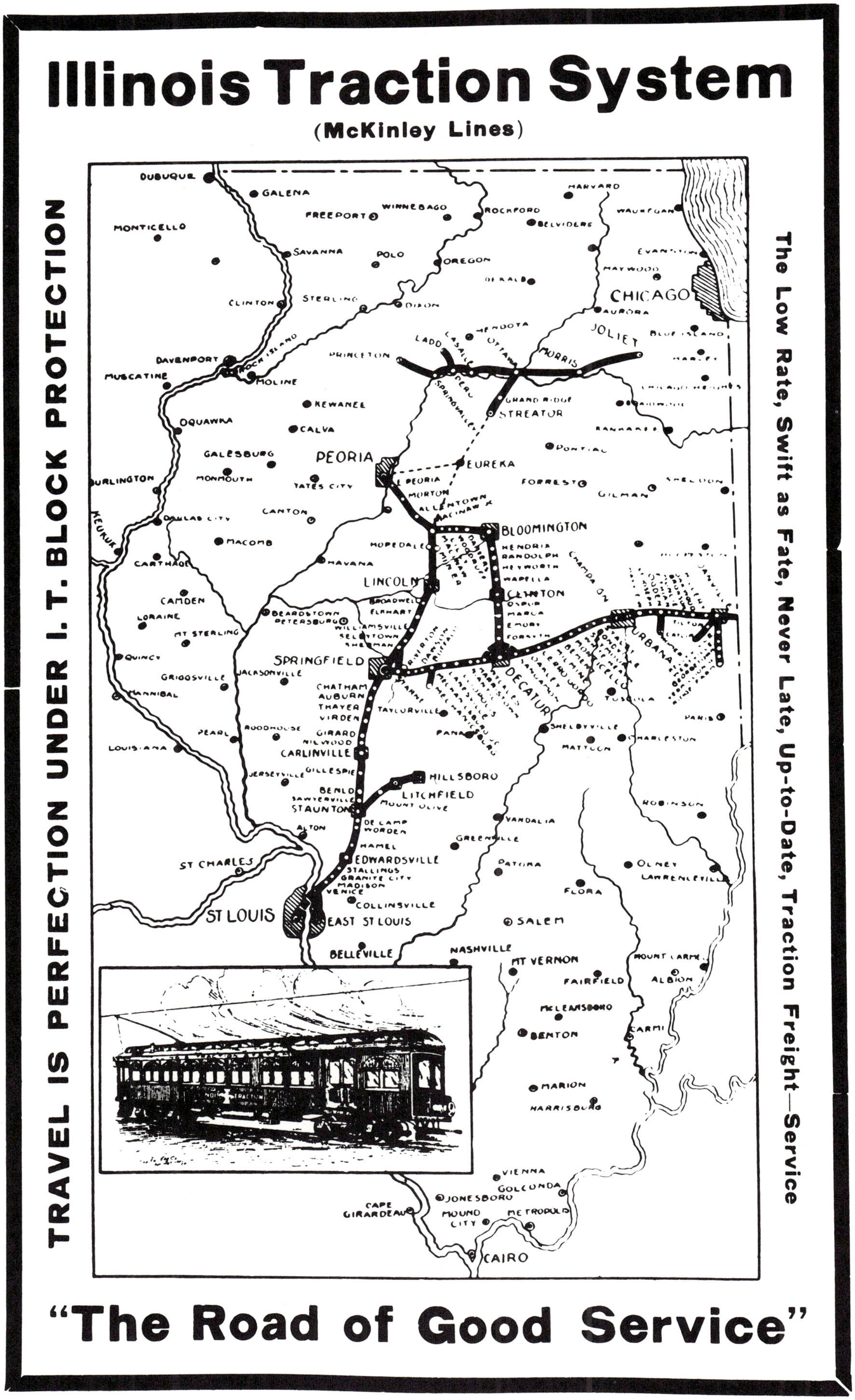
Illinois Traction System
(McKinley Lines)
TRAVEL IS PERFECTION UNDER I. T. BLOCK PROTECTION
The Low Rate, Swift as Fate, Never Late, Up-to-Date, Traction Freight—Service
CHICAGO
JOLIET
PEORIA
BLOOMINGTON
LINCOLN
CLINTON
SPRINGFIELD
DECATUR
URBANA
CARLINVILLE
HILLSBORO
LITCHFIELD
STAUNTON
EDWARDSVILLE
ST LOUIS
EAST ST LOUIS
BELLEVILLE
CAIRO
"The Road of Good Service"

THE AUTOMOBILE

Autos were still a wealthy man's toy in 1905 when nine cars from the Bloomington Auto Club made a widely-publicized run to Chicago to promote better roads. The "Illini Boulevard," now I-55, and the 'Meridian Road," now U.S. 51, were among the results.

Cars came within reach of the common man within a few years, however, and Ford dealer Floyd Iseminger and Overland dealer C.U. Williams were selling new autos as quickly as they could haul them from the depot and assemble them. Williams built a two-story showroom (now Paxton's Office Equipment) and an adjacent six-story warehouse (the Castle Theatre), the upper four floors designed to hold 400 cars, half of them suspended from the ceiling.

Blacksmith shops throughout the county were converting to repair the new machines. Distances were shrinking.

Taxi cab wreck, March 26, 1910, Bloomington

Bloomington Auto Club, ca. 1903

Unknown McLean County garage, ca. 1910

"Bloomington to Springfield—79 Miles . . . You now have the four-arm telephone poles which you follow through Shirley to a point . . . where there is a railroad crossing with a white board fence running clear to the road . . .Passing through west side of Lincoln the road runs south down Salt Creek hill, crosses a wooden bridge and two iron bridges and runs west and south . . . From this point the four-arm telephone poles will take you to Springfield . . . but there are some hills, a particularly bad, sandy one after you cross the Sangamon river. To avoid these hills leave the four-arm telephone poles at this point and follow small poles to Elkhart two miles south. There are poles on each side of the road . . ."

— **Irwin's Illinois Automobile Routes** 1906

At Miller Park, ca. 1910

EDUCATION

Bloomington people took pride in their new "half-million dollar high school" when they built it in 1917, and the modern building on East Washington Street showcased a change in educational methods. The McGuffy Readers were out, and learning by doing was in. Education became vocationally oriented.

Youngsters learned to grow their own tomatoes, and later proudly showed them off. Schools were turning out cooks, printers, woodworkers and musicians. Audio-visual aids were introduced, companies producing classroom-model Victrolas and promoting the educational use of their new machines.

Support organizations were forming under the banner of a group Bloomington's Letitia Green Stevenson helped found in Washington while her husband was serving as vice president—a group that became the PTA.

Bloomington High School, 1918

Gardening in Bloomington, 1915

"For several years we have been growing about three thousand Grand Pacific tomato plants for distribution among school children, giving to each a single plant or at most but two. The children were to set the plants in their home gardens, cultivate them and care for them in every way, and in September bring the finest of the fruit of the vines for tomato exhibits at the different ward schools. Prizes were awarded for the finest tomatoes.

This worked finely for several years, but last spring we thought we might do well to attempt something on a larger scale. So after a talk with our teacher of Agriculture and Nature-Study, we decided to have the pupils try to raise fifteen thousand Grand Pacific tomato plants for the purpose of giving ten plants to each of fifteen hundred pupils in the grammar grades for home cultivation. Full instructions were to be given on the cultivation and care of tomatoes in the home garden.

Fifteen thousand tomato plants are a good many, but the teachers and pupils entered into the work enthusiastically, so I felt sure the plants would be grown."

— J.K. Stableton, 1915

A class in cookery, 1905. Bloomington High School

The printing press, Edwards School, 1905

HIGH SCHOOL
PARENT-TEACHER CLUB
BLOOMINGTON, ILLINOIS
1915–1916

ORGANIZED MARCH 5, 1912

EDWARDS SCHOOL PRESS

High school manual training shop, 1905

Listening to the Victor, 1911

Bloomington High School Band, 1911

FOR THE COMMON GOOD

Letitia Green Stevenson was the presiding officer in 1907 when a group of women met at the Illinois Hotel to establish a day nursery. Social consciousness was growing, and citizens looked for ways to aid working mothers, orphans, the poor and the aged.

A mass meeting in the new Second Presbyterian Church a few weeks before the big fire led to the formation of Associated Charities, a grouping of eight of the major charitable organizations, for one annual fund drive. The Bureau of Social Service grew out of that first organization, forerunners of today's United Way.

Victory Hall for boys was purchased on Hovey in Normal in 1919, and the Girls' Industrial Home on Bloomington's South State Street (later the Lucy O. Morgan Home) had already been in existence nearly a quarter-century before that. The Baby Fold began providing a home for homeless babies in 1904, seeking permanent homes for its charges with good families.

The Jessamine Withers Home, meanwhile, provided comfortable living for older women. The McLean County Home for Colored Children, Fairview Sanitarium and the Salvation Army were also active charitable organizations in the century's early years.

Jessamine Withers Home, ca. 1915. 305 West Locust

Girls' Industrial Home

POLITICAL REFORM

Women in McLean County were voting in local elections before they were voting for president. Prohibition forces secured their franchise in Illinois, and their support against demon rum.

Campaigns were spirited and candidates numerous. Local candidates ran on the Progressive and Socialist tickets, in addition to Republican and Democratic. When Bloomington's Frank Funk joined Teddy Roosevelt on the Progressive ticket in 1912, he came within a few thousand votes of finishing second in Illinois's governor's race. In McLean County, Roosevelt, the Progressive, totaled 4,350 votes; but Wilson, the Democrat, carried the county with 5,336 votes.

Ballot box key tag, ca. 1915

SPECIMEN BALLOT

For use in the City of Bloomington, Illinois, and in the Town of the City of Bloomington.

ELECTION, TUESDAY, APRIL 6, 1915

Issued by the Board of Election Commissioners of the City of Bloomington, Illinois.

Dwight E. Drink
Chief Clerk.

FOR WOMEN

◯ REPUBLICAN	◯ DEMOCRATIC	◯ PROGRESSIVE	◯ SOCIALIST
For Supervisor	**For Supervisor**	**For Supervisor**	**For Supervisor**
☐ WM. SCHMIDT 601 E. Locust St.	☐ ________	☐ ________	☐ FRANK DONOVAN 1303 W. Locust St.
For Assistant Supervisors (Vote for Four)	**For Assistant Supervisors** (Vote for Four)	**For Assistant Supervisors** (Vote for Four)	**For Assistant Supervisors** (Vote for Four)
☐ JOHN G. WELCH 512 E. Chestnut St.	☐ CHAS. GOELZER 603 E. Jefferson St.	☐ ________	☐ LOUIS J. SALCH 1004 Summit St.
☐ W. H. FLESHER 606 E. Olive St.	☐ W. W. SHARPLES 1410 Franklin Ave.	☐ ________	☐ V. RAY SMOCK 410 Willard Ave.
☐ W. H. GENEVA 114 E. Moulton St.	☐ BENONI S. GREEN 1102 N. Main St.	☐ ________	☐ ________
☐ A. J. HOUCHIN 1012 W. Moulton St.	☐ ROBERT ORR 708 S. Lee St.	☐ ________	☐ ________

FRANK H. FUNK

OF BLOOMINGTON, ILLINOIS

Candidate For

GOVERNOR

ON THE PROGRESSIVE TICKET

Was born in 1869, in McLean County. His grandfather, Isaac Funk, settled in McLean County, in 1824.

He is a graduate of Yale, class 1891. He is a successful business man and has been a farmer and stockman for 21 years.

In 1901 he organized Funk Bros. Seed Co., the largest seed corn growers in the world.

He is a member of the widely known Funk family of McLean County, the leading cattle feeders in Illinois.

He was a member of the Illinois State Senate in 1909, 1910, 1911 and 1912.

As State Senator he voted for the Nominee of the people for United States Senator, against Lorimer.

He was a member of the new organization in the State Senate which defeated the old notorious senatorial combination. **He Voted For** the Progressive Bills in the 46th and 47th General Assemblies. **He Voted Against** the bills desired and pushed by "big business."

Examine his record in the State Senate.

He is pledged to fight against graft and corruption.

He is pledged to fight for honesty and efficiency and human rights.

He is not a politician. He has no political debts to pay. He has not made and will not make any promises in order to get votes.

He is greatly interested in the development of the agricultural and industrial interests of his state.

He fully realizes the vast importance that the agricultural and live stock interests play in the prosperity of the state of Illinois as well as the nation at large.

A Vote for this Honest Farmer is a Vote Against Corrupt Political Methods and a Vote for the Best Interests of All the People

LABOR UNIONS

From railroad workers to cigar makers, from butchers to coal miners, McLean County workers were organizing, and most prominent among them was John B. Lennon, national officer of the Journeymen Tailors' Union and treasurer of the American Federation of Labor.

The inevitable disagreements over union recognition reached their most violent when street car motormen struck in 1917. The community was fully polarized a month after the strike began when famed labor organizer Mother Jones addressed the Bloomington strikers. An inflamed mob left the meeting, confronted non-striking motormen, and within a short time, people were beaten and shots were fired. National Guard troops arrived by dawn, and the motormen had a contract within a week.

The TAILOR
OFFICIAL ORGAN OF THE JOURNEYMEN TAILORS' UNION OF AMERICA

VOL. XX. BLOOMINGTON, ILLINOIS, NOVEMBER, 1909. No. 4

Offices of John B. Lennon, secretary, Journeymen Tailors' Union
Eddy Building, Main & Market, ca. 1907

". . . BE IT RESOLVED: That the Citizens' Alliance of Bloomington, Illinois, unanimously and emphatically approves the course of the said Company in refusing to sign said proposed contract, and that this Alliance will give to the said Company in its effort to operate its cars for the service of the public, their earnest moral and financial support.
RESOLVED FURTHER: That it is the duty of every member of the Alliance to ride upon the street cars upon every possible occasion and to encourage all others to do the same, to the end that lawlessness, coercion and disorder may cease, and right and justice triumph."

— **Minutes of Bloomington Citizens' Alliance**, January 5, 1904

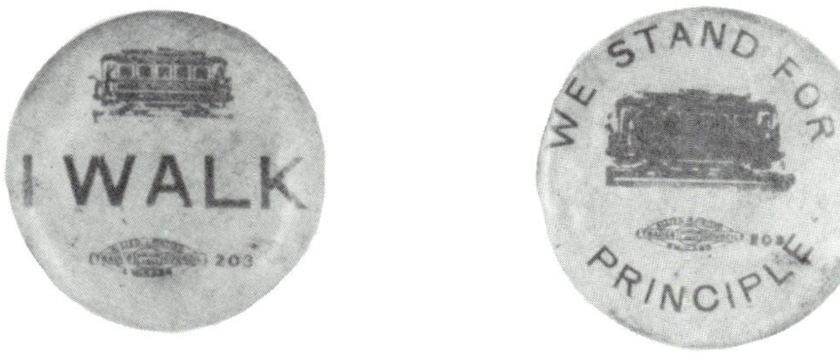

Buttons worn by supporters of the strike

National Guard tents on courthouse square

South side of square, July 1917. Bloomington streetcar strike

THE BLACK MIDDLE CLASS

Dr. Samuel Witherspoon had been the first black person in McLean County to cast a vote, back in 1870, and was the most prominent professional man in the black community at the turn of the century.

It was in 1900 when the Wayman AME congregation, already 54 years old, built its new church at 806 North Center. The Third Christian Church, also organized that year, at 303 South Western, was led by Rev. George Hoagland.

Rev. Hoagland built Bloomington's most prominent black-owned business, manufacturing Oil of Gladness furniture polish and mops, and selling them across the Midwest.

Wayman AME Church, ca. 1900

Address
Hoagland's Oil of Gladness
Geo. Hoagland
Prop.
Bloomington.
Ill

HOAGLAND'S
Oil of Gladness Mops

The Sanitary, Modern, Scientific
Dustless Method

Makes less Work, Worry, Time
No Sweeping of Floors
No Washing with Soap and
Water

"Oil of Gladness" factory, West Washington Street, 1912

BILLY SUNDAY

When Billy Sunday arrived the day after Christmas, 1907, Normal was dry, but there were pubs aplenty in Bloomington. But in six weeks of fiery preaching in the specially-constructed tabernacle just south of the business district, and frequent trips around the courthouse on his "water wagon," Billy changed a lot of thinking.

More than 375,000 people heard the ex-baseball player during his stay, and when it was over, 4,000 new members were on the rolls of Bloomington churches. The press said it was the most converts ever for an event of its kind. And within six years, Bloomingtonians voted themselves dry.

North side of square, on Jefferson Street

Interior of the tabernacle, South Main Street

ENTERTAINMENT FOR ALL

In the 1800s, much of the entertainment to be had in McLean County was behind closed doors—at private parties. But now, low-cost or free entertainment was available at a number of public facilities. People from all social strata were mixing on the square and at Houghton's Lake, the borrow pit from a rural brickyard that later became Lake Park, then State Farm Park.

William Jennings Bryan led a parade to Houghton's Lake for McLean County's first chautauqua in 1901, and was the headline speaker. Campers from throughout the area set up a tent city, speakers lectured, bands played and children went on nature hikes. The Bloomington-based George Goforth Black and Gold Orchestra and the Vera Pearl Kemp Ensemble became quite popular around the chautauqua circuit.

1886 TWENTY-FOURTH YEAR 1910

FIRST CONCERT

GIVEN BY

DeMolay Commandery Band

MILLER PARK

Sunday, June 11, 1910 3:30 P. M.

PROGRAM

FRED T. ASHTON, *Director*

Bloomington Band Mardi Gras, east side of square, ca. 1920

MILLER PARK

The arch over the gate at Morris Avenue read "Tourists Welcome," and enough of them came to make Bloomington's Miller Park one of the most popular public parks in the Midwest—a model for those in other cities.

The original lake, formed by damming a creek, was more than doubled in 1902, with a large earthen dam built on the west and south sides. Miller Park Lake was said to be Illinois's largest man-made lake by 1920.

Street cars brought citizens to visit the zoo, the dignified pavilion and the band stand. They walked past the new soldiers' monument, built to replace the crumbling monument in the center of Franklin Park.

The shaft from the original Franklin Park monument was removed, and the base now sits on private property along Dawes Place.

Erecting the soldiers' monument, 1912

Miller Park Pavilion, 1906

Free fishing at Miller Park Lake, ca. 1905

OTHER PARKS

Bicyclists at Franklin Park, ca. 1900

A day at the races, ca. 1912

Official Program of the

Bloomington Chautauqua

LAKE PARK

JULY 18, 19, 20, 21, 22, 23, 24, 1917

THATCHER'S SYMPHONY ORCHESTRA---ONE OF THE GREATEST MUSICAL ATTRACTIONS EVER APPEARING ON THE PROGRAM

Sunday, July 24.

9:30 a. m. . . . . Sunday School

10:30 a. m. . . . . Ladies' Orchestra

11:00 a. m. . . . . Dr. G. A. Scott
"The Carpenter of Nazareth."

12:45 p. m. . . . . Mrs. C. C. Loch
"The Children's Hour."

2:00 p. m. . . . . Ladies' Orchestra

2:30 p. m. . . . . Father L. J. Vaughn
"The Power of Love."

7:00 p. m. . . . . Miss Elma B. Smith

7:30 p. m. . . . . Ladies' Orchestra

8:00 p. m. . . . . Moving Pictures

BOATING SCENE—HOUGHTON'S LAKE.

Monday, July 25.

10:00 a. m. . . . . Ladies' Orchestra

10:30 a. m. . . . . Rev. J. H. Sowerby
"The Two-fold Nature of Man."

12:45 p. m . . . . Rev. M. M. Varney
"Our Jewels—Children's Rights and Wrongs."

2:00 p. m. . . . . Ladies' Orchestra

2:30 p. m. . . . . Rev. T. N. Ewing
"The Under Side of Things."

7:00 p. m. . . . . Miss Mabelle C. Church
"Up-to-Date Saleslady."

7:30 p. m. . . . . Ladies' Orchestra

8:00 p. m. . . . . Moving Pictures

When the future Bloomington-Normal Hall of Famers Charley Radbourne and Clark Griffith were pitching for the Bloomington Reds back in the 1880s, the town's ball park was at the foot of South Center Street, about where Wood Street is. "Old Hoss" Radbourne, they say, worked on his new-fangled curve ball here and became the first major league pitcher to use it successfully when he won an incredible 60 games for Providence of the National League in 1884.

But by the new century, it was the Bloomington Bloomers of the Three-I League, and businesses closed on opening day to allow the men to hop a streetcar to Fans' Field on LaFayette Street, just off Main. The 26-inning game Bloomington lost to Decatur there on Decoration Day, 1909, was the longest completed game played in professional baseball for nearly seven decades.

I. I. I. BASE BALL SCHEDULE, '08

WALTER ARMBRUSTER'S

Barber Shop

Three Chairs, No Waiting
Kinloch Phone 1259 R

110 E. Front St.

AGENCY TROY LAUNDRY

BLOOMINGTON AT HOME

APRIL	30	Peoria
MAY	1	Peoria
	4-5	Clinton
	6-7	Rock Island
	8-9	Dubuque
	10*-11	Cedar Rapids
	16-17*-18	Springfield
	30**-30**	Decatur
	31*	Peoria
JUNE	1-2	Peoria
	8-9-10	Decatur
	11-12-13	Rock Island
	14*-15	Clinton
	16-17-18	Cedar Rapids
	19-20-21*	Dubuque
JULY	2-3	Springfield
	5*-6-7	Peoria
	10-11-12*	Decatur
	13-14-15	Cedar Rapids
	16-17	Dubuque
	18-19*-20	Rock Island
	21-22-23	Clinton
	24	Springfield
AUGUST	5	Springfield
	6-7	Peoria
	18-19-20	Dubuque
	21-22	Cedar Rapids
	23*-24-25	Clinton
	26-27	Rock Island
	28	Springfield
SEPTEMBER	6*-7**	Springfield
	7**-8	Decatur

*Sunday **Holiday

NIMROD MACE PRINT,

I. I. I. BASE BALL SCHEDULE, '08

BLOOMINGTON ABROAD

MAY	2-3*	Peoria
	12-13	Springfield
	14-15	Decatur
	19-20-21	Rock Island
	22-23-24*	Clinton
	25-26-27	Dubuque
	28-29	Cedar Rapids
JUNE	3-4	Peoria
	5-6-7*	Springfield
	22-23	Dubuque
	24-25-26	Cedar Rapids
	27-28*	Rock Island
	29-30	Clinton
JULY	1	Clinton
	4**-4**	Decatur
	8-9	Springfield
	25-26*	Clinton
	27-28-29	Rock Island
	30-31	Cedar Rapids
AUGUST	1	Cedar Rapids
	2*-3-4	Dubuque
	8-9*-10	Decatur
	11-12-13	Peoria
	14-15-16*	Springfield
	29-30*	Cedar Rapids
	31	Dubuque
SEPTEMBER	1	Dubuque
	2-3	Clinton
	4-5	Rock Island
	9-10-11	Decatur
	12-13*-14	Peoria

*Sunday **Holiday

C-A-Fenn

BEFORE BUYING

Base Ball and Sporting Goods

114 E. FRONT ST.

Bloomington ball club, 1911

THEATRES

Movies, automobiles and, finally, radio teamed to doom the chautauqua circuit, but the theatres continued to prosper. Acts arrived from all over on the interurban and took their turn at the Castle Theatre, where State Farm's downtown building stands today. Also included on the card was a concert from the Castle's pipe organ and, at the end of the program, a movie, often of questionable technical quality. "Chasers," they called them. They were really devices to get the people out of the theatre at the end of the program.

C.U. Williams relocated the Castle Theatre a block to the east a few years later, but by that time, new entertainment houses abounded.

Northwest corner, Washington & East Streets, ca. 1914.

Castle Theatre

BLOOMINGTON'S SOCIETY PLAYHOUSE

Week Beginning Monday, November 18, 1907.

Ladies will confer a favor to patrons and management by kindly removing their hats.

HOUSE STAFF

M. GOLDBERG LEW M. GOLDBERG	Proprietors	ELMER RIEBE	Doorkeeper
GUY MARTIN	Manager	HARVEY PETERSON	Stage Carpenter
		CHRIS JACKSON	Advertising Agent

FRED STANSFIELD, Musical Director

Performance Every Evening at 8:15. Matinees Tuesdays, Thursdays, Saturdays at 2:15. Doors open at 7:45 p. m. and 1:45 p. m.

Patrons of this house may claim lost articles at the office by proper identification. All articles picked up in the house must be left at the office.

Both Phones, Old 573-K, New 1243-L. Seats reserved will not be held after 1:45 p. m. for matinee performances and 8 p. m. for night performances.

The attaches of this house are not permitted to accept fees nor gratuities of any kind. It is intended that the admission fees shall cover all the advantages afforded by the superior equipment of the Castle Theatre. Ladies' retiring room will be found upon the East Street side of Theatre immediately behind first stage box. The management request physicians and others in the audience who may expect a summons by telephone or messenger during the performance to register at the box office.

PROGRAM

Week of November 18
(Subject to change)

A OVERTURES

Headquarters Restaurant

CORNER WASHINGTON AND CENTER

The Best 20c Meal in City. 21 MEALS $3.50

ROOMS IN CONNECTION.

PROMPT SERVICE. OPEN ALL NIGHT.

Kitchell's PHOTOGRAPHS

THE UP TO DATE KIND.

Special Rates to Students and Professional People. S. W. Corner Square.

THE HENSEL

214 West Jefferson St.

A GENTLEMAN'S EUROPEAN HOTEL

JOE E. HENSEL, Proprietor

G MARNO TRIO
Eccentric Acrobatic Comiques.

H CASTLESCOPE PRESENTING LIFE MOTION PICTURES.

MATINEES—Tuesday, Thursday and Saturday
Ladies and Children 10c. Any Seat in the House

Go to CHRIS. HOFFMAN'S Barber Shop under 1st National Bank for First-Class Barber Work.

FURNISHED ROOMS FROM $1.50 TO $3 PER WEEK
BATH AND STEAM HEAT. 306 N. Madison St.

Stump & Wilson

Blacksmiths

213 E. Front New Phone 1223 J

Chatterton Opera House

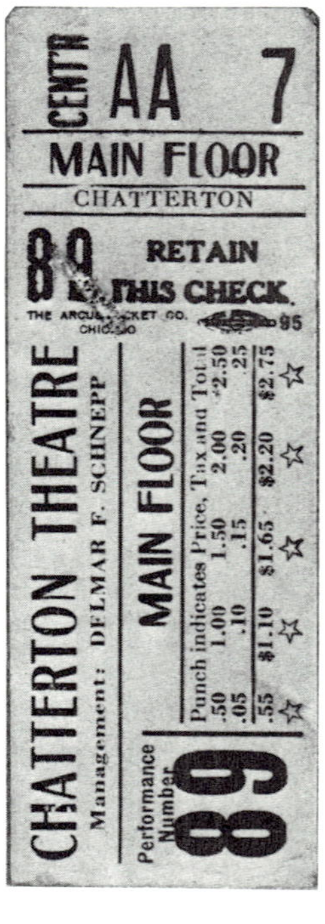

The Chatterton on East Market opened in 1910 and featured Lillian Russell, Ed Wynn, the great violinist Rubinoff and a very young Mae West, wowing, the press said, "the Bloomington boys on bald head row."

Bob Hope, Jack Benny and Will Rogers appeared three blocks south, at the Majestic Theatre, where Bloomington Federal's main office now stands. The Marx Brothers cooked goulash on a canned heat stove in the Majestic's basement to save themselves the price of a meal.

But Clarence Irvin's new movie house on Jefferson Street was touted as the "finest modern photo play house in the Midwest, outside Chicago," offering a floor slanting toward the screen and "a near perfect sight line to each patron."

Southwest corner, Washington & East

Harry Lauder & Davis Ewing, Bloomington depot, 1918

THE COUNTY'S MUSEUM

Interest in the preservation of McLean County history began early. The History of Bloomington Society started saving the recollections of the county's pioneers in 1856, a year before the Chicago Historical Society was formed. But it was in 1892 when a trio of Bloomington men got down to business and formed the McLean County Historical Society.

George Perrin Davis, the financier; Ezra Morton Prince, the collector of written material, and John Howard Burnham, the military historian, were the moving spirits. Initial memberships were by invitation only, and members were required to write and present papers, most of which were printed in the *Bulletin* and *Pantagraph*.

Museum space was provided on the top floor of the new courthouse and, in 1923, in the McBarnes Building. Milo Custer served as custodian during 11 of those years and busied himself gathering the nucleus of today's pioneer collection.

Historical Room, 3rd floor of courthouse, ca. 1915

"Captain Burnham and E.M. Prince of the McLean County Historical Society, will pilot a party of men over the site of the supposed Indian battle ground near Arrowsmith to-morrow. The gentlemen will leave here on the Lake Erie train in the morning, and will be met at the Arrowsmith depot by Douglass Dement, at whose invitation the visit is made. The exploration will consume the day, with the exception of the dinner hour, which will be spent at the hospitable home of Mr. Dement."

— **Sunday Leader**, May 16, 1897

West Township, ca. 1912. Milo Custer on monument

Historical Society members at Indian burial ground, Old Town, 1912

GERMAN DAY

Ethnic groups, particularly the German and Irish immigrants and their families, filled leadership roles all over McLean County as the century began, and one of them chose an October weekend in 1913 to celebrate how far it had come.

By then, Bloomington had a German-language newspaper, school and churches, and retail stores advertised their German-speaking clerks.

Newspaper accounts estimated the crowd at 20,000 for German Day. It was a weekend for a demonstration of ethnic pride—a weekend that would be unthinkable in McLean County after the Lusitania was sent to the bottom just two years later.

Washington Street, east from Main

500 block, North Main Street

German Day parade

Band concert, East Washington Street

THE CORN PALACE

Many communities built corn palaces for harvest-time celebrations, and Bloomington people were no exception. As early as 1903 and as late as 1916, workmen hammered frames on the face of the Coliseum at Front and Roosevelt, and decorated the place with corn ears, shucks, stalks and tassels.

The Pantagraph called it the "most pretentious corn palace in the Midwest" and people paid a dime to go inside for the corn and vegetable displays, the canning demonstrations, and the merchandise displays featuring everything from haberdashery to the new gramophones. A carnival outside helped lure folks to Bloomington from all parts of the county.

Northwest corner, Front & Roosevelt

Corn Palace exhibit, 1916

"Corn Dollar" made by William Brigham,
Corn Palace exhibit, 1916

RURAL CONCERNS

The groves and prairie grass that marked McLean County's early years were disappearing under the plow by the first years of the century, and the old-timers who remembered how things had been decided to save some of it for future generations. Simeon West's donation of 20 acres of woodland, West Park, continues three-quarters of a century later to preserve for McLean County a part of what was once its largest timber. Old Town Timber covered nearly 15,000 acres at one time—about 23 sections of land.

West was looking to the future, too, and authored during his term in the Illinois legislature in the early 1880s "West's Hard Road Law," which enabled counties to vote to levy a tax to construct "rock, gravel, macadam or other hard roads . . ."

Rural road near Bloomington, ca. 1915

Simeon H. West at northwest corner of West Park, 1908

"I have just let a contract for the erection in West Park of a monument of beautiful Monticello granite, for the purpose of a permanent record of date of donation and intended purpose of the park. I think this will be a matter of interest in ages to come.

The monument will contain this inscription:

On reverse side:
"This Monument was erected by the donor in 1908."

On east end:
"The groves are God's own Temples."

On west end:
"Let us worship at the shrine of Nature."

I get the impression that the placing of this permanent record in the park is the proper thing to do, and that the sentiments on the ends of the monument are in harmony with the surroundings."

— S.H. West
March 12, 1908

GASOLINE TRACTORS

The "Rumley Tractor Special", C&A R.R. near Lexington, ca. 1912

West also pushed through the legislature in 1884 a bill that strictly regulated farmers' ability to move steam-powered engines over public roads from field to field. Horses continued to provide most of the in-field power and would do so into the 1930s. But until slowed by the World War, the move toward gasoline tractors was on.

A special train brought dozens of the new tractors into the county for inspection, and a demonstration arranged by the Chamber of Commerce four years later drew 16,000 people.

Within a few years, a young farmer from Merna was calling on farmers through the area, selling tractors. George Mecherle would drive up the same lanes a few years later to offer policies from his new State Farm Insurance Company.

The "Rumley Special" from the front

Gasoline tractor demonstration near Bloomington, August, 1916

EDUCATIONAL ADVANCES

Many of the classes in the county's schools had for years simply been taught by the oldest student. But the new office of the county superintendent of schools was making progress in standardizing education. Teachers' institutes, summer school, hot lunches and buses all became a part of the scene.

Arthur Pillsbury designed the Ben Funk School to eliminate the light and ventilation problems that had plagued one-room schools, and other McLean County towns hurried to hire their own architects and build their own spacious school buildings.

Chenoa Grade & High School, 1912

Hot lunch program at Spaulding School, Dale Township, 1918

Corn exhibit, County Teachers' Institute, 1909

McLean County's first public school transportation, 1917

ORGANIZED SPORTS

Improved transportation brought rural and urban athletes together, often to play on the same teams. But each town took pride in its own team, too, and the competition was spirited, on dusty pastures during baseball season and around pot-bellied stoves in drafty gyms during basketball season.

Coaching, however, was at a premium. Star Wesleyan athlete Fred Young would hop the train or interurban to various towns to help with a practice session. During one McLean County high school basketball tournament, Young coached no fewer than five of the participating teams, and refereed the games.

Catholic Order of Foresters baseball team, ca. 191

Saybrook High School basketball team, 1914

LIBRARIES

LeRoy built its library with funds willed by James T. Crumbaugh and Lexington built the Smith Library with tax funds. But many of the libraries built after the turn of the century were helped by funds from the Carnegie Foundation.

The new buildings were a source of community pride—a signal to passersby that the smaller towns could provide all the amenities of big-city life.

Interior, McLean Library

Public Library and Community Hall, McLean

AERONAUTIC ENTERTAINMENT

Airplanes and blimps were still entertainment, not transportation. And several thousand Bloomington people rode buggies and street cars to White's Place in 1905 to watch Captain George Yager pilot the first controllable aircraft to appear in the county. The small gasoline engine at the rear of the blimp wasn't strong enough to buck a stiff wind the first day. But Captain Yager piloted "The Comet" around the courthouse dome for a surprise landing on Klemm's roof the second day.

Famed barnstormer Lincoln Beachey brought big crowds to the LeRoy Fairgrounds to watch some loop-the-loops eleven years later.

"The Comet" atop the Klemm Building, 1905

Lincoln Beachey at the LeRoy Fair, ca. 1916

CELEBRITIES

It was no secret that McLean County had sent more than her share of interesting people out into the world. Bloomington's Gordon Lillie was one of them, becoming a prominent ranchman, opening the Oklahoma Territory, and later taking to the road with a "Wild West Show."

One of his featured attractions was Hudson native Charley Jones. Jones supplied food for the builders of the Union Pacific Railroad—they said he killed more buffalo than any other man before he changed direction in later years and worked to prevent the extinction of the species. Buffalo Jones became a close friend of Teddy Roosevelt and was depicted as the hero in several of Zane Grey's western novels.

Gordon "Pawnee Bill" Lillie

Charley "Buffalo" Jones

MARGARET ILLINGTON

Maud Light left her childhood home at 302 East Front in 1900, armed with a music education from Wesleyan and dramatic training from a Chicago drama school, plus a letter of introduction to famed producer-director Daniel Frohman. Within three weeks, she was starring in a New York show, and within three years, she was married to Frohman, 30 years her senior.

She used a contraction of her home

Cast of "The Lie", 1915

town and state as her stage name, and Margaret Illington was destined to become America's foremost actress for a quarter century.

Margaret returned to play Bloomington's Grand Opera House in 1906 and the Majestic Theatre five years later. When she died in 1934, a national radio network broadcast a memorial service and a message was read from President Roosevelt.

SELWYN & COMPANY
Present

Margaret Illington

In

"THE LIE"

A New Play of English Life in Four Acts
By Henry Arthur Jones

— CAST —

HAMP	THOMAS O'MALLEY
MISS PINSENT	VIRGINIA CHAUVENET
GIBBARD	BERTHA KENT

Program Continued on Second Page Following.

Margaret Illington, left center

RACHEL CROTHERS

If there was a lady during those 25 years whose name was more nearly synonymous with theater success than that of Margaret Illington, it must surely have been Rachel Crothers. Ms. Crothers left Bloomington for New York in 1895 and became the greatest woman playwright the nation has known.

She wrote 37 plays, 20 of which played Broadway, and directed nearly all of them herself. Rachel won a Pulitzer Prize and wrote often of women's liberation, and her works were still being performed in the 1980s. "Like Neil Simon today," the *New York Times* said in 1980, "Rachel Crothers filled houses."

Minnie Saltzman spent her girlhood years in a basement apartment below Jefferson School, where her mother was a janitress. But her marriage in 1899 to wealthy Bloomington druggist A.N. Stevens gave her the financial means to travel to Paris to study with the famed Jean DeReszke.

Within a short time, Mme. Saltzman-Stevens was one of the world's most acclaimed dramatic sopranos, drawing rave notices at the ease with which she handled tough Wagnerian roles at houses like London's Covent Garden.

When she returned to perform at the Chatterton Opera House on Market Street, she was greeted by what a newspaper account called "one of the greatest audiences ever seen in this city."

MINNIE SALTZMAN-STEVENS

ELBERT HUBBARD

Hudson claimed Elbert Hubbard, at least for a few years, and by the turn of the century, Hubbard was one of America's most distinguished literary figures. He founded an off-beat periodical called *"The Philistine"* and penned an editorial in 1899 that became a national sensation. Accounts said more copies of the essay titled *"A Message to Garcia"* were sold than any other printed work except the Bible.

Hubbard promoted everything from fine books to glass lamps to a laid-back lifestyle through his East Aurora, N.Y. company, the Roycrofters Press.

When the "Lusitania" sailed in 1915, Hubbard and his second wife were aboard, hoping to write from first-hand experience about the European war. Their lives ended off the coast of Ireland, their ship torpedoed by a German submarine.

". . . I have carried a dinner-pail and worked for day's wages, and I have also been an employer of labor, and I know there is something to be said on both sides. There is no excellence, per se, in poverty; rags are no recommendation; and all employers are not rapacious and high-handed, any more than all poor men are virtuous. My heart goes out to the man who does his work when the 'boss' is away, as well as when he is at home . . ."

— ELBERT HUBBARD
A Message to Garcia

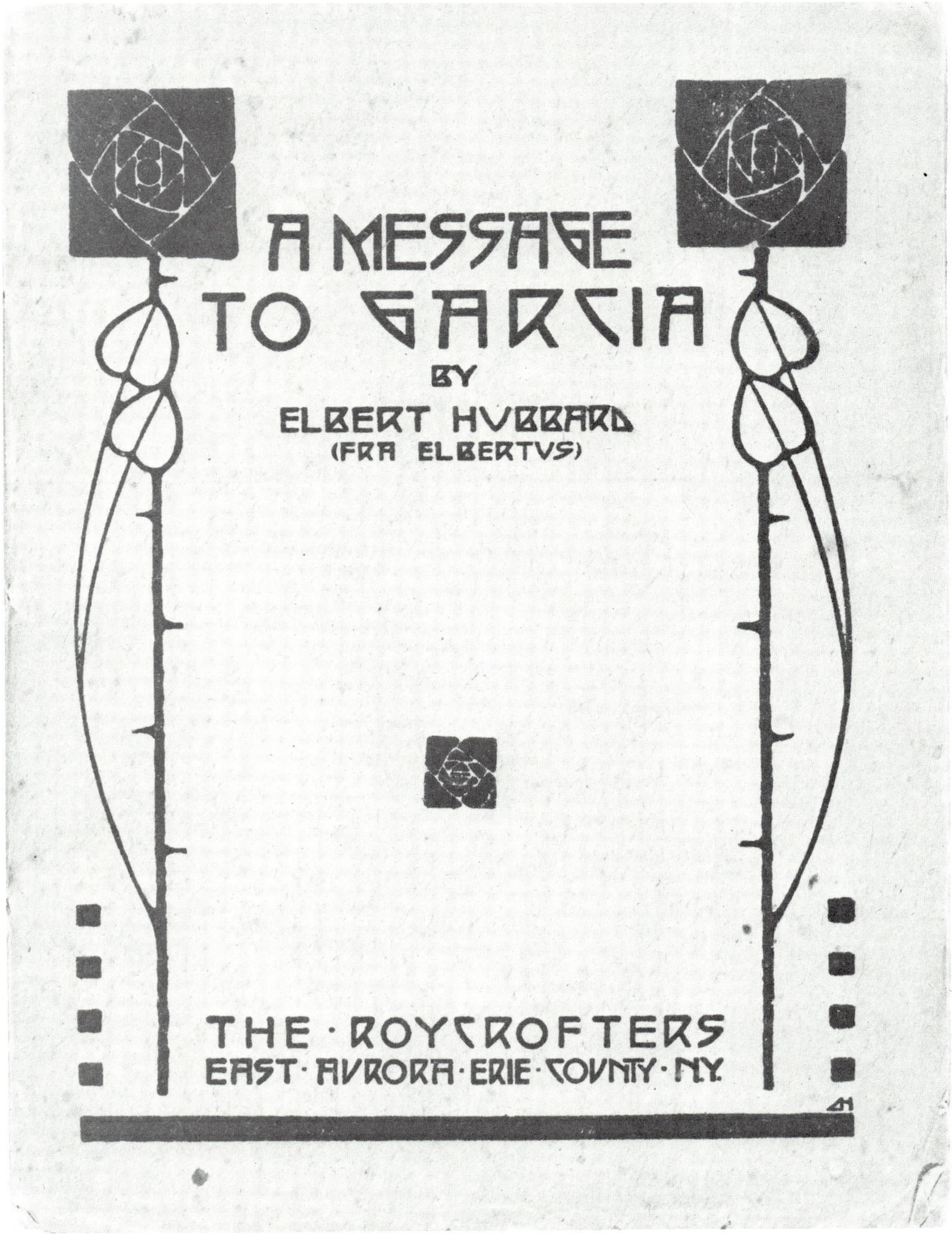

WORLD WAR I

While the official United States position on the European war was one of neutrality, the question in McLean County was not so much whether we would enter the war as when. The Bloomington chapter of the Red Cross began in February, 1917, to organize on a war basis, and Company D of the Illinois National Guard was mobilized and drilling in the streets by March 28. The United States declared war on Germany ten days later, and 14 recruits signed up at the local recruiting station three days after that.

In all, 2,500 volunteers left McLean County for the war, while another 2,500 draftees boarded trains for boot camps.

Troop train leaving Bloomington

Draftees marching to train station, South Main Street, September 5, 1917

Reading war bulletins, Pantagraph Building

Battalion drill, Camp Warden McLean, Tennessee

Mess in cantonment building

PATRIOTISM

It was a popular war on the Central Illinois home front, the curiously posed picture from the Chicago and Alton shops notwithstanding. The shops were a center of some amount of socialist sentiment and provided an unlikely setting for a propaganda picture. But the Council for Defense was hard at work locally, promoting extra effort from "the man behind the man behind the gun" and resisting all things German.

The council ordered the Gummermans to cease printing their *Bloomington Journal* newspaper in German, and the publishers complied. Use of the German language was banned in the schools and in public places, and the German-American Bank changed its name to the American State Bank.

People filled the sidewalks along Madison Street to read the latest war news from *The Pantagraph*, and dug into their pockets to loan the government more than $11 million, some 30 times the cost of the courthouse only 15 years earlier. By war's end, an 8,000-ton freighter named "Evergreen City" plied the Atlantic, a floating symbol of the local contribution. By then, McLean County Red Cross volunteers had made and contributed 440,000 articles for use by troops in the field.

1,000 men of the C&A shops gathered at noon hour to sing patriotic songs, 1918

THE HOME EFFORT

Victory garden, Danvers 4-H Club

Canteen hut, C&A depot

"Knitted articles and supplies, February, 1917, to December, 1919: Sweaters, 7,571; Socks, 6,576 pairs; Mufflers, 1,964; Helmets, 804; Wristlets, 3,649 pairs; Trench caps, 60; Total number, 20,624. Total value, $66,839.75. Surgical dressings, from March, 1917, to December, 1918: Number dressings, 331,732; Value of dressings, $11,262.68 . . ."

— McLean County in the World War

Bloomington's Carl Vrooman, President Wilson's assistant secretary of agriculture, organized a plan that visualized "a million war gardens" across the nation, and McLean County's Home Improvement Association urged the planting of gardens on every vacant lot.

Women flocked into the war kitchen on North Main Street to learn the secrets of cooking healthy meals using the least possible amounts of critical foods, while more than a thousand women attended lectures at the municipal canning kitchen, learning how to preserve their newly harvested garden foods.

Interior, Red Cross Canteen, 214 West Jefferson

Two Stores

Phillos Candy Shop, 108 N. Center St.

Princess Confectionery Store, 106 W. Washington St.

BLOOMINGTON, ILL.

Red Cross Ladies in front of Phillos' Candy Shop, July 24, 1918.

Entire receipts $335.00 were donated to the Red Cross by Mr. C. D. Phillos.

Co. B, 124th Machine Gun Battalion in France

Awaiting the attack

Illinois's 33rd Division was formed during the war's first months, primarily from National Guard units, and McLean County men made up almost the entire roster of Company B, 124th Machine Gun Battalion. The company suffered 85 casualties while capturing 112 prisoners during campaigns in France.

Saybrook and Blooming Grove native James Harbord, meanwhile, was chief of staff to General John Pershing, commander of American forces. Major General Harbord, in turn, headed the mammoth supply force serving the American Doughboys and commanded the defense of Paris.

FLU EPIDEMIC

It was an incredible thought in the twentieth century that a common disease like influenza could kill more people than hostile bullets in Europe, but it happened. The first case of the deadly Spanish influenza appeared in September, 1918, and Bloomington's first death occurred on the 29th of the month. Within two weeks, the disease reached epidemic proportions.

Bloomington-Normal hospitals quickly filled and a Wesleyan fraternity house was pressed into service as an additional hospital. The Bloomington Country Club club house was offered next and was filled with 72 patients in two days. Additional victims were bedded on the third floor of the Bloomington Club and in the Vrooman residence.

The Spanish flu claimed 29 McLean County lives in September, 99 in October, 54 in November and 60 in December.

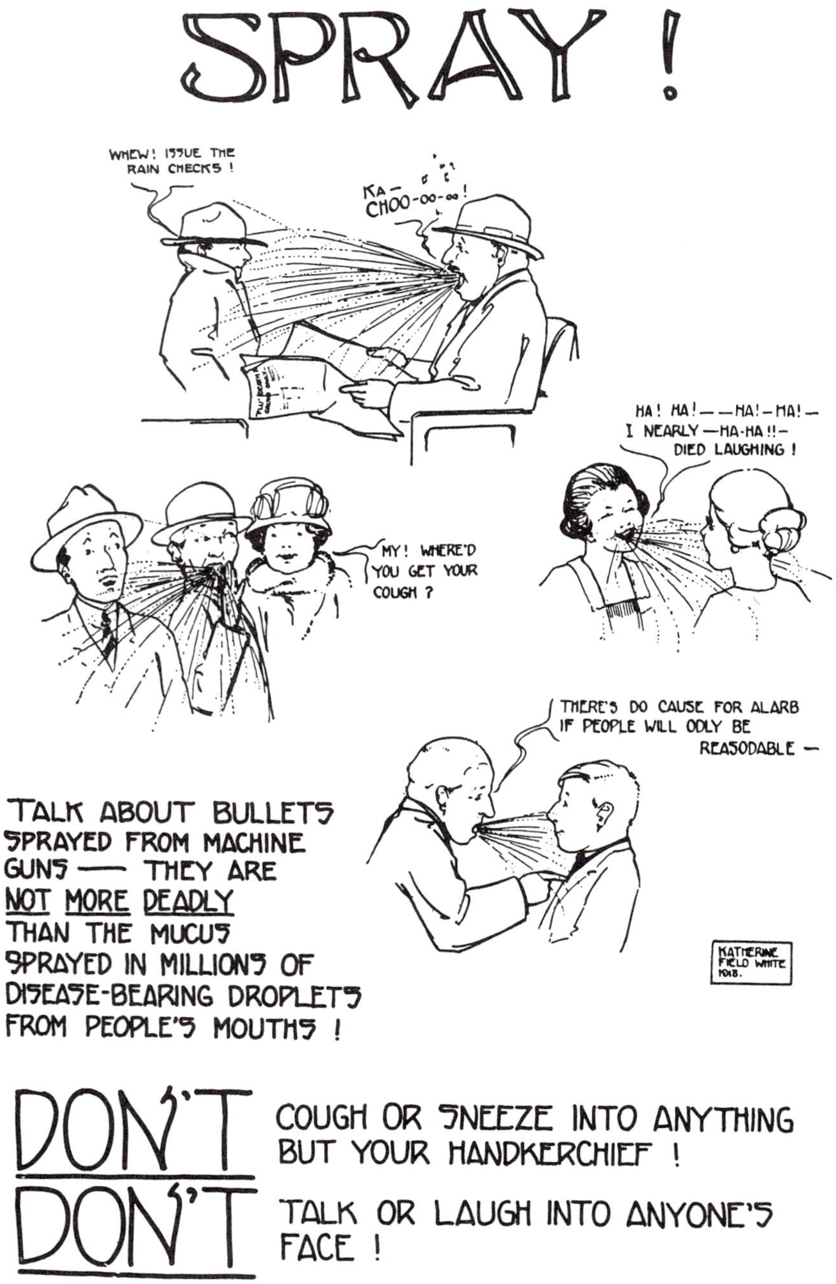

Vrooman residence, 701 East Taylor Street

AT AN END

Company B, 124th Machine Gun Battalion, was assaulting German positions in front of the Troyon sector in France when a general shout up and down the lines accompanied the end of the fighting at 11 a.m., November 11, 1918. McLean County soldiers were on their way home, marching first through part of Germany, then into Luxemburg. They stepped onto troop ships at Brest five months later.

More than 150 McLean County men did not return. Many more were wounded and gassed.

"It was about 3 a.m. The whistling locomotives and the clanging first bells were awakening the community and the enthusiasts were making their way up town to join the jubilee. For a few minutes there was a lull in the ear splitting noise. This proved to be a golden opportunity for a cornetist, somewhere in the northeast section of the city. Stepping to the porch of his home, he played the 'Star Spangled Banner,' throwing his whole soul into the inspiring strains. It was a beautiful and appropriate interpolation and thrilled all who were priviledged to hear it. The player, Dr. A. F. Strange, will never know the effect of the selection upon his widely scattered auditors, but it was an inspiration to all within hearing of the silvery notes. It seemed as if again, 'bombs were bursting in air' and all knew the 'flag was still there.' Patriotism was strengthened and the jubilee given a finer meaning to those who stood reverently in hearing. There was a universal sigh of regret when the final note died away. It was a benediction of the early morn of peace."

— **Pantagraph,** Nov. 12, 1918

Veterans' parade, Main Street, east side of square, 1923

9. RETURN TO NORMALCY

Candidate Harding called it a "return to normalcy," but jailed Socialist opponent Debs's campaign button seemed to modify the term to "would-be-normalcy." The veterans were organizing after the war and so was the Klan. Inflation was a problem, and while times were good for the people with money, the 1920s weren't much different than the '30s for the many without.

But, for a few pennies, Bloomington people could take home some Chinese food from the second-floor Grand Inn Chop Suey Cafe on Center Street, or hop off the streetcar for a ten cent sandwich at the Aljo in the 600 block of North Main.

Meanwhile Thompson's Cafe, a fast-food pioneer, threw away the key to its front door and announced it would be open 24 hours a day. Thompson's was a "must" stop after a movie or a night at a speakeasy. "Everybody" showed up there at one time or another.

Campaign buttons, 1920

Center Street, north from Washington, 1928

Interior, Thompson's Cafe, 208 North Center Street, ca. 1926

Fresh Strawberry Sundae
Whipped Cream 25¢

MENU

FANCY SUNDAES

Banana Split	30	Banana Chop Suey	30
Funny Sundae	20	B. H. S. Special	25
St. M. H. S. Special	25	Boston Nut Sundae	25
Wesleyan Delight	25	Chocolate Bud	25
Goody Goody Sundae	25	Aljo Special	25
Gold Dust Twins	25	Fruit Sundae	25

MILK SHAKES AND MALTED MILK

Chocolate Milk	10	Green River Milk	10
Strawberry Milk	10	Butterscotch Milk	10
Pineapple Milk	10	Grape Milk	10
Orange Milk	10	Mint Milk	10
Cherry Milk	10	Vanilla Milk	10
Lemon Milk	10	Root Beer Milk	10

Malted Milks 15c

MENU

TOASTWICH SANDWICHES

Sar-a-Lee	10	Olive Butter	10
Peanut Butter	10	Pimento Cheese	10
Chicken Salad	20	Ham	10
Salted Almond	15	Luncheon Spread	10
Minced Ham	15	Ham and Cheese	15
Cheese and Pecan	15	Date and Nut	15
Buttered Toast	10	Ham and Olive	15

MISCELLANEOUS

Milk	5	Green River	5
Half and Half	15	Grape Juice	15
Clicquot Club, pint bottle	20	Root Beer	5
Gingerale	10	Bromo Seltzer	10
Phosphates (all flavors)	5	Lemon Seltzer	15

While **Aljo Sweet Shop** is not to be held responsible for loss or exchange of personal property every precaution is exercised for the safety of patrons effects

Unlike so many other improvements, the radio found acceptance in the rural areas almost as rapidly as in town. Montgomery Ward filled mail-orders for the battery operated sets and McLean County people were taken closer to the entertainment centers. Bloomington's Earl Goforth led the house band on WLS in Chicago, while brother George Goforth's Black and Gold Orchestra played at the Harding inauguration.

Dancers became familiar with Tiny Hill's band and those of Bix Beiderbeck, Cab Calloway and Earl "Fatha" Hines via radio, then turned out to see them in person at Bon-Go Park, the Coliseum, the Green Mill Cafe and the O'Neil Park Pavilion. 5,000 people crowded into Funk's Grove to witness a classic "battle of the bands" between Isham Jones and the Coon-Sanders Nighthawks.

Airline Conqueror Model "A"

Earl Goforth's WLS Band, ca. 1925

Funk's Grove Dance Pavilion, ca. 1928

HARD ROADS

Railroad strikes and a shortage of railcars after the war alerted the public to the advantages of shipping by truck, and by 1920 an Association of Commerce bulletin in McLean County announced "we are now on the eve of the greatest program of road construction the state has ever seen."

Within a couple of years, workers were pouring concrete for the Meridian Trail Road (now U.S. 51) and the Illini Boulevard (now Interstate 55). Both routes led directly through Bloomington and Normal, and engineers designed the Main Street overpass to keep traffic moving and enhance safety at the busy railroad crossing.

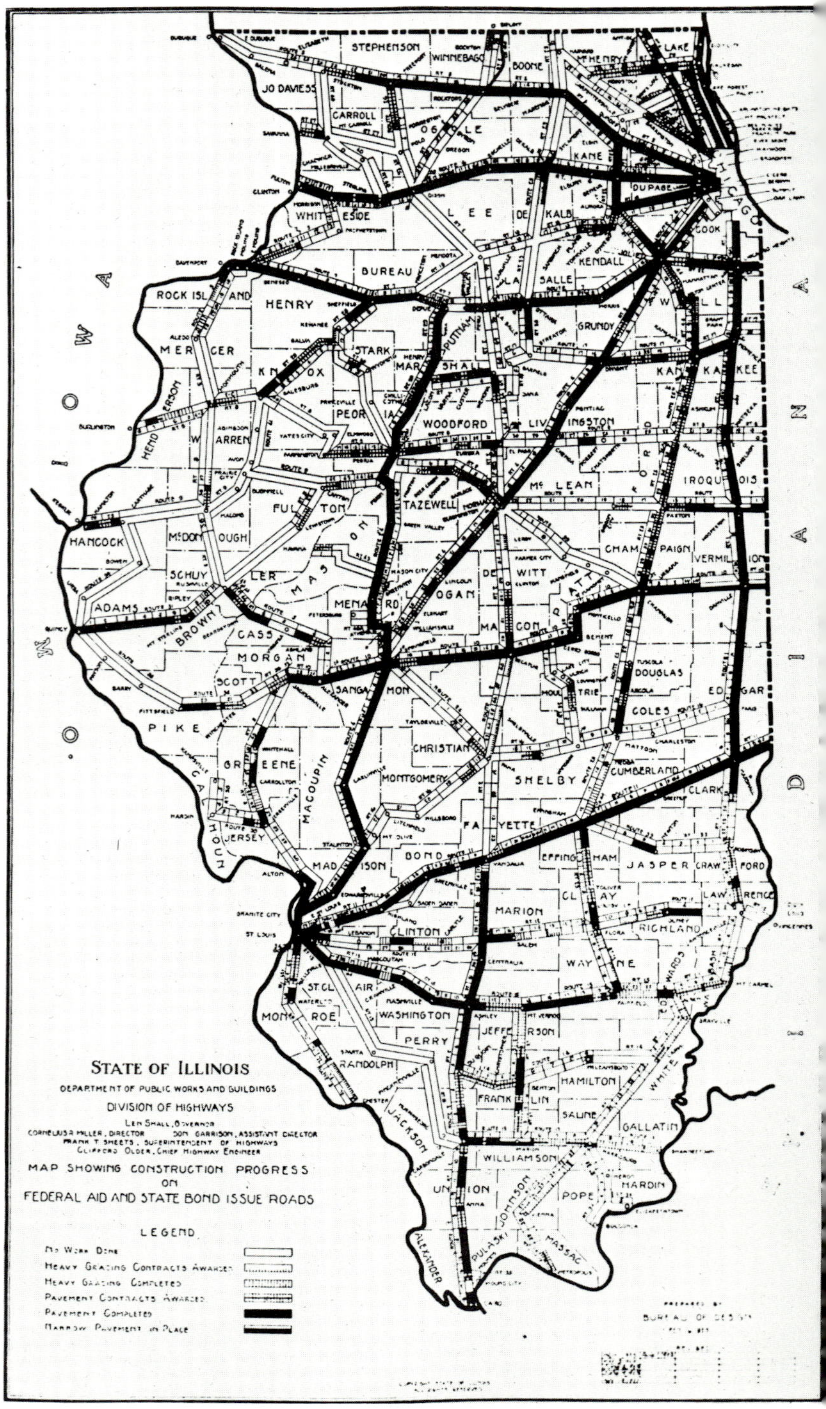

Clearing timber through Funk's Grove

"Illini Boulevard" through Funk's Grove

South Main Street Viaduct, looking north, ca. 1925

TRAVEL BY AIR

Although it would be nearly three decades before Ozark Airlines would provide the area with scheduled service, the 1920s were years for thinking of airplanes less as a barnstormer's novelty at the fair and more as a legitimate means of transportation.

Aviation pioneers Harvey Wurtzburger and Art Carnahan flew their open-cockpit "Jenny" and Curtis biplanes from the new municipal airport north of Normal beginning in 1927 and from the WPA-built airport east of Bloomington seven years later.

An unknown Charles Lindbergh surprised the boys in the Covell general store one foggy, sleety night in 1926 when he walked in and told them he had stepped over the side of his sputtering mail plane and parachuted onto a barbed wire fence. Lindy's out-of-fuel plane crashed a half mile away.

"Travel Air" at Bloomington Airport

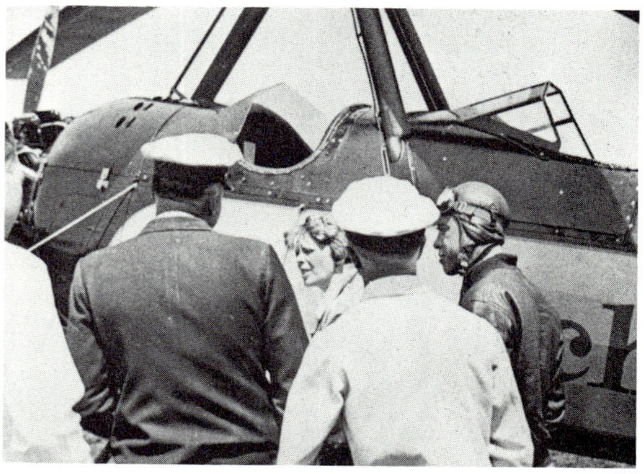

Amelia Earhart at Bloomington Airport

Airport north of Normal on U.S. 51

A NEW SOURCE OF WATER

Jesse Fell looked at the Mackinaw River back in 1850 and predicted Bloomington would go there for her water some day. That day never came, however, as a few years later an underground stream was accidentally discovered by some coal miners.

But the backyard wells and the cisterns were no longer doing the job by the 1900s, and plans were developed for McLean County's largest construction project ever—the $1.5 million Lake Bloomington. The lake was dedicated on the county's 100th birthday, in 1930.

A thousand acres of timber had been cleared, and the dam across Money Creek impounded enough water to quench Bloomington's thirst for years to come, a task thought to be more necessary by the passage of the Volstead Act (Prohibition) a decade earlier.

Laying the pipeline

Lake Bloomington under construction

The Spillway, Lake Bloomington

PRO-HI TIMES

Keeping in business

Those with a thirst for something stronger than water found ways to satisfy it during prohibition. Normalites regularly carted the stuff home on the streetcars from Bloomington for years before prohibition and enough residents of dry Lexington had done the same that the locals called the 5:30 evening train from Bloomington "the booze train" or "Whiskey Dick."

Now, everybody was improvising. Prohibition had been voted in while many who might have opposed it were in the trenches in Europe. And many of the veterans led the way in making berry wine at home, and buying 100 percent grain spirits from the druggist, then cutting it at home with fruit juice. The cocktail became a way of life.

Improvising extended to the Blatz Beer Company. It took up the distribution of tobacco and candy for the duration. Innocent-looking houses on West Hovey and East Jersey became speakeasies. And the sheriff's men lined up a successful haul behind the jail at Madison and Monroe, knowing all the time they were fighting a losing battle.

A successful haul, 1926

An evening out . . .

". . . I knew who was making moonshine as my father's general store was the only store that stocked bulk Fleishman yeast. At the end of each order would be

3 pounds of Fleishman yeast
100 pounds of sugar
100 pounds of bran (bran was used to cap the mash.)

A trained McLean County deputy could smell the sour mash cooking for a mile when the wind was right . . ."

— MORRIS JONES, 1969

. . . at a speakeasy . . .

. . . was a crime.

HOME BUREAU

The war-time Home Improvement Bureau became simply the Home Bureau in later years and Clara Brian served as the county's home advisor for 25 years, turning around an initial "I don't want any outsider snooping around my kitchen" attitude.

Classes in meal-planning, pressure cooking, canning and sewing quickly filled, and homemakers were learning about the nutritional value of milk and the harmful effects of what was then-prevalent coffee drinking among their children.

Farmers brought fresh produce into the city and rented booths at the market inside the Farm Bureau Building, still standing at Monroe and Madison. It was a depressed time on the farm, but 9,503 dressed chickens, 24,574 pounds of butter, 18,198 pounds of sausage and 14,075 dozen eggs nevertheless changed hands here in 1921.

"Difficulties to be overcome"

Northeast corner, Monroe & Center streets

Leisure activities, 1926

A cooking demonstration, 1926

CHILDREN'S CONCERNS

New generations of famous names were dotting the McLean County scene by 1924. Vice-president Stevenson's son, Lewis, had been Illinois's Secretary of State a few years before. And now, Florence Fifer Bohrer became the state's first woman senator. Her father, the former governor, once whispered to his wife "I declare, my dear, and I didn't think she was worth educating!"

Bloomington's new senator went to work in Springfield, pushing through legislation to prevent using young children in the labor market. Senator Bohrer became a strong initiator of child welfare laws, but did perhaps her most unusual convincing on the morning after an official visit to the state mental facility in Moline.

The superintendent and his wife were away when Senator Bohrer walked into the building one evening and introduced herself. She was given a meal and led to a Spartan room. She noticed upon entering that the attendants, dressed in white, locked the door from the outside.

After she had a good night's sleep the superintendent released her and apologized, explaining "You know, we have had patients who thought they were Abraham Lincoln or Jesus Christ, but we never had a WOMAN before who thought she was a senator!"

Florence Fifer Bohrer at her desk in Springfield

Boys' playground, ISSCS, 1925

The Illinois Soldiers' and Sailors' Children's School, established in 1867, was serving more than 500 children by the early 1920s. Some of them were orphans of military veterans, but others were youngsters who would otherwise be sent to county alms houses.

Barrel rolling contest, 1925

"Shanty Row," boys' playground, 1925

MEDICAL ADVANCES

Bloomington-Normal boasted three hospitals by the 1920s, the Mennonites having purchased the Kelso Sanitarium in 1920. St. Joseph's Hospital had been on the corner of Morris and Jackson since the 1880s, nestled among beautiful oak trees. And Brokaw Hospital had been built along the streetcar line, out in the country between Normal and Bloomington, "avoiding the dirt and noise of a city." As the towns advanced their boundaries toward the hospital, advances were also being made on medical fronts.

New X-ray machines were being used. Bloomington doctor Watson Gailey was gaining an international reputation for his techniques of eye surgery, particularly in the treatment of cataracts. And local doctor E. P. Sloan led the world-wide fight to eliminate goiter, an abnormal swelling of the thyroid gland. Dr. Sloan became president of the Illinois State Medical Society.

Fairview Sanitarium, meanwhile, concentrated on treating another feared affliction of the time—tuberculosis. When it was completed in 1919, Fairview was the second county-owned sanitarium in Illinois.

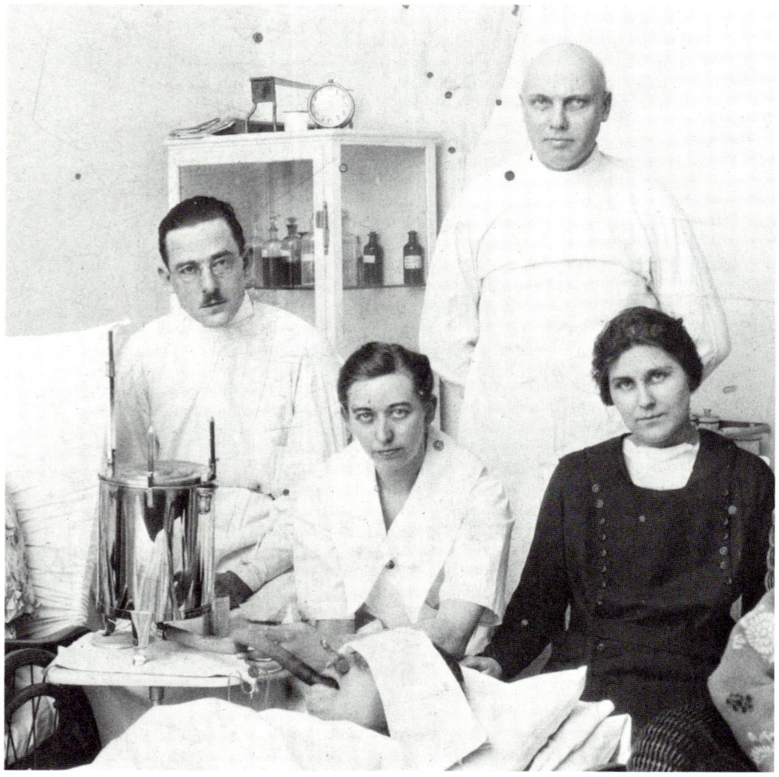

Goiter Clinic, 1922

Fairview Sanitarium, 900 block North Main Street, Normal, ca. 1925

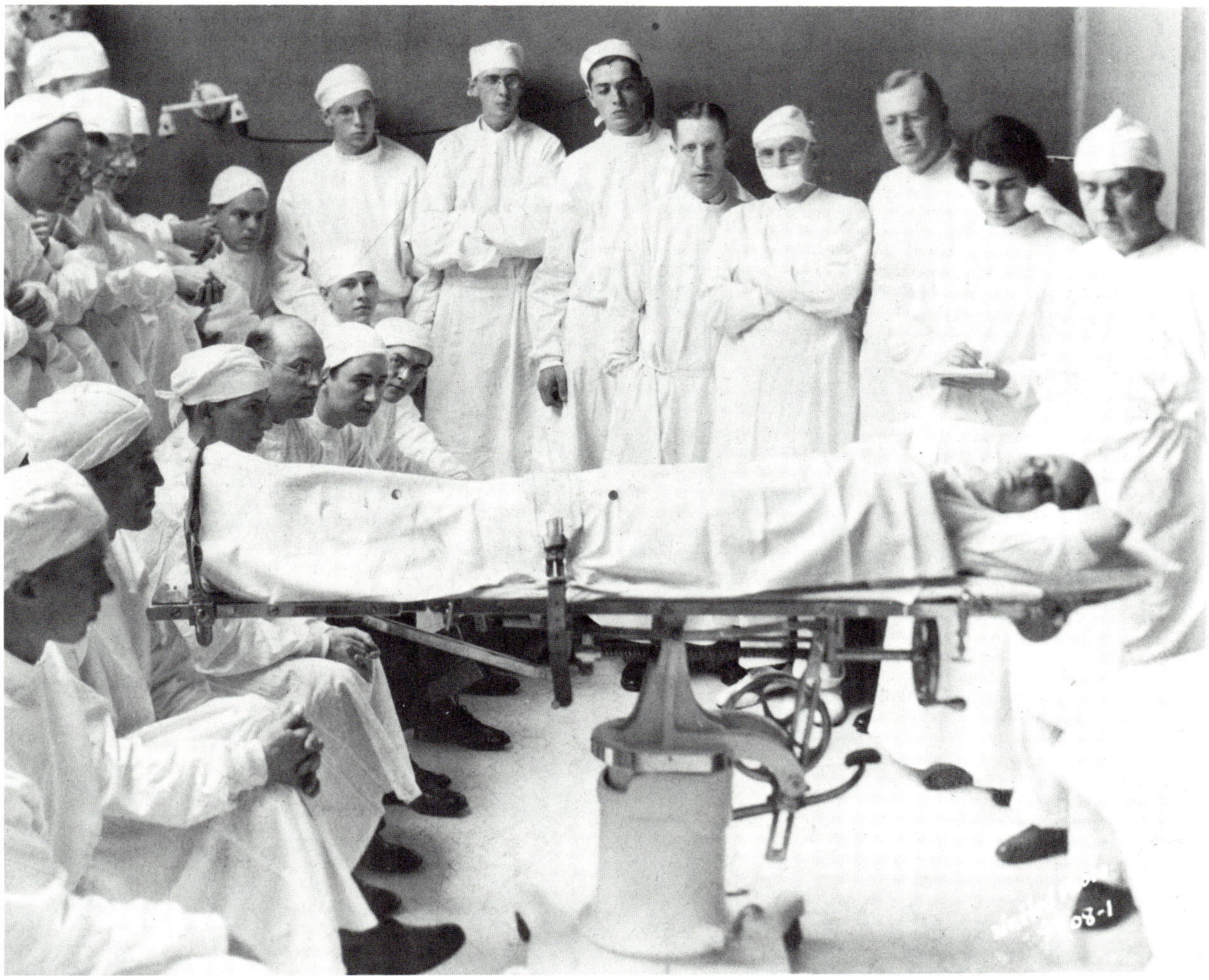

Medical class in operating room

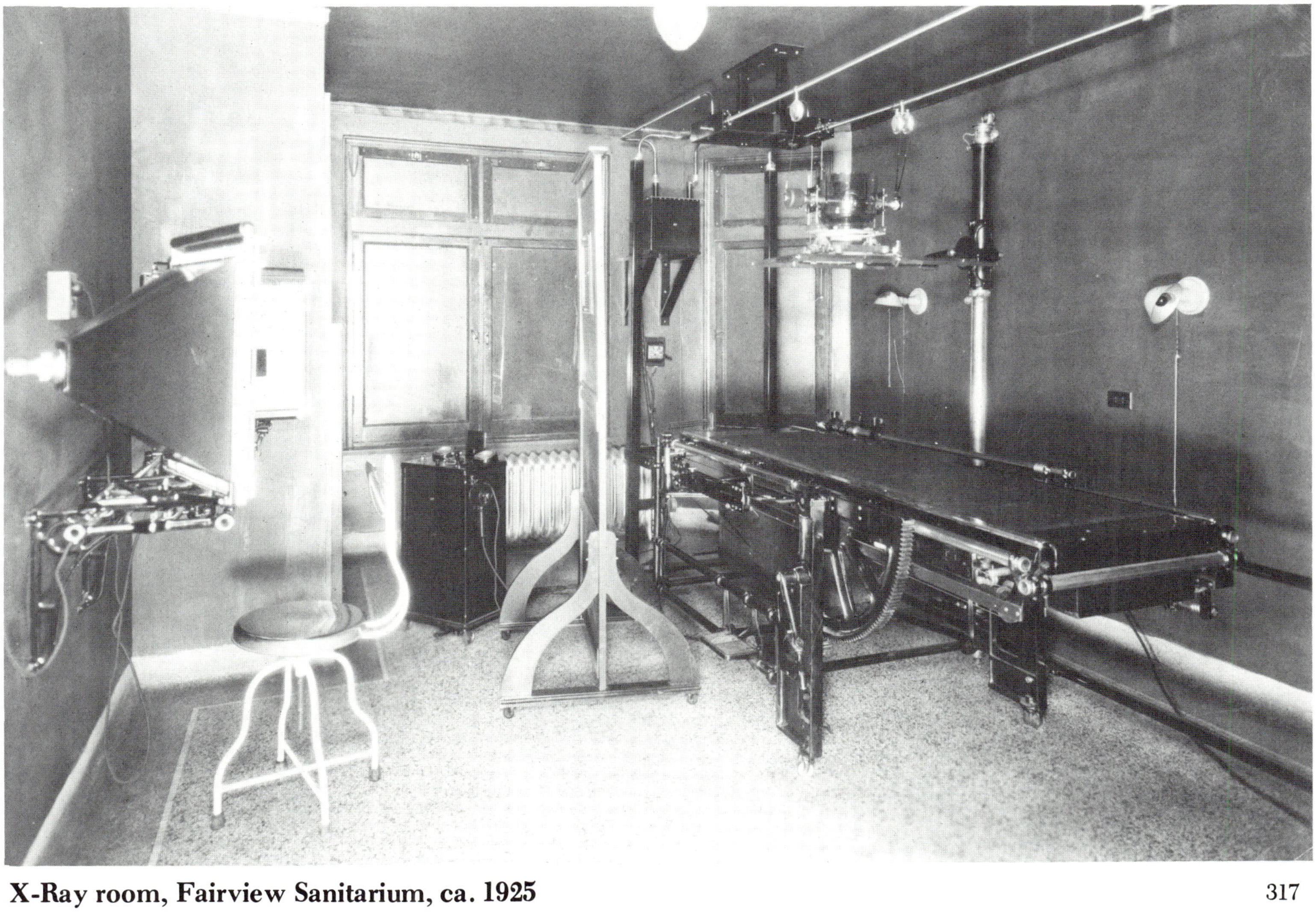

X-Ray room, Fairview Sanitarium, ca. 1925

The PASSION PLAY

The Cast

The House of Joseph:

Jesus of Nazareth	Frederick A. Hitch
Mary, His Mother	Clara Koogle

The Twelve Disciples

John	Andrew W. DuBois
Peter	Fred L. Muhl
Andrew	Simon R. Salzman
James, Son of Zebedee	Charles O. Johnson
Philip	Harry L. Stone
Thomas	Lon K. Anthony
Matthew	George H. Johnson
James, the Less	Burl H. Sealock
Thaddeus	John V. Hileman
Simon	Fred Blum
Bartholomew	Harmon S. Munro
Judas	Louis L. Williams

Intimate Friends of Jesus

Mary Magdalene	Grace Freitag
Martha	Frieda Muhl
Mary, Sister of Lazarus	Daisy Birney
Joanna Chuza	Maedie Brazelton
Susanna	Lou V. Smith
Lazarus	Fred G. Taylor
Malachi	George W. Marton

Women of Jerusalem

Lezzetta Bowmaster
Isla B. Brown
Carrie L. Thompson
Cora L. Tay
Marguerite Bayless
Nora E. Wilson
Anna Marie Altes
Myrtle Grimm
Ethel Green
Pearl Seibel
Caroline Jennings
Laura Green
Bess Marquardt

Scene from first Passion Play, 1922

Scottish Rite Temple, 1920

The Masons built a temple in the 300 block of East Jefferson Street in 1908, and young Wesleyan professor Delmar Darrah was active in its planning. Darrah was an organizer, starting Wesleyan's Drama Department and, by the end of the World War, working on a play about the passion of Jesus Christ — a play much like the famous passion play in Oberamergau, Germany.

What was needed was a fitting building in which to perform Darrah's American Passion Play, and by 1920, the Darrah-designed Consistory was finished. The community took pride in its participation in the performances, and in the workmanship in the new building. Much of the intricate stonework was done in place by an Italian artisan, Joseph Petarde.

Delmar D. Darrah

"WE'RE IN THE MONEY..."

McLean County folks celebrated their centennial some 10 months after the stock market crash of 1929, but the mood was still optimistic in Bloomington. Thousands thronged the city for a daytime parade to kick off the event and thousands more stood in the rain four nights later for the finale.

In between, there were boat races and vaudeville acts at Miller Park and a nightly historical pageant at Highland Park.

Newspaper ads promised a building boom in the 1930s. But most of the buildings — and the prosperity — were not to be.

Centennial Parade, west side of square, 1930

From Centennial Edition, Daily Pantagraph, 1930

ABOVE—Grace M. E. Church, Bloomington
AT RIGHT—Law School Bldg. for Illinois Wesleyan University

ABOVE—Nurse's Home for Brokaw Hospital
AT RIGHT—Sunday School Addition to First Christian Church

Buildings to be erected in Bloomington in the near future. LUNDEEN, HOOTEN, ROOZEN & SCHAEFFER, Architects.

ABOVE—Addition to Mennonite Hospital
AT RIGHT—Sigma Chi Fraternity at Wesleyan

Southeast corner, Main & Washington

Centennial Parade at night, looking southeast from courthouse

10. THE GREAT DEPRESSION

Farms, homes, businesses and savings were quickly lost and farmers were reduced to grinding their own wheat to feed their families. Bloomington issued its own Barter and Exchange Scrip. Fewer people could afford to ride the trains and layoffs plagued the Chicago and Alton shops.

When the C&A offered special excursions to Chicago for the "Century of Progress" in 1933 at a dollar a ride, some 3,000 people took the offer, filling three trains from Bloomington. But many others attempted to ride for free. Hobo camps sprang up along the McLean County railroads and surveillance in the yards was stepped up. Railroad employees often looked the other way, however, at the sight of a man hopping a freight car. The outgoing passenger meant one less name on the local unemployment roles.

Among the unemployed was Bloomington's Charles Morgan. Before the Depression, he had been a carpenter, but now, with little demand for his services, he recorded the feelings and experiences that many people shared.

". . . Thousands of hobos go back and forth. Each freight train brings them in and takes them out. You can see them every where you look."

— Charles Morgan
May 23, 1932

". . . Then about four thirty I started for home. On the way I met Mr. B. . . and he told me that we must move out . . ."

— Charles Morgan
July 17, 1933

Hobo camp, north end of C&A Yards

THREE MYSTERIOUS FIRES

Plenty of people were out of work and many of them were angry about it. But nobody was ever arrested for the three arson-related fires that frightened Bloomington in 1932.

City firemen, using outdated equipment, were no match for any of them, the first of which started with an early-morning explosion inside the Bon-Go Park pavilion. Hundreds of spectators watched that March 4 as the dance hall, a restaurant and a bowling alley burned to the ground. Only the roller-slide was left, sticking out of the lake.

Two mornings later, in near-zero weather, firemen watched Jefferson School—the old Bloomington High School—burn to the ground. And, in the largest blaze of them all Holy Trinity Church burned down the next morning.

Antique pumper pressed into service

Bon-Go Park, March 4, 1932

Jefferson School, March 7, 1932

Holy Trinity Church, March 8, 1932

THE UNEMPLOYED REACT

The Unemployed Councils of Bloomington actively agitated for unemployment insurance, free water for the out-of-work and free swimming and fishing at Miller Park. But it was when the group took its case to Normal in February, 1932, that trouble developed.

Normal's mayor had publicly deplored the council's avowed connection to the Communist Party and turned down the group's request for a street-corner rally. More than 200 unemployed marchers nevertheless gathered at North and Fell. Fists and police billy clubs flew and firemen hosed down the demonstrators. The unemployed grabbed the end of the hose and stretched it down Broadway a couple of blocks before forming in ranks again and beginning a soggy march back to Bloomington.

Unemployment march, Fell Avenue, Norm

Demanding unemployment insurance, 214 North Madison, 1933

bruary 1932

Picketing the Emergency Relief Office

Confrontation at the Relief Office, corner of East & Jefferson

RELIEF EFFORTS

Relief was available, but it was a sign of the times that workers were expected to create the resources for it. The Kiwanis Club was active in beginning a 70-acre community garden, and trucks of unemployed men left early in the morning to hand cultivate the land.

Other plots were made available to individuals. The old canning factory on Normal's Ash Street provided free cans, supplied by the government. Gardeners of low income could preserve their harvest for the winter months. Those with jobs could get free canning if they would agree to furnish half their crops for relief.

". . . at this time things look very cerious to me. Practially every thing in this vacinity for a large scope are doomed to nothing. And the rising prices on all necessities continue to rise. With still no work to speak of Or any methods to get money a poor fellow out of a job has a mighty hard row to hoe. The only one that says times are getting better is the man that is lucky enough to have a job. Our relief allowances has not raised. There for we can not get as much by a fourth as we have bin getting. So we have to resort to a cheaper grade. And that practice may result in sickness or some other malady . . . Bakery goods are all raised twenty five per cent in price. Meats and potatoes are now exerbant. Potatoes at present are selling at the rate of two dollars and ten cents per bushell. Butter around thirty cents per lb. A raise of twelve cents per lb."

— Charles Morgan
July 22, 1933

Leaving for work at the community garden

Harvesting in the community garden

"Clear and a fine day. Hot and sultry in the sun. But a cool brisk north east wind made it more pleasant. I worked out in the community garden this morning . . ."

— Charles Morgan
July 26, 1933

Making saurkraut from the harvest

Other efforts to provide food for the needy were as basic as that of "Uncle Billy" Shelper, who organized a group to salvage potatoes after a freight car overturned. The good spuds were given to those on relief. People with jobs could buy their potatoes in the new Piggly Wiggly supermarket at 123 North Street in Normal.

Through it all, folks managed to scratch out a subsistence, extending their credit lines, trading their scrip notes, and when all else failed, joining other unemployed at the St. Joseph's Hospital soup kitchen. Billy Shelper served free meals to some 6,000 hungry folks at his Home Sweet Home Mission during one two-month period.

". . . Hundreds get scanty allowances through charitys and well fares. Hundreds of acres gardened by unemployed Factories closed. Run out of money to do buisness on. Hardly any one has the cash to buy nessecaries at all. Begging. Bartering and trading in different ways to get along . . ."

— Charles Morgan
May 23, 1932

". . . I went up to the civic relief this morning. Brought out a sack of flour . . ."

— Charles Morgan
July 28, 1933

Salvaging potatoes from an overturned freight car

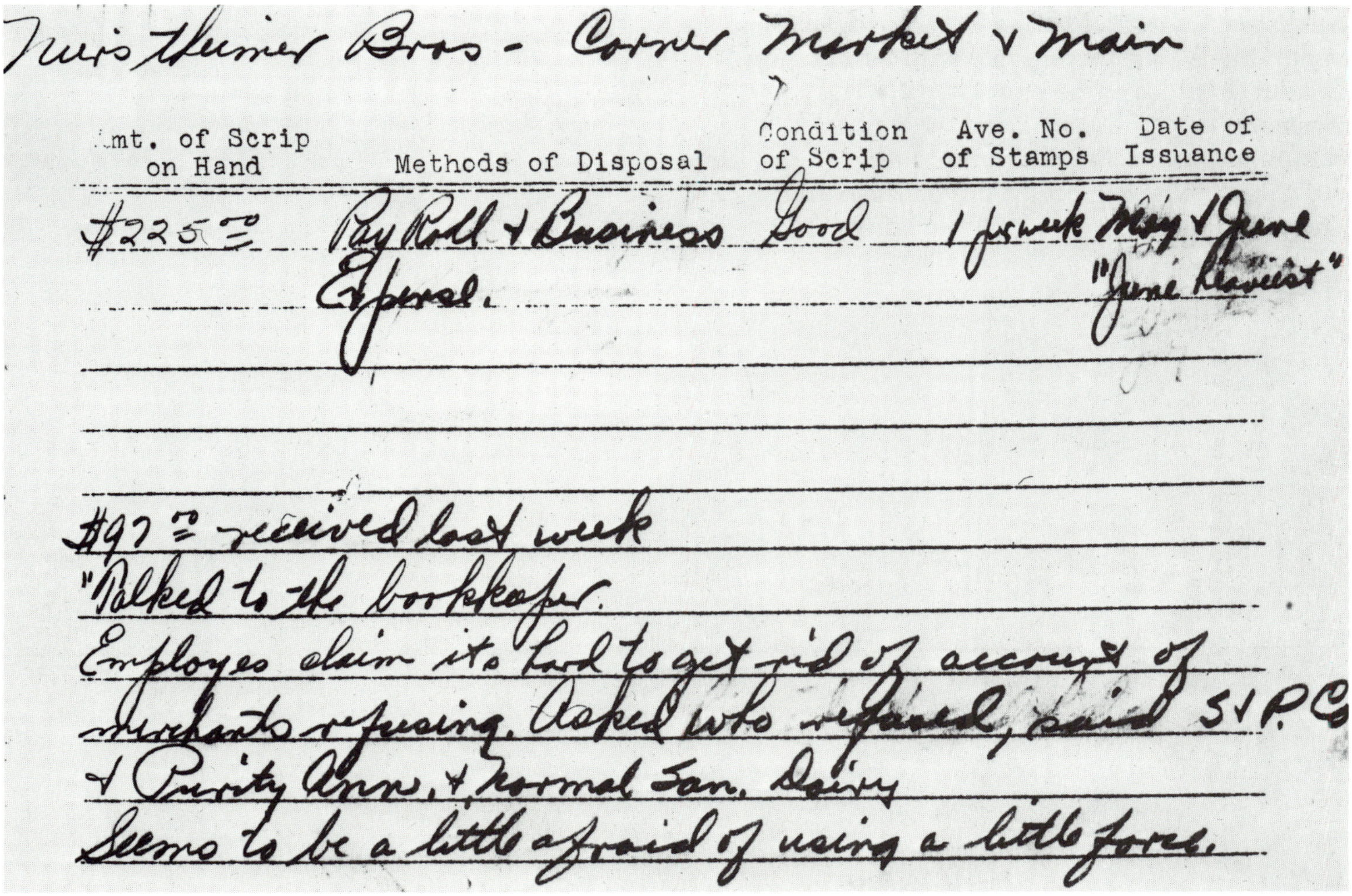

Meis Heimer Bros - Corner Market & Main

Amt. of Scrip on Hand	Methods of Disposal	Condition of Scrip	Ave. No. of Stamps	Date of Issuance
$225.00	Pay Roll & Business Expense.	Good	1 per week	May & June "June Heaviest"

$97.00 received last week
"Talked to the bookkeeper.
Employes claim it's hard to get rid of account of merchants refusing. Asked who refused, said S & P. Co & Purity Assn. & Normal San. Dairy
Seems to be a little afraid of using a little force.

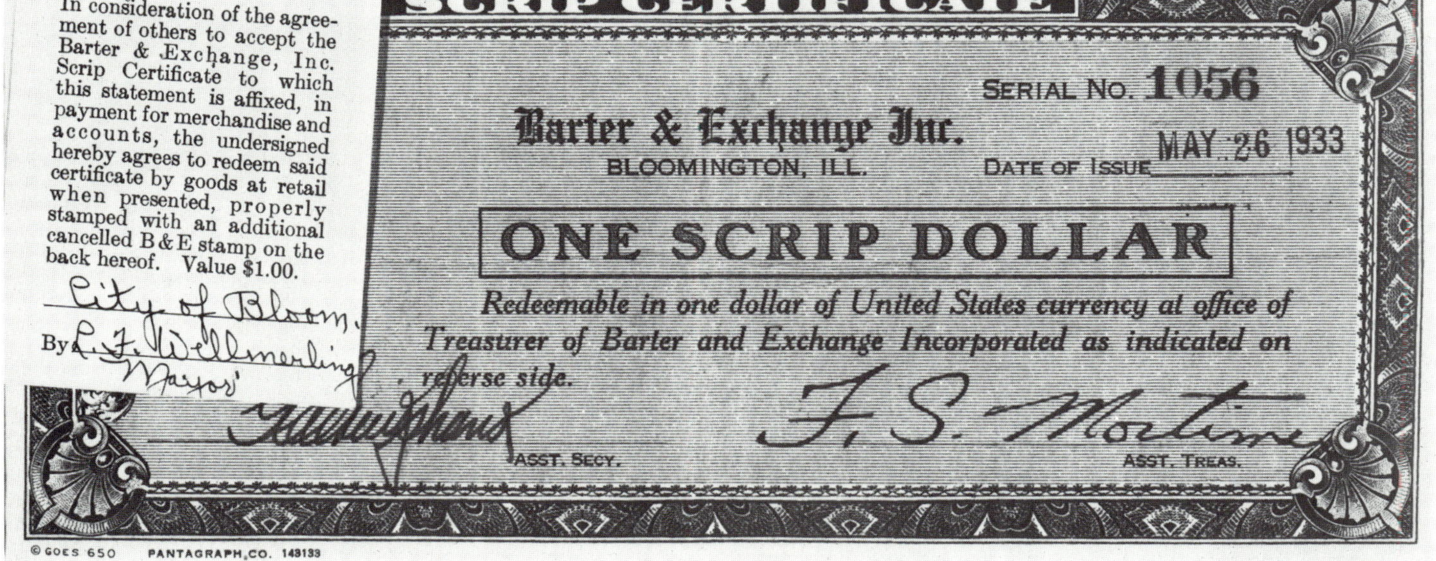

In consideration of the agreement of others to accept the Barter & Exchange, Inc. Scrip Certificate to which this statement is affixed, in payment for merchandise and accounts, the undersigned hereby agrees to redeem said certificate by goods at retail when presented, properly stamped with an additional cancelled B & E stamp on the back hereof. Value $1.00.

City of Bloom.
By L. F. Wellmerling
Mayor

SCRIP CERTIFICATE

SERIAL NO. 1056

Barter & Exchange Inc.
BLOOMINGTON, ILL.

DATE OF ISSUE MAY 26 1933

ONE SCRIP DOLLAR

Redeemable in one dollar of United States currency at office of Treasurer of Barter and Exchange Incorporated as indicated on reverse side.

ASST. SECY.

F. S. Mortimer
ASST. TREAS.

© GOES 650 PANTAGRAPH CO. 143133

REPEAL

Bloomington had been wet again, dry again for a number of years, voting booze out in 1914, back in during 1916, then back out in 1918. There were said to be 80 saloons in the city during one of the wet years. A lot of barkeeps were standing in line when relicensing began in 1933.

Fred and John Baldini joined them in 1936. Brothers from Lucca, Italy, they served a full-course plate lunch for 25 cents and displayed live lobsters in the front window. The original mahogany bar still dominates the grill, and at the end of it sits the first pizza oven in Central Illinois.

Window display, National Liquor Store

National Liquor Store, 203 South Main, ca. 1939

Lucca Grill, 116 East Market, 1936

THE ROAD TO RECOVERY

When President Roosevelt ordered all United States banks closed on March 4, 1933, several Bloomington institutions used the following ten days to reorganize as the National Bank of Bloomington. Peoples Bank of Bloomington and First National Bank of Normal were the first to open when the presidential order was lifted, and the community was relieved when there was no rush among depositors to withdraw their funds.

President Roosevelt's "alphabet soup" approach to turning the economy around was primarily one of organization. Local efforts and local groups became national programs to fight a national depression.

Several thousand people stood along the tracks at Bloomington's C&A depot seeking encouragement when FDR appeared there, and the familiar American eagle symbol of the National Recovery Act began to appear in store windows.

Young men of the Civilian Conservation Corps camped outside LeRoy and planted tens of thousands of trees in the area. The combination was a good one—unemployed men put to work to prevent a local recurrence of the western states' "dust bowl" soil losses.

Franklin Roosevelt, Bloomington, 1936

WPA

Evidence of the Works Progress Administration was everywhere. WPA workers built roads and buildings, and found employment in such diverse undertakings as painting the mural in the Normal Post Office to putting on a show at the LeRoy Fall Festival to indexing past issues of *The Daily Pantagraph*, which is now on file at the Bloomington Public Library.

WPA workers improved the fairways at Highland Park golf course, built a community football and baseball stadium at Wesleyan and , using mostly real horsepower, constructed a new airport.

WPA sewing project, 1937

Street improvements

Work at Highland Golf Course

THE COMPANY WILL APPRECIATE SUGGESTIONS FROM ITS PATRONS CONCERNING ITS SERVICE 1201-S

CLASS OF SERVICE

This is a full-rate Telegram or Cablegram unless its deferred character is indicated by a suitable sign above or preceding the address.

WESTERN UNION

(57)

R. B. WHITE, PRESIDENT — NEWCOMB CARLTON, CHAIRMAN OF THE BOARD — J. C. WILLEVER, FIRST VICE-PRESIDENT

SIGNS

DL = Day Letter
NM = Night Message
NL = Night Letter
LC = Deferred Cable
NLT = Cable Night Letter
Ship Radiogram

The filing time shown in the date line on telegrams and day letters is Standard Time at point of origin. Time of receipt is Standard Time at point of destination.

Received at 210 West Washington St., Bloomington, Ill. Telephone 3000 1937 NOV 19 AM 11 03

C55 28 GOVT=SN WASHINGTON DC 19 1133A

MCLEAN COUNTY HISTORICAL SOCIETY=

WORKS PROGRESS ADMINISTRATION ADVISES OF APPROVAL OF ALLOTMENT OF $1,096 TO PROVIDE EMPLOYMENT FOR NEEDY PERSONS TO INDEX AND CATALOG RECORDS ETC. FOR MCLEAN COUNTY HISTORICAL SOCIETY=

JAS HAMILTON LEWIS US SENATOR.

A NEW AIRPORT

Grading for the Bloomington-Normal airport, 1934

Finishing the runway, 1934

PEST CONTROL

White grubs, cutworms and, particularly, chinch bugs began to destroy large stands of corn in 1932, and by the following year, at the peak of the depression, the chinch bugs wiped out 3,000 acres of McLean County's crop and damaged thousands more.

1934 was a drought year, and farmers built 3,000 dusty miles of barriers onto which they poured six carloads of government-supplied chinch bug oil.

Chinch bug barrier, ca. 1934

Waiting for government chinch bug oil, 1934

THE SUMMER OF '36

If the "winter of the deep snow" and the "winter of the sudden freeze" were the bases for stories surviving from the 1830s, 1936 must go down as the most intolerable of summers. Record highs for 12 consecutive July days still stand—from 105 degrees on July 4th to 114 on July 15th.

Residents slept in their yards, waded in the Miller Park Lake, increased their usage of water by about 20 percent and quickly bought out the stores lucky enough to receive shipments of electric fans.

". . . We stayed around the rooms all day. Intirely to warm and sultry to venture out anywhere. We all swelter in the terrific heat all day. Each day there is some breeze. But very stifeling and calm and close at night time. People lay around everywhere in back yards On porches. In the parks anywhere to keep cool. Anywhere people are allowed to sleep without moslestation The temperature run up to 109⁰ today. Crops and gardens and pastures all all burnt up. For the past two weeks it has dayly run up from 105 to 112⁰ degrees several fatalties from the heat now. And increacing dayly. Farmers do their work at night time. In order to save what is left . . ."

— Charles Morgan
July 12, 1936

Evening field work near Hudson

HYBRID CORN

Farmers had for decades saved their best ears of corn for next year's seed, but the chinch bugs, root worms and drought of the middle-1930s changed their thinking. Dr. James Holbert of the Funk Brothers Seed Company had been experimenting with hybrid corn for years and had developed varieties resistant to dry weather.

The yield success of hybrid corn versus open-pollinated seed was evident, and McLean County was on its way to becoming the "hybrid corn capital of the world." Adults gave way to teenagers years later, but the perennial summer job—detasseling—changed little.

Detasseling crew, Funk Farms, 1932

DOWNTOWN

Even if you didn't have a lot of money, you could still afford to window shop, and McLean County shoppers dressed for the occasion—white gloves for the ladies. You could take the streetcar downtown (until the buses took over in 1936), have a bag of popcorn, and enjoy a matinee featuring the latest Bing Crosby movie.

The increasing number of women in the job market might lunch at the popular Village Inn or Rolands' Tea Room, advertised as a "tea room of refinement." Some with cars gassed up with high-test "Magic Ethyl" at the station next to the Irvin Theatre and took an occasional noon-hour drive to Normal's South Main Street to sample Gus Belt's 10-cent "Steakburgers" and ten-cent milk shakes at the Steak-n-Shake.

Irvin Theatre, ca. 1939

Southeast corner, Jefferson & Main streets.

Northeast corner, Monroe & Main streets, ca. 1938

Village Inn interior

Northeast corner, Jefferson & East streets, ca. 1939

OTHER DIVERSIONS

For a dime, in the late '30's, you could play a round of miniature golf at the popular course on Wood Street in Bloomington. And you could watch for free as Edward B. "Buddy" Rust played in the state amateur golf tournament or Russell Shirk won the men's city tennis crown.

All-Americans Tony Blazine and Bob Neuman were leading Wesleyan to an unscored-upon conference football season in 1932, while straw-hatted fans were cheering for the Bloomington Bloomers in the Class B Three-I League.

As many as 300 circus performers were spending their winters in Bloomington, and the town was the national home for trapeze acts. When Art Concello quit performing to manage the Ringling Circus, his wife, Antoinette, carried on as a featured performer, and was known as "the greatest lady flyer ever." Their catcher, George Valentine, formed his own troupe, and it was honored by *Billboard* magazine as the nation's "greatest outdoor flying act."

Mary and Roy Valentine and Reiner

Bones Brown

"Tilbury Flash" at Bloomington Airport

Art Carnahan was engaged in a different sort of flying, though not much farther off the ground. Carnahan piloted a plane around the pylons on a five-mile course, swooping below his competitors, only feet off the ground, to win the Polish Trophy at the International Air Race in Chicago in 1933.

His "Tilbury Flash", with an 18-foot wing span and a motorcycle engine, hangs from the ceiling in the McLean County Historical Society Museum.

South of Bloomington, behind National Guard Armory

ART SHOW

Perhaps the most ambitious McLean County diversion came in 1939 when Rolands' owner Raymond Wakely and Pantagraph publisher Loring Merwin led a drive to bring to Bloomington what Chicago Art Institute official Chauncey McCormick called "the best show, outside of the three or four leading museums in America, that I've seen."

Originals by Rembrandt, Rubens, Monet, Toulouse-Lautrec and Grant Wood were carted in. And *Time* and *Newsweek* ran feature stories. *Life* magazine said "This week in Bloomington, art history is being made. For the first time, a top-rank show of paintings is being held in a small midwestern city."

A critic

"*. . . Last December . . . we were recalling the various stunts that had been tried for bringing visitors to Bloomington. These covered all the regular things from amateur boxing matches to corn guessing contests . . . Last winter, for instance, we had Betty and Benny the 'Sky-Dancers' . . . who gyrate 200 feet above the city's tallest building on an 18-inch disc and drink, in this order, a bottle of Coca-Cola, a bottle of Carnation milk and a bottle of Blatz beer for the edification of the crowd . . . Somebody suggested an art show . . .*"

— Loring Merwin, 1939

American Legion guarding the paintings

WAR PREPARATIONS

The coming war had already arrived in Europe and the Far East. Few doubted United States involvement was imminent. Preparations were underway.

U.S. 66 had long served as the major highway between St. Louis and Chicago, but it threaded its way through each town along the way. Workers in 1938 put the finishing touches on the four-lane bypass around Bloomington-Normal, designed to carry non-stop military traffic. No stop lights were planned. Cross traffic hurried across at its own risk. Curves on Bloomington's southeast and southwest corners were designed for 100-mile-per-hour traffic.

Bloomington's National Guardsmen, a quartermaster outfit attached to the Illinois 33rd Division, recruited heavily, pointing to the strong likelihood of a soon-to-come wartime draft.

Building the Beltline

Co. D convoy north of Rockford, 1937

Bloomington National Guardsmen at rifle practice

11. ANOTHER WORLD WAR

The draft came a year before Pearl Harbor and numbers were assigned to all males in McLean County ages 21 through 35. The numbers were posted on the Pantagraph's outdoor bulletin board and in the courthouse. Twelve-thousand people gathered that same day to listen to presidential candidate Wendell Wilkie speak at the Alton Station.

President Roosevelt was in Washington and presided two days later when the lottery numbers were drawn to decide the order in which the registrants would be called. There was some weeping in the courthouse rotunda when it was learned who would go first, but the county's first three draftees, farmer John Dale Smith of LeRoy, State Farm Executive John Workman of Bloomington and auto mechanic Harold Johnson of Normal took it in stride.

Bloomington's National Guard battalion rolled out of town in convoy in March of '41 for a year's training at Camp Peay, Tenn. Draftees, meanwhile, left town by rail for boot camp while parents and girlfriends waved goodby from "heartbreak bridge," the Front Street overpass at the Alton Station.

Unlike the wars before, this one would allow for no state indentity. Illinois soldiers were placed in units with recruits from other states in a massive cultural mixing.

Reading draft numbers at the courthouse, October 27, 1940

City
Bloomington
Only

TRAINING

The re-education began at the induction center when the omnipresent overweight sergeant took over, making clear to former masters of McLean County households that they were to begin living as numbers, by the numbers.

The sarge showed them their perfectly made bed was wrinkled and their spit-shined boots were smudged. He harassed them out of bed at 5 in the morning and tore apart their foot lockers at night.

Home was often not even wooden barracks. Quonset huts went up quickly in overcrowded training camps but the American engineers put their own touch on the British huts. The American version often had a front porch.

Quonset huts built for barracks

Camp library

Parade Rest

Port Arms

Right Shoulder Arms

BIVOUAC IN HAWAII

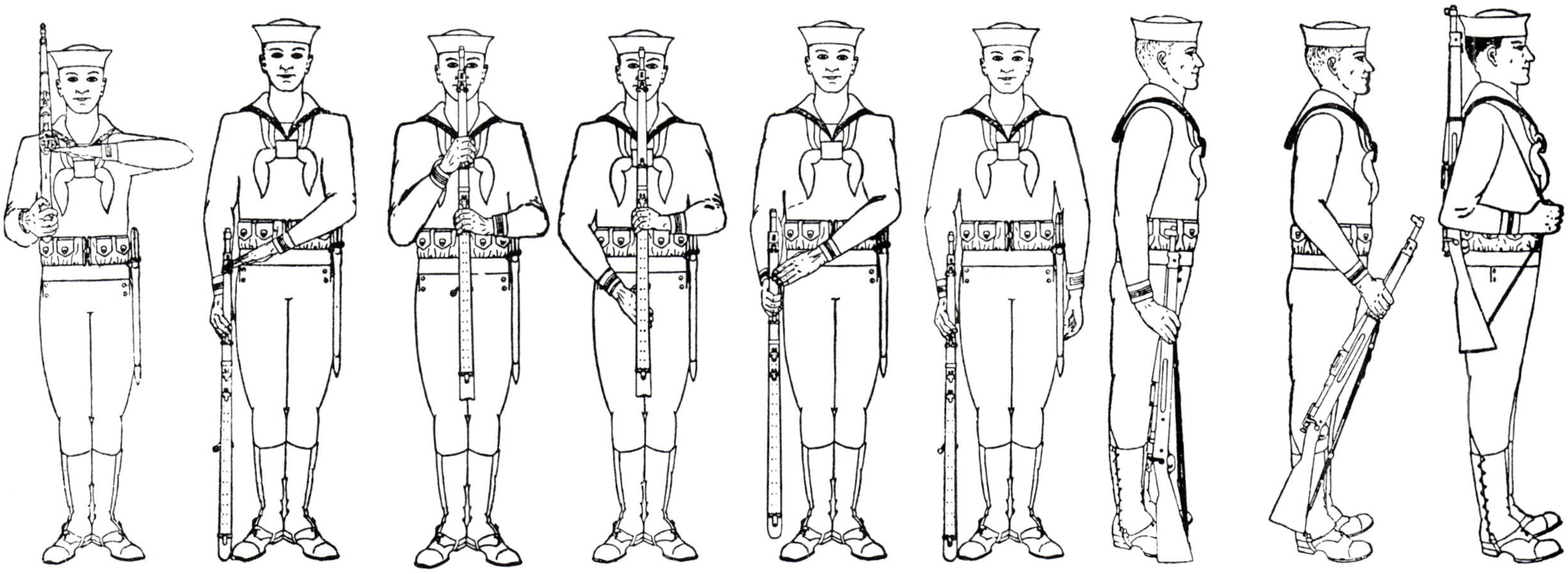

Rifle Salute Present Arms Order Arms Trail Arms Sling Arms

CIVIL DEFENSE

Those remaining at home became involved in Civilian Defense or the Civil Air Patrol, helped the Red Cross or became air wardens. Those wanting to wear a uniform had no trouble finding one to wear.

Within a year, the county was conducting its own drills, such as a mock air raid testing Civil Defense efforts after pretend incendiary bombs fell on St. Joseph's Hospital and the Alton Station.

Chanute Air Base officers declared Bloomington and its Moulton Street "red light" district off limits, and Mayor Mark Hayes vowed to clean up the entire Wood Hill area.

Shutting down the lights proved a tougher task, but Bloomington joined with the rest of the state in successfully doing it one July night in 1943.

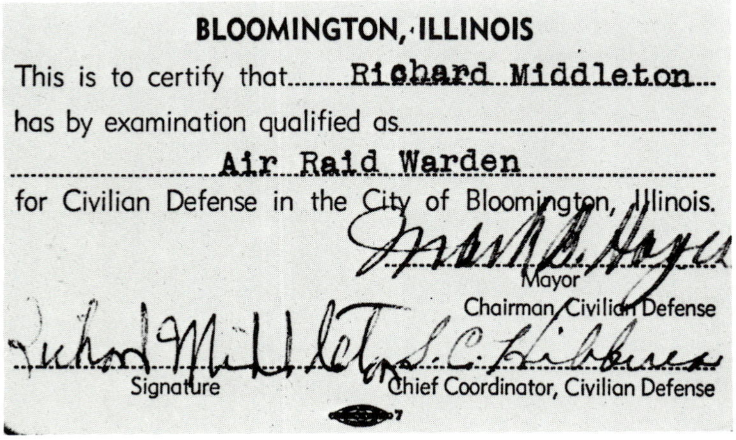
BLOOMINGTON, ILLINOIS

This is to certify that Richard Middleton

has by examination qualified as

Air Raid Warden

for Civilian Defense in the City of Bloomington, Illinois.

Mark B. Hayes
Mayor
Chairman, Civilian Defense

Richard Middleton
Signature

S. C. Gibbens
Chief Coordinator, Civilian Defense

Civil Defense Control Center, December, 1942

Before

Blackout

After

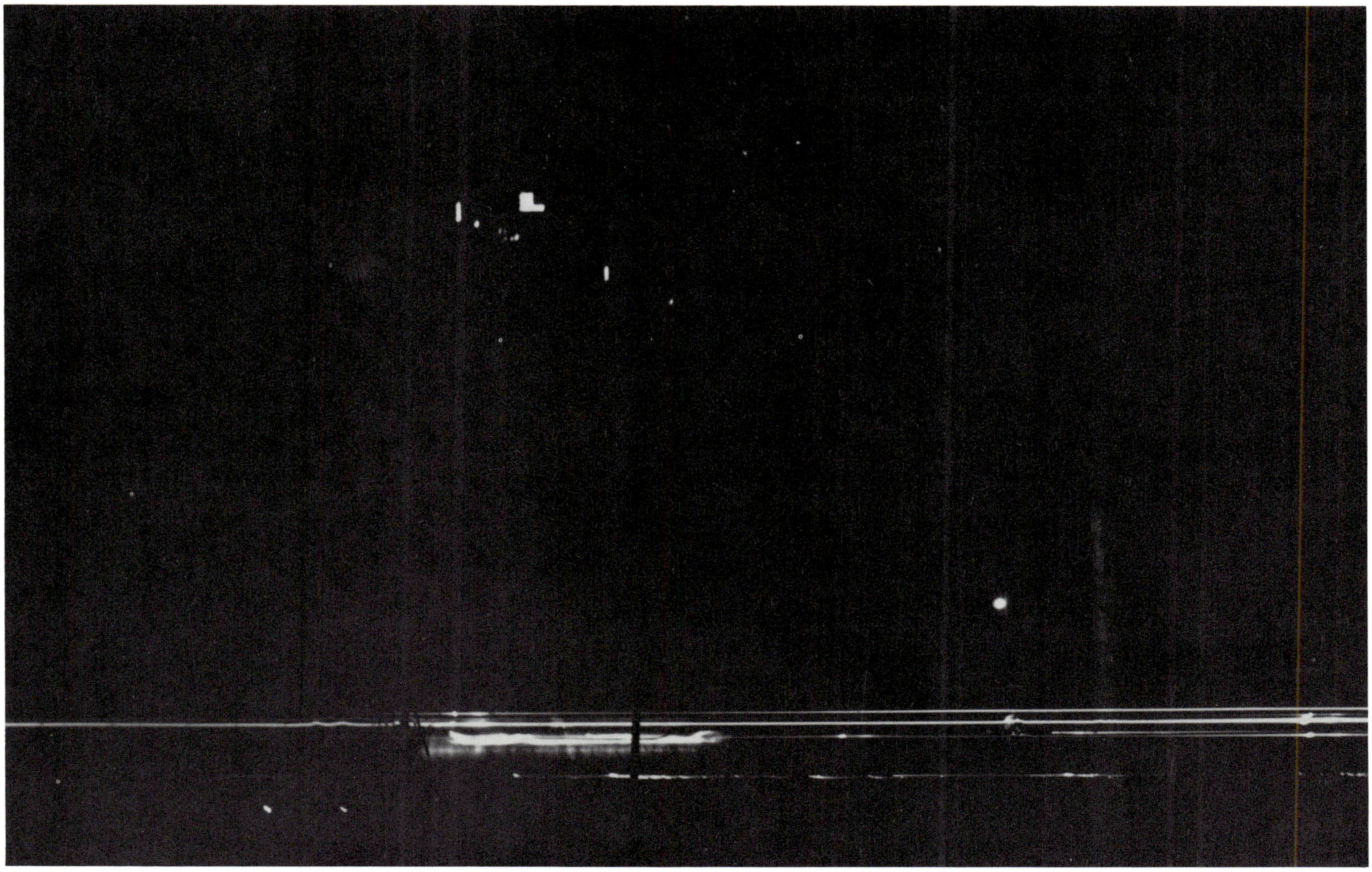

FOR THE DURATION

Girl Scouts collected grease, Boy Scouts organized paper drives, county residents collected more than 300,000 pounds of tin cans, and the Pantagraph, in a burst of patriotism, donated its first press to the war effort. Officials preached conservation on all sides, and even provided for the transmission of photographically-reduced messages in tiny envelopes through the V-mail service.

Gasoline and tires were rationed first, food later. By 1945, McLean County folks applied for 7,000 tires, but the Ration Board was allotted only 1,418.

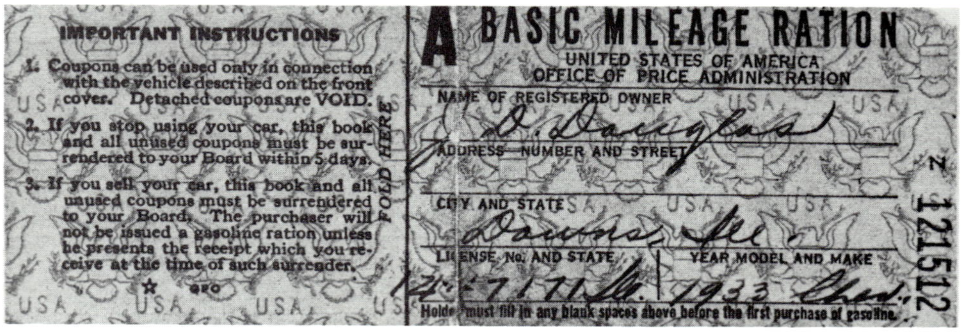

The farmers were also doing their bit for the war effort. Harry Fritz and others were putting in a new crop at the government's request—marijuana, for hemp fiber. And a special plant was built east of Lexington to process it.

With shortages affecting nearly everything, the McLean County farmer was insuring that there weren't going to be major food shortages. Bill O'Hara, a Hudson farmer, serving on the draft board, knew that deferments were needed to keep the farms going. Somebody had to stay at home to bring in the crops.

Those who served knew that when it was over, there would be something to come home to.

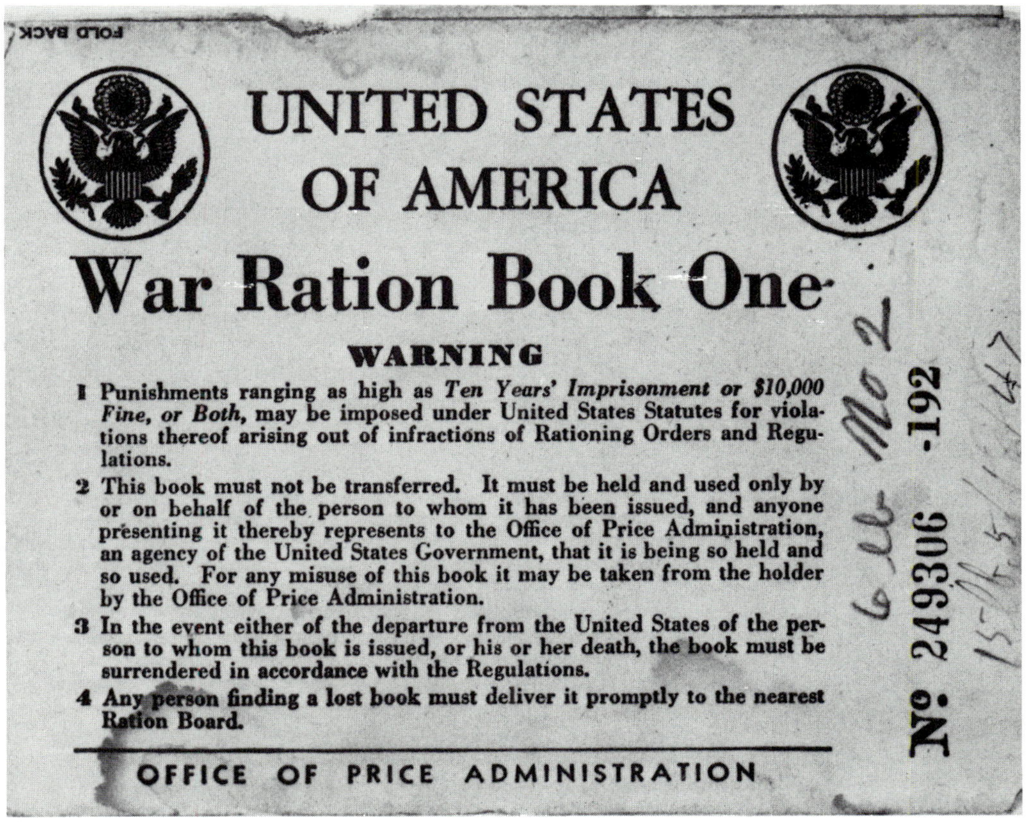
FOLD BACK

UNITED STATES OF AMERICA

War Ration Book One

WARNING

1 Punishments ranging as high as *Ten Years' Imprisonment or $10,000 Fine, or Both,* may be imposed under United States Statutes for violations thereof arising out of infractions of Rationing Orders and Regulations.

2 This book must not be transferred. It must be held and used only by or on behalf of the person to whom it has been issued, and anyone presenting it thereby represents to the Office of Price Administration, an agency of the United States Government, that it is being so held and so used. For any misuse of this book it may be taken from the holder by the Office of Price Administration.

3 In the event either of the departure from the United States of the person to whom this book is issued, or his or her death, the book must be surrendered in accordance with the Regulations.

4 Any person finding a lost book must deliver it promptly to the nearest Ration Board.

OFFICE OF PRICE ADMINISTRATION

Nº 249306 -192

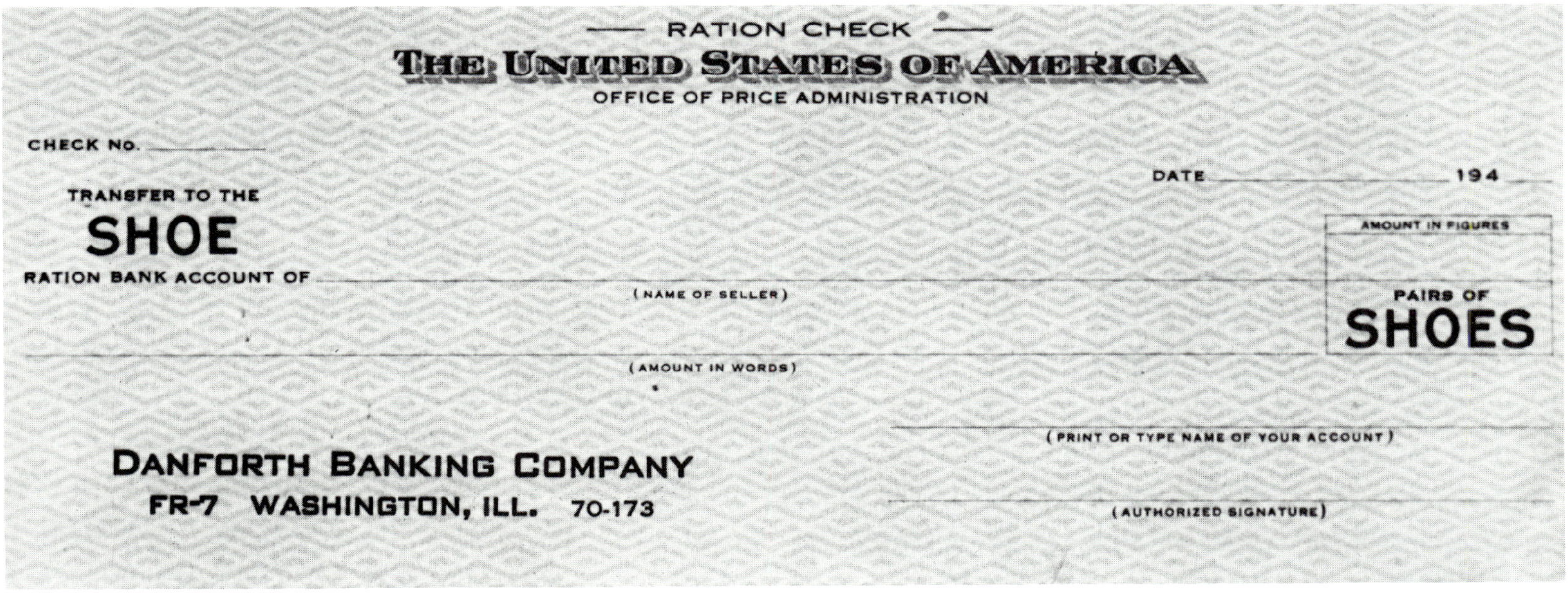
RATION CHECK

THE UNITED STATES OF AMERICA

OFFICE OF PRICE ADMINISTRATION

CHECK NO. ______

DATE ______ 194__

TRANSFER TO THE SHOE RATION BANK ACCOUNT OF ______ (NAME OF SELLER)

AMOUNT IN FIGURES

PAIRS OF SHOES

______ (AMOUNT IN WORDS)

______ (PRINT OR TYPE NAME OF YOUR ACCOUNT)

DANFORTH BANKING COMPANY

FR-7 WASHINGTON, ILL. 70-173

______ (AUTHORIZED SIGNATURE)

PILOT TRAINING SCHOOL

Members of Art Carnahan's Civil Air Patrol command included some of the county's leading citizens, David Davis and Dr. E. M. Stevenson among them. But Carnahan was also furnishing military pilots. His pre-war Civilian Pilot Training program furnished Lieutenant Colonel Robert Steinkraus, a Marine combat pilot who distintuished himself in that war and in Korea and Vietnam, and Major George Marquardt, who followed the Enola Gay by 40 miles and took the official photos after the first atomic bomb was dropped.

The Navy contracted with Carnahan in 1943, and more than 1,000 young men received their elementary flight training at the Bloomington Airport in the next year.

Naval cadets at Bloomington Airport, 1943

Pushing training plane into the hangar

Fueling up

Instructors' conference

Final flight check, Art Carnahan & cadet

WAR DRIVES

"A bomber a month" was the goal of McLean County's sale of Defense Bonds. It would take the sale of $10,000 worth each day, and rallies and drives were quickly started. Captured enemy hardware was displayed, and public praise given the buyers of bonds. Bloomington's Charles Kirkpatrick won national publicity by winning one such contest, buying $151,000 worth of bonds.

Citizens weren't the only ones mobilizing. The Williams Oil-o-Matic Company re-tooled for military production and so did the Watlington Company on North Linden, turning out parts for airplanes.

Mock plane crash, northeast corner of square

West side of square

WOMEN AT WAR

This was the first war in which large numbers of women served in uniform, and many of them were deployed near the front lines. One such was Heyworth's Lieutenant Ruth Munson, an Army Corps nurse who waded ashore in southern France with a pack on her back and later tended to combat wounded, working from bombed-out hospitals and living in tents.

Lieutenant Munson administered one of the first military doses of the new wonder-drug, penicillin, helping an Army colonel recover from pneumonia.

Many women served on the home front, too, as factories looked for replacements for men lost to military service. The movement of women into the workplace became a permanent one.

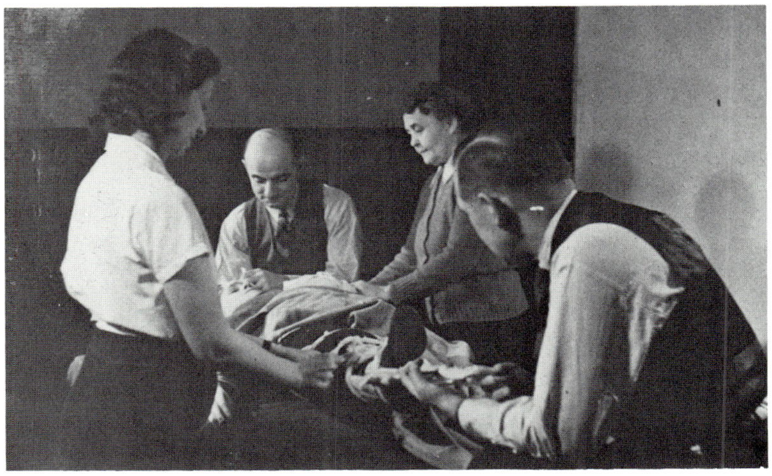

Community First Aid training at Tilden Hall

Women's Army Corps on North Main Street

IN COMBAT

The line between survival and death was a thin one. Chenoa's Dr. Charles Kerr was captured in the Pacific and died during the Bataan death march—the first county professional man to become a casualty. Corporal Jack Story of Bloomington was stationed in China and was taken prisoner the day after Pearl Harbor. His subsequent escape from a Shanghai prison and return to Allied lines became the subject of a book about war suffering.

281 McLean County men and women died in military service. Thousands more returned and adjusted as best they could, but nothing could erase the trauma of the years just past.

And nobody could predict the changes that would accompany the years and the generations to follow.

Breaking for K-rations, France, July 11, 1944

Passing supplies ashore, Leyte Island, the Phillipines, 1944

Enroute toward Paris, August 23, 1944

What the veterans wanted was relief from the just-past 15 years of social upheaval. They wanted things to get back to normal, to "build a bungalow and raise a family," providing for its needs with all the material things they'd had neither the money nor the time to enjoy.

What the veterans got was technological change, a consumer-oriented economy, and plenty of babies, many of whom learned about their world from their new TV sets. Some of the baby-boom children would watch a far-away war in Korea on television, and others would themselves fight another far-away war in Vietnam a generation later.

But the clock wouldn't move backwards. Things could never again be the same in McLean County, or any place else in a shrinking world.

. . . *AND NOW A WORD FROM OUR SPONSORS . . .*

AMERICAN STATE BANK

They fell heir to half the highly successful Meyer & Wochner Brewery when their father died in 1899. But Albert, Adolph and Herman Wochner were more interested in banking than beer. They sold their share of the brewery and, in conjunction with several other businessmen, founded the new German-American Bank. It opened in 1902 in the Leader Building, and under the direction of Albert, president, and his brothers, the bank prospered.

During World War I, the German-American Bank was renamed the American State Bank and was located in part of the Unity Building, downtown, on the east side of the Bloomington courthouse square. In the mid-1920s, the bank moved again, this time into much larger quarters, taking over the old Metropole Hotel Building just a few doors north.

The '30s brought the Great Depression, and in 1933, President Roosevelt declared a nationwide banking moratorium. Many banks were forced to fold, but American State soon reopened to pump nearly a million dollars back into our struggling economy. Even through the "lean years" the bank continued to grow and it assumed a role of leadership in our financial community with a commitment to progressive customer service.

In the '30s, American State was one of the first banks in the nation to offer drive-up banking service. In the '40s, it was one of the first to establish a separate department to provide installment loan service.

Officers & clerks, ca. 1910

In the '50s, recognizing the need to extend the old "bankers' hours" for busy customers, it opened one of the first sidewalk teller windows to accommodate downtown pedestrians. And in the early '70s, it was the first area bank to establish an auto/truck leasing program.

As a charter member of the Association for Modern Banking in Illinois, American State worked hard through the '60s to obtain legislation allowing banks branch facilities to serve expanding markets. The crusade was finally successful and in 1969, the bank's "Jewel Box" at Washington and McLean streets was one of the first to open in downstate Illinois. Then in 1979, a much-needed expansion of the main bank took place with the acquisition of the Cole Building next door north. That former site of Kresge's dime store was transformed into one of the most beautiful and most complete banking lobbies in central Illinois. In 1980, a third facility, the "Executive Banking Center," was established on the east side of town for customers' service.

By 1982, American State Bank could boast $80 million in total assets and 80 years of service to McLean County.

You Need Not Enter Our Bank to Make a Deposit

Just Use Our Modern Window Depository

Driving around the square seeking a place to park, finally parking out several blocks and walking in—that is all eliminated at our bank. All you need do is turn into the alley-way north of our building, pass your bank book and deposit through the depository window there and drive on.

AMERICAN STATE BANK

BEER NUTS INC.

In the mid-30s, Mr. and Mrs. Edward G. Shirk and their son Russell purchased the Caramel Crisp Shop, then located at 115 E. Jefferson.

The original Caramel Crisp Shop was located in leased quarters in the Odd Fellows' Building where the Shirk family sold popcorn, peanuts and orange drink to customers of all ages, but especially to the patrons of the Irvin Theater which was located diagonally across the street. The glazed Virginia Redskin peanut sold by-the-scoop was a favorite of regular patrons of the Caramel Crisp Shop. The Shirks enhanced the peanut's popularity by giving a liberal sample to all who purchased their homemade orange drink. In 1938, State Farm Insurance Company of Bloomington bought the Odd Fellows' Building for the expansion of their Home Office Building and the Caramel Crisp Shop was moved to 413-15 North Main. At this location short order foods were added to the line of confectionery items.

In 1952 Russell Shirk and Eldridge Brewster, a Blue Star potato chip distributor of Bloomington, arranged for the first volume production and distribution of the popular glazed Redskin peanut. They selected the trade name BEER NUTS® for the new packaged snack—1-1/2 oz @ 10¢. The BEER NUTS® peanuts caught on in central Illinois and nearby areas. A year later the Caramel Crisp Shop was closed and the Shirk family devoted its time to the new peanut product from Shirk Products. Russell Shirk incorporated the business in 1955.

Within a year the growing business required a larger facility and the equipment was moved again. This move was into a 7,000 square foot building at 505 North Prairie. During the next 17 years at this location the company increased production from 300,000 pounds to 10 million pounds of peanuts annually by way of several additions totalling 22,000 square feet of plant. Because of increased demand and cramped quarters, the company began construction in 1973 of a new production facility adjacent to the existing Prairie Farms Dairy building at 103 North Robinson. The new 100,000 square foot plant completed in 1974 provided production capacity in excess of 25 million pounds of peanuts annually.

BEER NUTS® products are presently sold in all types of retail food outlets in all 50 states and in several foreign countries.

At the present time, under the management of James A. Shirk, grandson of the founders, the firm employs 97 people from McLean County and continues to strive for excellence in its products, carrying on the tradition of quality begun by the Shirks in the early Caramel Crisp Shop.

Odd Fellows' Building, 115 East Jefferson

OTHER SUGGESTIONS

Buttered and Caramel Popcorn 5¢, 10¢, 15¢, & 25¢
Peanut Brittle 25¢ per lb.
Jumbo Red Skins 25¢ per lb.
Spanish Peanuts 20¢ per lb.
Caramel Apples 5¢ each, Family Special 6 for 25¢
Popcorn Balls on special order (in quantity)
* * Try some of our fandy nuts at popular prices * *
Pecans, Bridge Mix, Cashews, Almonds,
Special Bridge Mix, Brazils, & Blanched Peanuts

Wholesale & Retail Prices

The Caramel Crisp Shop
415 N. Main Street

BEICH CANDIES

109 East Front, ca. 1895

Beich Candies, 1982

The Paul F. Beich (BIKE) Company dates back to William A. Gerken, confectioner and baker, who came to the United States from Germany. One day in the 1880s a boy named Paul Frank Beich, who had left Prussia at the age of 16, married Gerken's daughter Catherine. Paul Beich was working as a salesman for a wholesale confectionery firm, the J.L. Green Company, which had its start in 1854.

Caramels, ca. 1935

Mr. Gerken helped Beich purchase the wholesale confectionery business across the street in 1892. During the period he met Milton Hershey who had need of a western branch of the Lancaster Caramel Company. When Mr. Hershey sold the Lancaster Caramel Company in Pennsylvania, Beich bought the Bloomington branch on the west side and moved his business from downtown.

The early product line was very wide, consisting of chocolate coated creams, nut clusters, jellies, pan goods, and nearly every other type of confection imaginable.

The only confection in production since 1916 is GOLDEN CRUMBLES, an open-fire-cooked peanut butter "pillow." One of the secrets is freshly ground peanut butter and sealing in airtight containers.

The WHIZ BAR, a marshmallow bar with peanut topping and enrobed in milk chocolate was started in the 1920s and remained in the line until the closing of the old plant at Front and Lumber streets during the 1960s. During World War II, the advertising slogan . . . "Whiz-z-z the Best Nickel Candy There Iz-z-z," was sounded off on radio spots for many, many years.

The origin of the Kathryn Beich line of candies dates from the early 1950s. Kathryn, the wife of President Paul M. Beich, thought of placing an ad in the Springfield *Churchman*, an Episcopalian monthly news magazine, for groups who would like to raise funds. A post office box number had been placed on the ad. Kathryn fell sick and after an extended illness, passed away. Some weeks after her funeral, Beich went to the post office to check on the ad replies. As he removed the letters from the post office box, the postman behind the boxes said, "Wait just a minute, I have another bag for you," and that was the start of Kathryn Beich Candies for sale as fund raising items. For many years it was strictly a mail order business. Today customers are serviced by mail, direct factory representatives, and a network of drive-in branch offices.

Employment has varied greatly from the period of 1900 to the 1960s, often reaching over 800 factory employees.

Today the company has endeavored to modulate production so that the work force is relatively stable. The past few years about 200 plant employees have been used and the dollar volume and tonnage have increased approximately 5-fold.

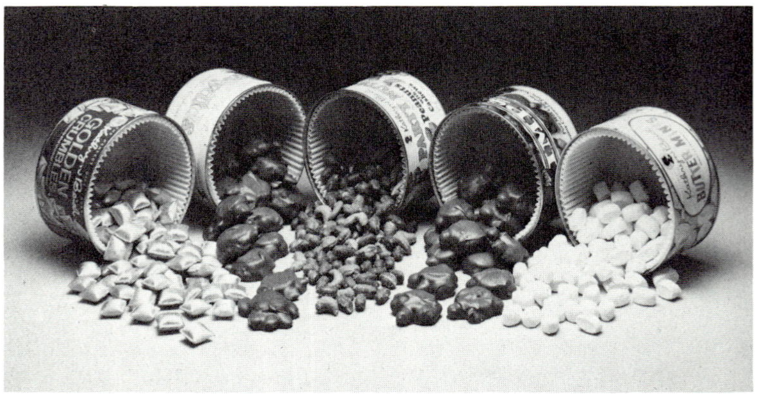

Kathryn Beich Candies, 1982

The BIKE plant is located on 50 acres southwest of Bloomington. The facility has just recently been expanded by one-third and included the installation of one of the most modern chocolate moulding lines in America to serve the goal of leadership in the production of high quality moulded chocolates.

BLOOMINGTON FEDERAL SAVINGS & LOAN

When Bloomington Federal opened the doors for business in May, 1941, it quickly joined the growth and progress of McLean County. By the end of that year, Bloomington Federal was already the leading lender among the four savings and loans in Bloomington-Normal.

First located at 105 N. Center, Bloomington Federal organized with share capital of $52,000. The directors determined the minimum monthly payment would be $10, and set dividends on savings at 3%, well above the 1% being paid by other local financial institutions.

CERTIFICATE NO. 1
ISSUED FOR $5000.00
Bloomington Federal Savings and Loan Association
INVESTMENT SHARE ACCOUNT
This Certifies That
G. J. MECHERLE IS A MEMBER OF BLOOMINGTON FEDERAL SAVINGS AND LOAN ASSOCIATION
and holds a FIVE THOUSAND DOLLAR Dollar INVESTMENT SHARE ACCOUNT of said association, subject to its charter and by-laws and to the laws of the United States of America.
Witness the authorized signature of officer or employee
this twenty-second day of May, 1941
BLOOMINGTON FEDERAL SAVINGS AND LOAN ASSOCIATION
By
Authorized Signature
CANCELLED
CANCELLED
INSURED

The first savings certificate was written for the founder of State Farm Insurance

105 North Center Street, ca. 1955

By 1955, Bloomington Federal was the largest financial institution in McLean County with assets of $55 million. The association had outgrown the Center Street office and purchased the Majestic Theatre site at Washington and East Streets for construction of a new office, occupied in November, 1957.

Assets reached $100 million in 1970 and Bloomington Federal continued to serve McLean County, handling over 60% of the savings and loan lending volume in the county. A four-story addition to the office was completed in 1976, tripling the space.

By 1977, Bloomington Federal was the largest financial institution in downstate Illinois with assets of $462 million. During the decade of the '70s, savings deposits increased from $75 million to $508 million and Bloomington Federal loaned over $800 million to Central Illinois homeowners.

By year end 1982, Bloomington Federal anticipates assets over $1 billion, with completion of a home office addition that will again triple the available space. This expanded office enables the association to provide vital support services such as product development, computer support and operational assistance for the growing statewide network of offices.

Open house, November, 1957 — over 12,000 people toured the uniquely designed building.

Based on a foundation of friendly, innovative and professional service to all its customers, Bloomington Federal looks forward to building a future of accomplishments as noteworthy as those of the past.

BROKAW HOSPITAL

In the early 1890s a need was felt for a Protestant hospital in the cities of Bloomington and Normal. Five doctors and $500 apiece marked the beginning of a community hospital, later to be known as Brokaw Hospital. Drs. J.L. White, D.H. Nusbaum, M.H. Hull, C.M. Noble, and Ernest Mammen began the fund to be used for the initial purchase of grounds, building and equipment.

The contract for a new building was let in 1895, at which time it was voted to name the hospital for anyone contributing $3,000. Local citizens rallied for the effort and over 400 individuals contributed money toward the project. Even the local businesses gave their shares; cement was donated at cost and railways hauled material free of charge. The hospital was quickly becoming a community concern. The Protestant churches of McLean County were asked to appoint two representatives to serve on the hospital's board of trustees.

Opening 1 year later as The Protestant Hospital, the name was later changed to Memorial Deaconess Hospital, then to Deaconess Hospital, before becoming Brokaw Hospital in 1901. At that time, Abram Brokaw gave $10,000 towards the hospital's first expansion program with the understanding that the hospital would be named after him. Mr. Brokaw stipulated a 12-member board of directors should be elected by the trustees to govern the hospital.

Built in 1895

Diagnostic equipment, ca. 1930

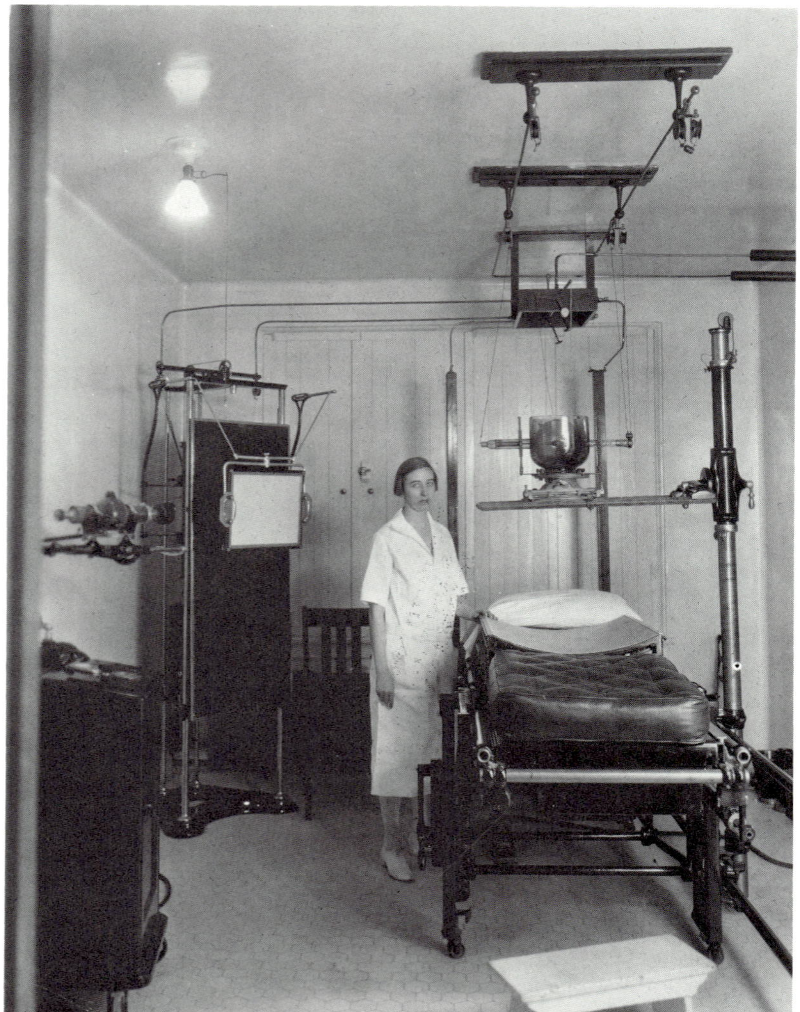

On May 3, 1896, the first patient was admitted to the hospital. A patient's perception of hospital care at that time was much different than ours would be today. Then, the hospital consisted of 22 beds, a kitchen, laundry, storerooms, dining rooms, and living quarters for the nurses. The weekly charge for a private room was $8 and nursing care was provided by deaconesses who received no wages, only room and board.

By 1899, 178 patients were treated and 104 operations were performed. Today, the staff at Brokaw Hospital cares for over 37,000 patients a year, performs over 4,600 surgical procedures, and has over 600 employees. Then, as today, the hospital relied on its volunteers and benefactors for support. Local people donated food, fruit, and flowers for the patients, and the Ladies' Aid Society met weekly to sew and mend the hospital's linen.

Due to continued financial support of the Protestant churches, Abram Brokaw, and other loyal benefactors, a second addition was completed in 1902. In 1913 a south wing was added to the hospital. This addition is now the oldest remaining building on the hospital campus.

Eighty years and 2 additions to the hospital later, Brokaw Hospital has prospered as a community effort to meet the ever-changing medical needs of the residents of McLean County. Brokaw continues to be governed by a board of directors who are elected from and by a board of trustees representing the McLean County Protestant churches. As medical and technological advancements occur, Brokaw will remain the stable, community-supported hospital responding to local health care needs.

CAPEN FRANK PROCTOR & BOWLES, INC.

The history of Capen Frank Proctor & Bowles, Inc. is really the history of several separate agencies developed independently until merging in 1977. But let's step back to the year 1876. The United States is celebrating its centennial anniversary. The same year Henry Capen leaves the crockery and glass business and founds an investment and banking firm in Bloomington. Through the years, community and business needs start to change. In 1897 the business moves into the insurance field, a newly emerging industry offering only Fire, Life and Ocean Marine coverage. The insurance endeavor grows slowly until about 1928 when it surpasses the mortgage loan business.

In 1938 Russell S. Proctor has just graduated from Illinois Wesleyan University. Directly out of college, he begins Russell S. Proctor, Inc., a combination insurance agency and loan business. Then in 1960 his son Page joins the firm to specialize in insurance.

Meanwhile, a University of Illinois graduate, C. William Frank, is about to start his own insurance agency. 1950 sees the beginning of the Frank Insurance Agency.

Very soon three separate paths cross. In 1954 John Bowles III joins his father-in-law, Henry W. Capen, in the insurance agency and assumes the leadership of the Capen Insurance Agency in 1976. Four generations of Capens in the insurance profession pave the way for the pinnacle year of 1977, when the firms merge to create Capen Frank Proctor & Bowles, Inc.

Henry Capen, ca. 1880

Capen insurance office, 1900

CITIZENS SAVINGS & LOAN

30 years after Normal's first town meeting on April 6, 1858, which gave the 6-square mile area called North Bloomington or "The Junction" (due to the railroads meeting) its first existence as the Town of Normal, our founders held their first meeting on a cold, blustery December night in the winter of 1887-88. It was in a building at 123 East Beaufort Street, now occupied by Kings Full Men's Hairstyling, the Underdog Restaurant, and, upstairs, Fidelity Union Life Insurance Company. This was then the office of William H. Schureman, who was the president of the Normal Exchange Bank of W.H. Schureman and Company. In those early days all meetings were held in and business transacted from the office of the secretary of our association and he was our first secretary. The "town and gown" idea of today was very evident back in those days, almost 100 years ago. Our first president was also president of Illinois State Normal University. By this time the university was going full swing, graduating hundreds of pupils possessed with sobriety (alcohol was not allowed on the premises), morality and humanity. It was believed the university would doubtlessly take rank with the finest of public institutions in the country.

For Citizens Savings Loan and Building Association of Normal, at this point in time, there was a desk, about $117.85 for supplies and a lot of imagination. Before long, however, reality began to catch up with dreams and 20 pioneering citizens subscribed to $31,000 in stock. The first loan closing was for $600 to Mrs. S.A. Thrall. A successful savings and loan was born. Unable to afford its own quarters in those early years, the association was located at several Normal addresses before moving to the McCormick Building at the northeast corner of North and Broadway. In 1937 we moved next door to 122 North Street. This was the first building that we owned, and was our home through all those hectic, wonderful years that brought us to our present location at 301 Broadway.

As we appeared in 1888

Following are the names of our first 12 directors and their occupations:

Dr. Edwin C. Hewett, president	President, Illinois State Normal University
J.Y. Thorp, vice president	Dealer in staple and fancy groceries
Jesse Blackburn, treasurer	Cabinetmaker, dealer in lumber, hardware and coal
William H. Schureman, secretary	President, Normal Exchange Bank
Levi Dillon (of Dillon Brothers)	Importer and breeder of Norman Percheron horses
Otto Seibert	Butcher, later mayor of Normal for 6 years
Joshua E. Baker	Stock-raiser
Charles R. Parke	Physician and surgeon
Henry Zimmerman (of Dodge & Zimmerman)	Small fruit orchard, real estate loan agent
H.J. Barton	High school principal
M.T. Burwell	Bloomington Canning Company
Thomas Sylvester	Brickmason and proprietor, Normal Milling Company

Shortly after we opened our doors, there were 14 building and loan and investment associations listed in the Bloomington-Normal Directory. We are the only surviving institution of that group.

O. Illman White, president
Bernice L. Hinthorn, executive secretary
Citizens Savings and Loan, Normal, Illinois

DIXIE TRUCKERS HOME

No sooner had the concrete dried on the two lane road between Chicago and St. Louis that J. P. Walters envisioned the need for a new kind of service for truckers and motorists. J. P., as his friends knew him, had been serving the fuel buying public with his independent oil jobbership, the Shirley Oil Co. It was only natural for him to think of providing another outlet for his products. John Geske, who married J. P.'s only daughter Viola, and J. P. bought out R. T. Lains and Charles Hutchinson's interest in the jobbership and started to move on this new project.

Service, they planned, would include gas, oil, tires and tire service, emergency mechanical service, overnight accommodations for truck drivers, and tourist cabins. But they knew for it really to go over, it would have to be open 24 hours a day. A good location was also needed and they knew that Rte. 66, which was rapidly becoming known as the "Main Street of America," was the road on which to locate.

So in the spring of 1928, with the front door keys buried in the new concrete drive, the Dixie Truckers Home opened in McLean, Illinois. Business started out slow, but the word soon spread. J. P. made sure it would spread. It wasn't unusual for him to drive all night to Kansas City to meet with truckers and tell them of the service he was offering in McLean, and to remind them that it was a perfect stop before that final haul into Chicago.

Business ideas expanded too. Coffee and donuts served on a cold night became plate lunches and dinners. A lunch consisting of meat loaf, potatoes and gravy, green beans and coffee would cost 50¢. Waitresses, then as now, would provide commentary on any number of subjects. In 1937, Social Security deductions caused waitress Rosalee Hardesty to yell across the room to another waitress that "We are not getting a dollar a day anymore. It's just 98¢ and they are taking out 2¢ for Social Security."

Hungry and thirsty (also slightly underweight) livestock were served their last meal in a special corral located nearby before going to the Chicago livestock markets.

J. P. Walters, out front

John Geske, at the cash register, 1957

By the late 1930s, a typical Saturday night crowd would amount to about 1,000 people, made up of truckers, tourists and locals, all listening to Polly of the Range and her string band, provided "courtesy of the management."

After J.P. died in 1950 John and Viola continued to bring customers to Dixie by criss-crossing the central United States calling on trucking firms and spreading the good word about Dixie resulting in a second truck stop in Tuscola and ownership of a third truck stop in Effingham.

Dixie has been a family business for four generations. In the 1940s Dean and Dorothy Walters assisted J. P., and now Chuck Beeler and his son Mark manage the business and carry on the family tradition of excellence.

What started with two employees, one day and one night person, at a dollar a day has now expanded into an operation of 300 employees with a payroll of $4,000,000 and sales of over $18,000,000.

Waitresses & cooks, ca. 1940. L. to R. Estell Spaulding, Florence Hafley, Blanche Baumgardner, Bill Norbits, Buella Criswell, Euella Mason, Lorena Criswell.

FELL FOUNDATION

"To each generation all things are new."

— Jesse W. Fell

Serving in the tradition of
Jesse W. Fell
(1808-1887)

"Friend of Education
Lover and Planter of Trees
Philantropist of Mighty Vision"

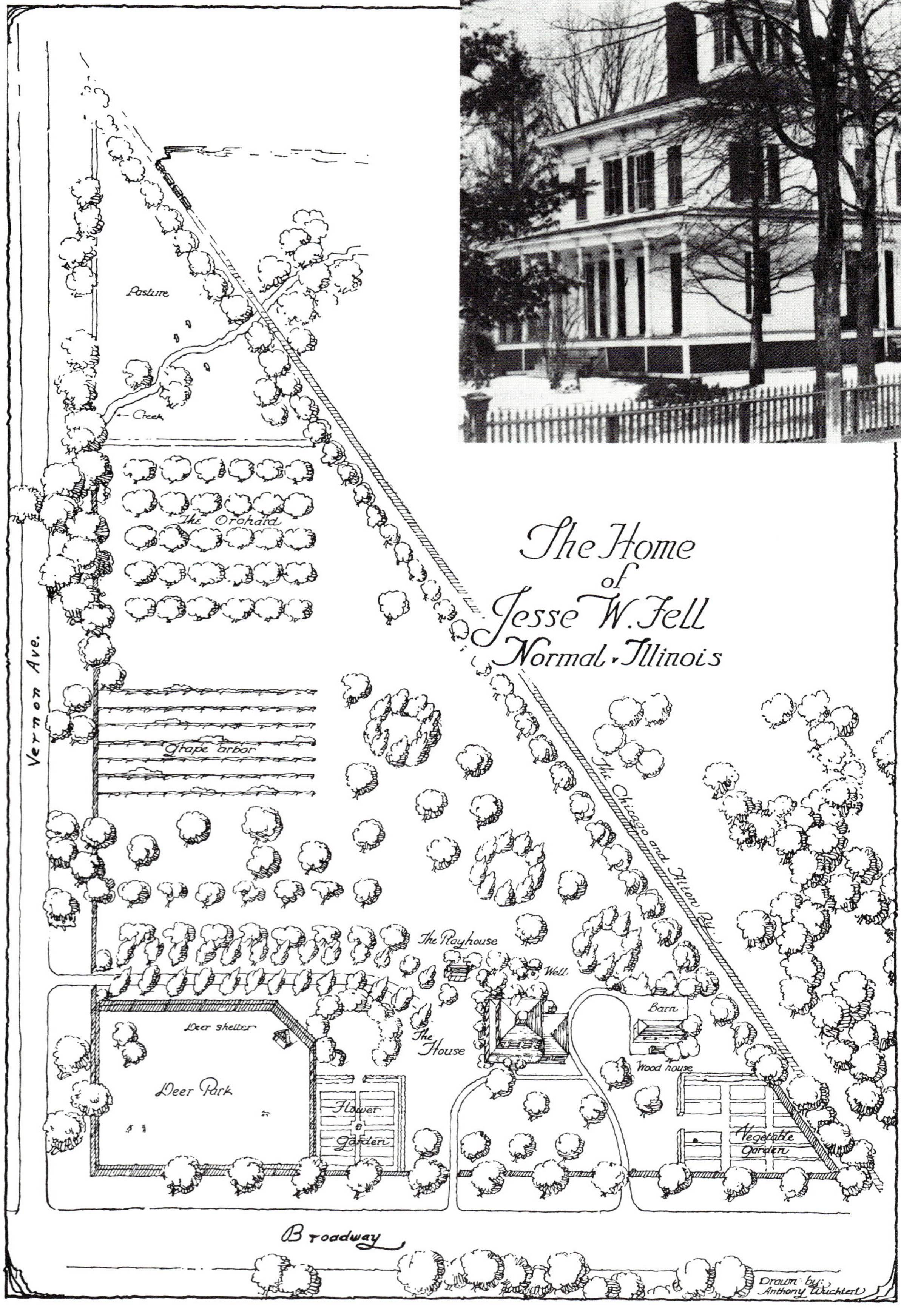

Towns founded by Jesse Fell:

Normal
Towanda
Clinton
Pontiac
Byron (now a ghost town)
Larchwood, Iowa

FUNK SEEDS INTERNATIONAL

In 1824, young Isaac Funk, weary from a long trek from Ohio, halted his ox team by a stand of timber now known as Funk's Grove. Here, he decided, was the spot he had been looking for.

From this early beginning, the relationship between the Funk family and McLean County has been very intimate.

The grandson of Isaac, Eugene Duncan Funk, became interested in providing high quality seed for his neighbors. After studying agriculture in Europe, E.D. (Eugene) returned home determined to start a family business of growing and selling seed. Joined by 14 members of the various Funk families, Eugene formed Funk Bros. Seed Co. It was incorporated in 1901, and Eugene would serve as president for the next 43 years.

The new company, with headquarters in Bloomington, Illinois, quickly established itself as a source of high quality seeds of all kinds, particularly corn. Funk's 90 Day and Funk's Yellow Dent became well known throughout the Corn Belt and in Europe. By 1905, Funk Bros. stated in their catalogue that they were "the largest seed corn growers in the world."

Under the leadership of Mr. Eugene Funk and the corn breeding genius of Dr. J.R. Holbert, Funk Bros. Seed Co. was instrumental in changing agriculture. They were convinced that hybrids were the answer to corn improvement. In 1916, a hybrid made up of a three-way varietal cross was marketed and was the world's first recorded sale of a hybrid seed corn.

As a member of President Wilson's Food Administration, Eugene Funk persuaded the USDA to establish an experiment station on Funk Farms and "loaned" Dr. Holbert to head the station in the study of corn diseases and hybrid corn. This station became internationally famous as the birthplace of commercial hybrid corn.

After World War II, with E.D. Funk, Jr. (Gene) as the new president, Funk Bros. Seed Co. helped re-establish agriculture to prosperity in parts of Europe by starting a hybrid corn business in Italy. This move was successful as Funk expanded to do business in Europe, Asia, South America and Africa.

In 1974, Funk Seeds was purchased by Ciba-Geigy Corporation. Today, the influence of Funk research worldwide is even greater. Now known as Funk Seeds International —with its U.S. headquarters still in Bloomington — Europe, Canada, Mexico, South America, Africa and Asia benefit from the products and people of McLean County.

FUNK'S G HYBRID ®

SEEDSMEN FROM McLEAN COUNTY FOR THE WORLD

FUNK TRUST PROPERTIES

Prairie Home built 1863-4, photo 1885

Isaac Funk and Robert Stubblefield settled in McLean County in 1824 at the edge of Funk's Grove.

They and their families established a tradition of leadership and they participated in the growth and development of McLean County for over 150 years.

The Prairie Home Museum, Funk's Grove Church and Cemetery have been preserved by these families and are open to the public. The home and museum can be visited by phoning Funk Prairie Home, Shirley, Illinois to arrange for a time and date.

The families of LaFayette Funk and his son, DeLoss, had lived in the home for over a hundred years. Many pieces of furniture dating back to the early 1870s can be seen there. Their lives are reflected in the dignity of these quiet surroundings.

The Rock Museum built in 1975 displays one of the largest private collections of rocks and minerals in the United States. This was made possible by the efforts of LaFayette Funk Jr. and his wife, Cleda. Their travels have taken them into over thirty states and several foreign countries. This museum also has a collection of buggies, sleighs, wagons, saddles, harness and tools. These have been collected through the efforts of Theodore, Paul, LaFayette and Eugene Funk, sons of Eugene D. Funk Sr.

Paul A. Funk wished to preserve the efforts of the Funk family and arranged for trusts to be formed that care for the home and museum as well as other civic and community organizations.

Further information is available at the McLean County Historical Society, 201 E. Grove Street, Bloomington, Illinois.

Gem and Rock Museum, LaFayette Funk

GENERAL TELEPHONE

Shortly after the turn of the century, nearly every city and town throughout Illinois had its own locally owned telephone company. In many cases, it was a secondary interest to the owner's primary business which ranged from general store proprietor to undertaker. The telephone heritage of McLean County began with the formation of the Home Telephone Company of Bloomington, the McLean County Telephone Company and the Central Union Telephone Company, all of which were combined later to form the Kinloch Bloomington Telephone Company. In 1931, this company, along with many others, joined together to form the Wabash Telephone Company which subsequently was merged into the Illinois Telephone Company in 1945. In 1956, Illinois Telephone Company became a part of General Telephone of Illinois.

Telephone switching equipment, ca. 1935

The old "number, please" days began to vanish in the late 1930s as companies converted to dial switching. Although the war effort temporarily affected this program, a partial conversion to dial phones in Bloomington was completed in 1943. In 1958, GenTel's Larry Gilbert won $50 on What's My Line because the panel didn't guess he was an operator. That same year Bloomington became the state headquarters for General Telephone of Illinois, and two years later, the city's 28,000 phones were converted to new Direct Distance Dialing Equipment.

General Telephone people were at the center of a major news story in 1965 when they provided telephone service to the government and press people attending the funeral of Adlai E. Stevenson. In 1973, three young repair clerks became the first women to attend pole climbing classes, the company hired its first woman communications consultant and June Tenckhoff of Western Illinois University was honored as the first woman elected to the company's board of directors. The state's first GTE Phone Mart opened in 1975 at a location on East Empire, and then moved to the College Hills Mall in 1980. The year 1977 was significant in the history of telecommunications as integrated circuits, digital switching and optical fibers were introduced to the public along with an FCC decision which allowed customers to own and maintain their own telephone equipment and connect it to the network.

In 1982, GenTel began installing a GTD-5 Electronic Automatic Exchange, incorporating the latest state-of-the-art digital technology, with a scheduled cutover in mid 1983. The GTD-5 provides a number of Custom Calling features, including Call Waiting, Call Forwarding, Three-Way Calling, and Speed Calling. Also, the equipment takes considerably less space, can be easily expanded to 150,000 customer lines and permits the company to centralize maintenance, administration and billing activities.

Wabash telephone switchboard operators, ca. 1935

IMMANUEL BIBLE FOUNDATION

VanLeer memorial bell tower

The Immanuel Bible Foundation, 1301 S. Fell Ave., Normal, was established by Mrs. B.C. (Margaret) VanLeer in 1944.

Mr. and Mrs. VanLeer, members of the Second Presbyterian Church, were deeply interested in Christian causes. Dating as far back as 1921, they planned and worked toward a goal of leaving their commodious and elegant home on Fell Avenue, their business — in fact, their entire estate to the Foundation. Mr. VanLeer, who operated the Keiser-VanLeer plumbing and hardware business on North East Street, Bloomington, died in 1933. Mrs. VanLeer died in 1949.

The first board, selected by Mrs. VanLeer, named her as president; Miss Constance Ferguson, vice president; L.W. Butler, secretary-treasurer. Kaywin Kennedy was appointed attorney. At the time of Mrs. VanLeer's death, the board added the names of Carl Niedermeyer, Miss Elizabeth Spicer (secretary), and Dr. Harold R. Martin as president. Russell Palmer, formerly with Montgomery Ward, was named director of activities in 1953.

When Mr. Palmer retired in 1969, Herschel W. Stuber was named director and assumed these duties in 1970. The present board members are: Dr. Harold R. Martin, president; David Polzin, vice president; Mrs. H.W. Stuber, secretary; H.W. Stuber, treasurer; Lorin Jump and John Wooledge. Mike Rudolph is maintenance engineer and general assistant.

Mrs. VanLeer had a bell tower built in North Italian Romanesque style, in memory of her husband. The bells, made and installed by the Meneely Bell Co. of Troy, N.Y., whose ancestors cast the first bells ever made in the United States, were played by Ray Olson for many years. The tower now contains a carillon that is played twice a day. At the dedication in 1940, a youth choir from Second Presbyterian Church presented a program and the president of Moody Bible Institute, Chicago, gave the address to a crowd of more than 1,500 persons.

The Foundation serves all churches and Christian organizations, providing a place for Bible classes, prayer groups, meetings and retreats. Three to 5,000 people use the Foundation for meetings during the year. A music lending library for small churches provides anthems for over 200 churches with a limited music budget. Initiated by Professor Richard D. Hoffland, Millikin University, Decatur, this library offers over 100,000 copies of anthems in 300 categories. In connection with the lending library, a music clinic is held annually for choir directors and choir members. It is directed by Professor and Mrs. Hoffland.

Each year, the Foundation sponsors a complimentary laymen's lenten breakfast at Illinois State University. An all-layman panel provides the program, emphasizing the Easter message. Six hundred attended the '82 breakfast.

In its outreach to help support Christian education and charitable purposes, the Foundation makes grants to Christian non-profit organizations. This does not apply to individuals, however.

"Broadview," 1906

INTERNATIONAL TAPETRONICS CORP./3M

International Tapetronics Corporation (ITC) was formed locally in 1969 to design, manufacture and sell professional audio tape recording equipment for radio and television broadcasting.

Today these professional tape machines are sold worldwide to commercial, university and government broadcast stations. ITC customers range from local professional and university stations (WJBC, WBNQ, WIHN, WRBA and WGLT) to the ABC, CBS, NBC and Mutual networks as well as CBS in Canada, England's BBC and other international broadcasters.

The extent of ITC's success in this market is illustrated by the results from a recent marketing research study which showed that ITC now sells over 60% of the audio tape cartridge machines sold in the entire world. With over 5,000 customers and over 40,000 machines in the field, it is little wonder that more than one out of every two radio and television stations in the United States now has ITC equipment in their studios.

ITC operates with 137 employees from three different buildings in Bloomington, Illinois. The main office and assembly plant are located at 2425 South Main Street, engineering research and development are at 2714 McGraw Drive, and the milling and sheet metal department is at 204 South McClun. A building site of approximately 20 acres has been recently acquired from the Bloomington-Normal Airport Authority in a contract to purchase with the intent to consolidate ITC operations on this site at some future date.

On January 1, 1982 ITC became a subsidiary of the 3M Company, St. Paul, Minnesota.

WGLT (Normal) goes "on the air" with ITC equipment

ITC cartridge & reel-to-reel equipment is found in over half the radio stations in the country.

McLEAN COUNTY BANK

McLean County Bank was established June 3, 1903, and chartered as a state bank. It was located on the south side of the courthouse square in downtown Bloomington where Sorg's Jewelry is presently located. The first McLean County Bank board of directors meeting was held July 1, 1903 with the following board members present: Joseph Beam, A.J. Barr, H.S. Dooley, B.S. Green, W.W. Hall, George McIntosh, George F. Dick, Robert T. Lain, H.W. McClure, Lee Rust and George W. White. Many of the founders of our organization were associated with agriculture in the community and initially the bank had it roots in this type of business. Although the bank has expanded into many other areas, McLean County Bank has continued its emphasis on serving the financial needs of agriculture.

The bank moved from its initial location on the courthouse square to the northeast corner of Washington and Main Streets in downtown Bloomington. The bank remained at this location until 1935 when growth necessitated larger quarters.

Teller Howard Rust, ca. 1910

In 1933 all banks were closed by presidential proclamation during the big economic depression and the bank moratorium. Banks were not permitted to reopen without an examination and approval of the supervising authorities. McLean County Bank was the second bank to reopen. It was allowed to open for business without waived deposits or consolidation or merger in order to be considered sound and safe for depositors.

In 1935 the bank relocated from the corner of Washington and Main to a banking house which was purchased from the receivers of the defunct Liberty State Bank at 119 North Main Street. Increasing needs of the banking public plus growth of the bank generated a decision in 1959 to acquire sufficient land for the construction of a new banking house and drive-in facilities. This was the only "bank from your car" facility in the area at the time. The present building, located at Towanda and Empire was completed in November of 1960, and continued expansion of departmental areas, five drive-up lanes and construction of the Mini-Bank with four additional drive-in windows was completed in 1975. In August, 1980, McLean County Bank opened its first branch facility, which is located inside the College Hills Mall, Normal, Illinois.

Bank interior, 1925

THE PANTAGRAPH

The Pantagraph has a long and distinguished history as the voice of McLean County and Central Illinois. It dates from Jan. 14, 1837, when Jesse W. Fell began The Bloomington Observer and McLean County Advocate.

That paper closed after two years, not to be reborn until 1845, when R.B. Mitchell began The McLean Register. His financial backer, Charles P. Merriman, took over when The Register failed in 1846. He changed the name to The Western Whig, but in 1851, having become disgruntled with the Whig Party, he again changed the paper's name to The Intelligencer.

The Sunday Pantagraph

The Daily Pantagraph

The final change came in 1853. A Greek scholar, Merriman took the new name, Pantagraph, from Greek words meaning "write all things."

The Pantagraph remained a family operation, and in 1980 it was purchased by another family, the deYoungs, owners of the San Francisco Chronicle.

Until 1973, The Pantagraph used linotype machines, shown in the 1930s photograph above, which used molten lead to set "hot type." Then came the conversion to computerized typesetting which uses cameras, film and computers, a process called "cold type." The Pantagraph was among the first newspapers in the country to convert to computerized typesetting.

Through the years The Pantagraph has been an aggressive and pioneering newspaper. It was the first to employ a full-time farm editor, and it remains a leader in agricultural journalism, publishing a farm news section seven days a week.

Winner of scores of local and state awards, The Pantagraph also has had its share of national recognition. Pantagraph newsroom alumni include former Presidential candidate and U.N. ambassador Adlai E. Stevenson II; the late Fred Young, nationally known sports writer and football-basketball official, and David Broder, Pulitzer Prize winning columnist and political author.

The universal desk, 1936

Building on its foundation as "the press" in Central Illinois, The Pantagraph became more than just a newspaper in 1981 when it entered the field of commercial printing and began the regular publication of books.

The following year it began a features syndication and mail order service and took its first solid steps into the future and the age of the electronic distribution of information.

The Pantagraph
Number One in Central Illinois
for a lot of good reasons

PEOPLES BANK OF BLOOMINGTON

On March 4, 1869, Governor John M. Palmer dipped his steel pen into an ink pot and scrawled his signature on House Bill No. 109. Peoples Bank of Bloomington, the oldest continuous bank in the county, came into being. Eleven Bloomington sponsors anxiously awaited the news; George W. Parke (who would be elected the first president), Captain John L. Routt, Laurence Weldon, Robert E. Williams, Lyman Ferre, Benjamin F. Hoopes, Dwight Harwood, Almon B. Ives, George F. Dick, Charles E. Dodge and Norval Dixon.

The incorporators of Peoples Bank bought Brokaw Corner, the southwest corner of Washington and Center streets. The first bank building on that site was opened February 1, 1871 (see page 144), a four story structure (an American adaptation of Second Empire) with a sandstone front, mansard roof, and carved walnut front door. Surviving the great Bloomington fire of 1900, the building was razed in 1909 to make way for the new seven story edifice designed by Arthur Low Pillsbury. This building is still Peoples' main banking facility, having been remodeled for a second time during 1982.

Steadily growing from first-year assets of $173,884, Peoples was the first bank in McLean County to report deposits of over $1,000,000 on February 26, 1900. Peoples Bank officials, knowing that their institution was in sound condition, were annoyed at the forced closing during the 1933 moratorium. It was the first of the four remaining Bloomington banks to reopen.

Peoples Bank has continued to progress with the ever-changing financial industry. During the 1960s Peoples introduced computers and TV Drive-in Tellers to Bloomington. The first automatic teller machines were installed during the '70s, along with the opening of the modern Peoples East banking facility at 2201 East Washington Street. As deregulation of banking becomes reality, Peoples looks back on its heritage with pride, knowing this successful past can help it to maintain a strong financial institution in the future.

Peoples Bank Building, 1916

"Hundreds of jubilant patrons of the Peoples bank . . . set about the business of transacting in a few minutes the monetary business they had been obliged to postpone during the 10 days moratorium. Deposits greatly exceeded withdrawals . . . Tellers were kept so busy attending to the wants of customers that no bookkeeping was possible before the 3 p.m. closing time."

— **Daily Pantagraph**
March 15, 1933

STATE FARM INSURANCE

1922: a time when farmers did much of their work by hand, and country roads were deep in mud much of the year. But Henry Ford was mass-producing the Model T, and retired farmer George J. Mecherle thought the time would soon arrive when almost everyone would own one. Mecherle dreamed of providing low-cost car insurance for Illinois farmers by establishing a company which would be owned by its policyholders and by introducing a six-month policy to make payments easier. Mecherle's dream became reality on June 8, 1922, one day after his 45th birthday, with the founding of State Farm Mutual Automobile Insurance Company.

Before the company was a month old, a farmer who wrecked his 1920 Buick filed the first claim. State Farm paid him $44.20 for a new fender and radiator, a few small parts, and 10 hours of labor.

The first "home office" was a small room in the Durley Building. Before the decade ended, the company had opened its first regional office in Berkeley, California, and moved into the first home of its own at Washington and East streets. In 1929, State Farm Life Insurance Company was established.

The '30s saw the birth of State Farm Fire and Casualty Company. The first and only regional office outside the United States was located in Toronto. Ramond Mecherle was elected president in 1937.

State Farm became the nation's largest car insurer in 1942 and issued its one millionth policy. World War II caused shortages in personnel, car parts, and tires and fuel for claim adjusters. Even some typewriters were "drafted" by Uncle Sam.

George Mecherle, known affectionately as "The Chief," died in 1951. His associate almost from the beginning, Adlai Rust, became president in 1954. He was succeeded by his son Edward in 1958. During this decade, 11 more regional offices were added.

In the '60s, State Farm became the nation's largest home insurer and offered health insurance policies for the first time. A new Corporate Headquarters complex was begun.

Occupants began trickling into the new complex during 1972, the 50th anniversary year. The 25th regional office opened in Texas during the '70s.

As the organization has grown to lead the industry, its business philosophy hasn't changed and is summed up in the theme: "Like a good neighbor, State Farm is there."

Durley Building, Main & Jefferson

Last addition, completed 1947

Roller skates sped up mail delivery in the '40s.

State Farm Presidents Adlai Rust and founder G.J. Mecherle

G.J. Mercherle and his Model T

"Any human organization absorbs and reflects the values and characteristics of its environment, of the community of which it is a part. Since State Farm was founded, the State Farm Companies have been nurtured by the ability, common sense values and virtues of Bloomington and Normal and the other area towns."

— Excerpt from 1974 speech by State Farm President Edward B. Rust

WJBC

Radio was hardly a novelty to McLean County people when WJBC moved to Bloomington from LaSalle in 1934 — but WJBC was nevertheless McLean County's first commercial *station*. WJBC had signed-on in a LaSalle furniture store ten years earlier, four years after radio first caught the public's fancy by broadcasting the Harding-Cox presidential election returns in 1920. During the Roaring 20's, residents from Bellflower to Stanford joined the rest of America in the sport of tuning-in far-away stations.

But WJBC was determined to get involved in its new community, opening studios on both the Wesleyan and Illinois State Normal campuses and in the Farm Bureau Building, and talking to passersby along the downtown sidewalks. By 1939, WJBC was broadcasting the big bands, boasting "full-time" service, and by 1941, the station was moving into spacious headquarters above Bloomington's Castle Theatre and sending its flashy news van to wherever news was being made. The local news was supplemented by war reports from Westbrook Van Voorhis on the American Broadcasting Company's Blue Network.

Mobile Unit, 1939

"Man on the Street" interview, ca 1936, in front of Griesheim Building, east side of square.

". . . In short, the success of WJBC is probably the most lopsided victory for the little AM versus the big guys . . . in modern broadcasting. How do they do it? WJBC's success is rooted in basic broadcasting skills: preparation, community involvement and honest hard work."

— **Radio and Records Magazine,** Oct. 30, 1981

Bloomington's Daily Pantagraph bought WJBC in 1947 and owned at least a part of the station until 1977. In between, a new FM station was added in 1947 (WJBC-FM would become the first downstate station to regularly broadcast in stereo a few years later), a station that would eventually become WBNQ-FM. In the 1950's a pioneering show called "Problems and Solutions" helped change the face of radio listener-involvement from man-on-the-street to telephone-talk.

Radio's pace was picking up on the heels of Elvis Presley's rock'n' roll and WJBC engineers adapted the new tape cartridge for broadcast use. The revolution they set off made possible what became known around the world as "Top 40 Radio."

By 1982, in an era of "live-by-the-ratings" in broadcasting, WJBC's audience share had, for several years running, been listed first or second highest in the United States by Arbitron, the major radio ratings service.

BLOOMINGTON & McLEAN COUNTY PHOTOGRAPHERS 1849-1940

According to historian Milo Custer, the first photograph made in McLean County was taken May 10, 1847, only eight years after the invention of photography. It was a daguerreotype of Dr. Isaac Baker. Since that time more than 150 commercial photographers have operated in the county.

The listing below, compiled from city and county directories, newspapers, and photos in the Historical Society's archives, is designed to be of assistance in dating photos readers may have in their own collection. Because the directories were not published every year, in many cases it has been difficult to determine exact dates, and so it should be borne in mind that the dates given may vary by several years.

These pages are respectfully dedicated to these pioneer photographers, without whom this book would not have been possible.

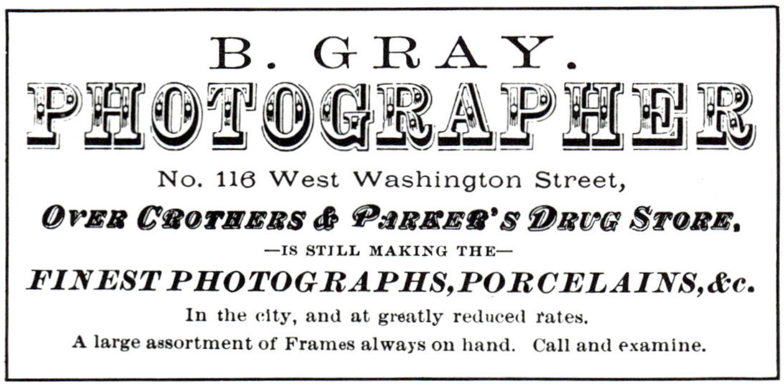

Dr. Isaac Baker, May 10, 1847

A.

Anderson, Charles. ca.1913
Anderson, Mr. & Mrs. 1852-ca.1857
Anderson, William & Alanson Thomas. ca.1859
Anderson, William. ca.1860 (?)-1866. Also ca. 1871
Arnold, ______. ca. 1913
Art Foto Shop. 1920-1930. Also 1934-1962

B.

Baker, C.E. (LeRoy) ca.1905
Barnes, J.A. ca.1891. Also ca.1899
Barnwell, E.A. & J.B. ca.1855
Bibel, Charles A. ca.1891
Bibel, William O. ca.1889
Bigelow, Theo. E. ca.1911
Bigelow, Thomas E. ca.1897
Biggs, L.A. (McLean) ca.1880
Bishop, W.M. (at Andrew Tullis's) ca.1870
Bloys Studio. ca.1911
Booth, Edward. ca.1870
Bronk, L.R. ca.1855
Browning, G.W. ca.1885
Bush & Kadgihn. ca.1886
Bush, W.E. 1887-1895. Also 1899-1905
Bush & Williams. ca.1897

C.

Camera Craft Studio. 1937-present
Camera Mart. ca.1940
Cole Brothers. ca.1909-1912
Cole, W.R. ca.1913
Cook, F.C. (at Gem Gallery) ca.1872-3
Cook & Fenwick. 1873-1877
Cope, Joseph A. (Lexington) 1912-1914
Corman, Hardin W. (?) ca. 1859

D.

Dennison, G.W. ca.1851
Denton, James W. 1889-1895. Also 1899-1902
Dillon, John. ca.1870
Dobyns, William. ca.1850
Doran, ______. (LeRoy) ca.1890
Downey, J.W. ca.1870
Drake, J.C. ca.1910
Dunn, James. (Belleflower) ca.1912

E.

Ellis, Mrs. A.O. (artist at Miller & Tankersley's ca.1873
Excelsior Photographic Gallery (B. Gray) ca.1872-3

F.

Fenwick, Richard. 1878-ca.1900
Finley, A.C. 1851
Finley, A.C. & R. Humphreys. 1852
Freeland, Law. 1902-1904. Also 1907
Fuller, J.O. (Danvers) ca.1915
Fullerton, James A. ca.1866
Funk & Kerr. ca.1889
Funk & Klauer. 1891-1893

G.

Garrett & Bell. ca.1880
Garrett, Thomas P. 1882-1905 (with C.U. Williams 1899-1902
Gem Gallery (B.Gray) ca.1872-3
Gibson, John S. 1873-1875
Godfrey & Son. (Saybrook) ca.1912
Goff, George. ca.1882
Gosselin, E.W. (photo colorist) ca.1870
Gray, Benjamin. 1864-1877
Gray's Gallery. ca.1871
Gross, Louis. 1917-1926

H.

Hammond, Johnson. (LeRoy) ca.1875-6
Hastings, Mr. ______. 1849
Hause, Dale C. ca.1932
Hawkins Studio. 1929-1977
Hays Brothers. (Saybrook) ca.1895
Hays, R.C. (Saybrook) ca.1900-1912
Helms, Reuben M. (at Excelsior Gallery) ca.1872-3
Henline, N. ca.1913
Hensley's Studio. (Colfax) ca.1905
Herron, George W. ca.1909
Hope, ______. (Normal) ca.1873
Horine & Ormsby. ca.1870
Howard, J.T. (Heyworth) ca.1865
Hunt, Elisha. (photo painter) ca.1870
Hurst, Miss Sylvira. (artist with R.G. LaMarr) ca.1873

K.

Kadgihn, Henry. 1887-ca.1890
Keeran, James W. 1878-1885
Kerr, C.N. ca.1895
Kitchell, James A. ca.1907
Klauer, C.W. ca.1894
Kyle, Julius. (Colfax) ca.1910-1917

L.

Lake, John W. 1904-1924

William Anderson, daguerreotypist

Lake, Mrs. Phebe J. 1932-1938
LaMarr, R.G. 1873-4
LaRush & Carns. (Heyworth?) ca.1885
LaRush, Charles. ca.1885
Leland, M.F. ca.1865
Leland & McClure. (?) 1857
Leland & Palmer. 1862
Lettelier, John G. & Frank White. ca.1866-1869
Lorraine Studio. ca.1926

Joseph H. Scibird, photo by John S. Scibird

M.
Macy & Macy. ca.1913
Macy Studio, ca.1917
Macy, Robert J. ca.1920-1926
Marton, Albert M. 1880-1932
Mayes & Bell. ca.1880
Mayes & Bush. ca.1895
Mayes, John J. 1880-1884. Also 1893-ca.1915
Mayes & O'Neill. ca.1895
McCabe, Charles. ca.1917-1930
McDonald, R.A. 1858
McIntyre, D.G. 1895-1897
Merrill, Stephen A. (Lexington) 1864-1912
Miller, Cyrus. ca.1870
Miller, Elias & John R. Tankersley. 1870-1875
Miller, J. Sidney (photographic chemist) ca.1870
Moore, Eldo M. (United Photo Shop) 1932-ca.1947 (may have been photographing as early as 1913)
Moore & Smith. (Normal) ca.1922
Morrell Brothers. ca.1886
Morrell, Isaac V. 1887-1889
Myers, F.C. ca.1911

N.
Neff, Sim. ca.1880-1885
Neff & Tiedke. ca.1875
Neher, William D. (Chenoa) ca.1910-1917
New York Daguerrean Gallery (William Dobyns) 1850
Nute, Charles N. 1870-1886

O
Oberkoetter, Frank F. 1935-1937
O'Neill, Owen B. 1895-1897

P
Pancake, Addison. 1868-1870
Perkins, Thomas B. ca.1872-3
Poole's Studio. (Lexington) ca.1912-1918 (Herman Poole)
Poole, Mrs. Nellie (Lexington) 1918-1921

R
Read & White. (postcards) ca.1910
Reese, Napoleon B. ca.1873
Rembrandt Photo Studio. ca.1932
Riggert, Herman J. 1907-ca.1915
Ros-Syl Studio. 1924-1932

S
Scibird Brothers. 1864
Scibird & Brother's Photographic Gallery. 1863
Scibird & Company. (J.S. & H.W. Scibird) 1856-1858
Scibird, Harvey W. ca.1859
Scibird, John S. 1858-ca.1866. Also 1871
Scibird, Joseph H. ca.1868-1870
Scibird, Joseph H. & George McC. Rex. ca.1865-1867
Scibird's Photographic Gallery. 1862
Scibird, Thomas & Anderson. ca.1857-8
Scott, J. Hedley. ca.1917-1926
Sethers, ______. (LeRoy) ca.1910
Shanklin, D.H. (Normal) 1899-1905
Silvius, J.L. (LeRoy) ca.1891
Simmons Brothers. 1895-1899
Skaggs, Frank. ca.1893
Skillman, C.A. (LeRoy) ca.1910-1913
Slason, M. 1850-1
Smith, C.O. (Saybrook) ca.1875
Spafford & Cable. 1902-1907
Spafford, R.I. ca.1909

Joseph G. Hawkins

Alfred M. Marton, self-portrait

Spafford's Studios. ca.1911
Stanefirth, Isaac. ca.1866
Star Studio. ca.1917-1928
Stimson, Joseph B. ca.1920-1923
Stimson Studio. ca.1917
Stipp, H.S. 1850-1
Swick, Prof. Milton. 1872-1875. Also 1880
Swick & Briggs. 1878-9
Swick & Stutsman. ca.1870

T.
Tankersley, John R. 1876-1885
Taylor, James. ca.1868-1871
Thomas, A. 1856
Ticknor, L.M. ca.1884
Tiedke, Otto. ca.1878
Tilton, ______. ca.1854
Tullis, Andrew. 1864-1870

U.
United Postal Company. ca.1911
United Photo Shop. 1913-ca.1947

V.
VanGorder, William P. 1909-1924
Vincent, Harry W. 1897-1909

W.
Webster, Miss F.J. 1858-9
Westerman, Otto. 1875-6
Westerman, Otto. (with J.S. Gibson) ca.1873
Whitehead, A.H. ca.1853
Williams, Charles U. 1899-ca.1915
Wills, A.M. 1852
Wright, ______.(?) ca.1857

ACKNOWLEDGMENTS

The collaborators of this work would like to give special thanks to the many who helped us with this task.

The following who served on the publication committee:

- Steve Arendell, Illinois Graphics
- Rex Bates, ACI
- Jim Bicket
- Fred Dolan, Pantagraph Printing & Stationery
- Barbara Dunbar
- Elmo Franklin
- Tim Ives, Chairman
- James Keeran, The Pantagraph
- Judy Stern Markowitz
- Gene Paxton
- Harriett Rust
- Dave Smith, ACI
- Walter Wright

And also Dianne Miller, librarian, The Pantagraph; Lois Woods, Illinois collections, Bloomington Public Library; Preston Hawks, archaeology lab director, ISU; Ron Smith Printing, brochures; Illinois Graphics, brochures; Bernie Gummerman, sage advice; Fred Brian, Pilot Rock Press, presentation page; Mary Michaels, photo archivist, Illinois State Historical Library; AASLH Publications Seminar; and to those who provided questions, answers, and ideas.

Bloomington firemen at leisure, 1871

AFTERWORD

The photos found in this volume were chosen as examples of the visual expression of the people and culture of McLean County. It was the compilers' intention that the reader (or viewer) be able to gain a sense of "what it was like" to live in the periods of time covered by this book. The subjects represented are examples of the common experience of the work and lives of those who preceded us. The choices made by the editors were based on the image's ability to convey the history of the county with visual continuity.

Local history is often confused with geneology and biography. The few individuals who appear in this work are representative of the type of people who made McLean County. Some are included simply because they are extraordinary. No effort has been made to include all prominent citizenry. Such an effort in a visual form would reduce itself to a mere portrait album.

What makes a photograph or an image "historic" is a combination of a number of attributes. In a publication of this type the most important feature is the way an image will assist another image in making a more coherent statement. The quality of an image is determined not only by who is in it, but more importantly by what the image can represent in terms of a narrative. The physical condition of an image is another concern in the production of a work. The mere ability to reproduce a photo may be obvious, but is an often unstated requirement. The third requirement in editing is the physical possession of the image. A photo becomes historic because it has survived and has been made available to the historian.

NOTES

Page

2 MCHS. Daguerreotype, 3-1/8 x 2-3/4 in. Taken during completion of the Federal style house. Elements of this house were later incorporated into the Oscar Wakefield house.

4-5 MCHS, Goforth Collection. Photo by Spafford.

7 *Art Work of Bloomington*, 1904.

Chapter 1. The First Settlers

9 a. MCHS.
  b. Courtesy Illinois State Museum.

10 a. Grooved axe. MCHS. Found by Dean Davis near Downs on Kickapoo Creek. Gray granite.
  b. "Lost Lake" type point. MCHS.
  c. Atl-atl weight. Courtesy ISU, Nuell Downs Collection. cat. no. 74-1/2172. Geniculate type. Banded slate. Used as weight on atl-atl or spear thrower.
  d. Chert knife. MCHS. Found by J.W. Moran, ca. 1910.
  e. Courtesy Illinois State Museum.
  f. Courtesy Illinois State Museum.
  g. Courtesy Illinois State Museum.

11 a. Hoe. MCHS. Cat. no. 722-244.
  b. Pipe. MCHS. Cat. no. 722-371.
  c. Celt. MCHS. Cat. no. 722-402. Found in Money Creek township.
  d. Clockwise from top: Adena leaf blade. MCHS, cat. 722-99.
  e. Waubesa/Adena point. MCHS, cat. no. 722-29.
  f. Lowe point. MCHS, cat. no. 762-568.
  g. Snyder point. MCHS, cat. no. 722-172.

12 a. Courtesy ISU.
  b. Points. Courtesy ISU. Chipped chert.
  c. Awls. Courtesy ISU.
  d. Shell hoe. Courtesy ISU.
  e. Pot. Courtesy ISU. Shell-tempered, cord-marked handled jar. Upper Mississippian. Excavated by Fred Brian.

13 a. Courtesy ISU.
  b. Courtesy ISU.

14-5 Courtesy Illinois State Museum.

16 a. MCHS. Brigham Collection.
  b. Courtesy *The Pantagraph*.

17 a. Courtesy National Archives of France. Cat. no. PH/1250/Reynards 1731 (DFC) 46e & 47e. Copy by Illinois State Historical Society.
  b. Given to J.H. Burnham, 1897. Collected by farmers near the site.

18 MCHS, photo by Hoppe, Horton, Kansas, 1906. Residence of Andrew Magonzee.

19 a. Courtesy Smithsonian Institution, Cat. no. 200510.
  b. Courtesy Charles Steen. Taken in Mexico, 1957. Archaeological remains of this type of structure found at Grand Village of the Kickapoo Site in 1974.

20 a. Iron hoe, MCHS, cat. no. 722-465. Found at Old Town.
  b. Knife blade. MCHS, cat. no. 792-866. Note blade markings.
  c. Trade axe. MCHS, cat. no. 722-510. Found near Arrowsmith, 1897.
  d. Scissors. MCHS, cat. no. 792-884 & 792-890.
  e. Bone hand. Courtesy ISU, cat. no. 73/327, A73-14K, site ML 21. Possibly worn as a talisman. The hand was an important symbol in Kickapoo religion.
  f. Silver cross. Courtesy ISU. Bulbar type, probably French. Mark unclear (BC?).

Page

  g. Gun cock. Courtesy ISU, cat. no. 5/1, KS.
  h. Iron arrow point. MCHS. Provenience unknown.
  i. Gun lock plate. Courtesy ISU, cat. no. 5/1, KS.

21 a. Map by Dave Mellen.
  b. Courtesy Illinois State Historical Library.

22 a. Amulet. MCHS. Found one mile west of Kickapoo Stockade site.
  b. MCHS. Copied from George Catlin by Florence Harris, 1906.
  c. MCHS. Copied from George Catlin by Florence Harris, 1906.
  d. Lid. MCHS. Found at Kickapoo Village site, 1911.
  e. Kettle. MCHS, cat. no. 722-497. Found at gravel pit, southeast of Old Town.

23 a. MCHS. Copied from George Catlin by Florence Harris, 1906.
  b. Courtesy Smithsonian Institution, cat. no. 178369.

24 MCHS. Photo by Hoppe, Horton, Kan.

25 MCHS. Photo by Hoppe, Horton, Kan.

26 MCHS. Photo by Hoppe, Horton, Kan.

27 MCHS. Photo by Hoppe, Horton, Kan.

28 MCHS. Photo by Hoppe, Horton, Kan.

29 MCHS. Photo by Hoppe, Horton, Kan.

30-1 MCHS. Photo by Hoppe, Horton, Kan.

32 a. MCHS. Copied from George Catlin by Florence Harris, 1906.
  b. MCHS. Copy by A.M. Marton, ca. 1917. Original ca. 1870.

Chapter 2. The White Settlers

33 Courtesy *The Pantagraph*. Top of chimney and general shape of structure are inaccurate, according to description by Lexington historian A.V. Pierson, 1902.

34-5 MCHS.

36 MCHS, SW 1/4, sec. 2, Funks Grove twp. Appears on page 17, 1874 Atlas of McLean County. This was Funk's second cabin, built in February, 1830.

37 a. MCHS. This type of crib was later built with milled lumber. A few examples remain.
  b. MCHS.

38 MCHS. Original map ca. 1900. Photocopy by R.W. Arnold, ca. 1915. Shows parts of Olio, Palestine, Kansas, and Montgomery townships, Woodford County, and White Oak township, McLean County.

39 a. Rifle. MCHS, cat. no. 726-12. Late 18th century. Converted from flintlock to percussion. "Roman nose" tiger maple stock. Lock marked "Roop."
  b. Powderhorn. MCHS, cat. no. 726-280.
  c. Photo by R. Fenwick, Bloomington, ca. 1890-5.

40 a. MCHS. Photo taken on George Perrin Davis farm near Gridley, ca. 1896. Oxen were used for winter cattle feeding. E.H. Hyneman (w/beard), John Hyneman (w/goad).
  b. Ox shoe. MCHS.

41 MCHS, cat. no. 725-6. This plow used for MCHS logo.

42 a. Sickle. MCHS, cat. no. 725-85. Blade marked "L. Shohalter."
  b. Pitchfork. MCHS, cat. no. 725-34.
  c. Flail. MCHS, cat. no. 725-12.
  d. Scythe. MCHS, cat. no. 725-8. Blade marked "W. Kimbal, Fitchburg, Mass."

43 a. Kettle. MCHS, cat. no. 723-123. Copper. Marked "L. Stutzman."
  b. Pin, MCHS, cat. no. 723-115. ca. 1837. Flame maple.

Page

43 c. "Dutch" oven. MCHS, cat. no. 723-99.
  d. Iron pot. MCHS, cat. no. 723-100.

44 MCHS. Barn loom. 4-harness, counterbalanced. Restored by Shauna Clark, 1977, and Joanne Meister, 1979. Dressed by Marilyn Townley.

45 a. Flax hackle. MCHS, cat. no. 725-120. Punched tin decoration.
  b. Flax wheel. MCHS, cat. no. 773-415. Marked "I. Smith." so-called "German" wheel because type orginated in Saxony. Walnut.
  c. Scutching knife. MCHS, cat. no. 725-189. Used to clean and pull flax fiber after breaking.
  d. Wool wheel. MCHS, From Heyworth, Ill.
  e. Yarn reel. MCHS, cat. no. 724-81. Oak Mechanism in back clicks, allowing accurate measurement of yarn.
  f. Wool cards. MCHS, cat. no. 725-140 & 725-146. Used to straighten fiber.

46 a. Mortar. MCHS.
  b. Photo by A.R. Nicholson, Lincoln, Ill., 1902. Probably taken at Atlanta, Ill. fairgrounds.

49 MCHS. Drawing by R. Sidney Smith (creator of Andy Gump and Old Doc Yak) Done from information supplied by Ezra M. Prince, 1900.

50 a. Drawing by Dwight Frink, 1898. Published in *Transactions of the McLean County Historical Society*, Volume I, 1899.
  b. Drawing by Dwight Frink, 1900. Published in *Transactions of the McLean County Historical Society*, Volume II, 1902.

51 a. From ambrotype taken ca. 1860 of painting done in 1821. Original painting in Bartholomew County Courthouse in Indiana, as of 1900.
  b. Drawing by Dwight Frink, 1899. Published in *Transactions of the McLean County Historical Society*, Volume I, 1899.

52 MCHS. Photo by Henry Miller, 1900. NW 1/4, Sec. 32, Mount Hope twp.

54 MCHS. Sec. 15, Hudson twp. photo ca. 1900.

55 a. Sec. 11, Hudson twp. Photo ca. 1900.
  b. Photo ca. 1910. The house is a vernacular interpretation of the Federal style of architecture.

56 MCHS. Photo ca. 1900. Southwest corner Main and Olive, Bloomington.

57 MCHS. Ambrotype, ca. 1860. 4-1/4 x 5-1/2 in. plate. First reproduced in Carl Sandburg's *The Prairie Years*, 1926.

58 a. MCHS. Carte de visite by L.A. Biggs, McLean, Ill., ca. 1880.
  b. MCHS. Photo 1903. Originally on the southeast corner of Main and Olive, Bloomington. Later moved to the corner of Mill and Madison. Note removal of corner door at left.

59 MCHS. Photo ca. 1900. Outlot 18, Village of Hudson.

60 MCHS. Ambrotype, ca. 1860.

61 MCHS. Daguerreotype, ca. 1868 (?). Possibly copied by J.H. Scibird.

62 a. MCHS. Ferrotype, copied from earlier image.
  b. MCHS. Ferrotype, ca. 1870.
  c. MCHS. Daguerreotype, ca. 1850.
  d. MCHS. Ambrotype, ca. 1856.

63 a. MCHS. Daguerreotype, believed taken in Peoria, 1844. "Scovills" on plate, "E. White" on case, 1/4 plate size. Miss Briggs would be 7 or 8 years old.

NOTES

Page

63 b. Daguerreotype, 1852. "W.H." on plate. 1/4 plate size.
c. Daguerreotype, ca. 1855. "Scovills" on plate. 1/4 plate size.
d. Ferrotype, copied from earlier image. Note photographed brass mat from earlier image.

64 Courtesy *The Pantagraph*.

Chapter 3. The Yankees and Their Towns.

65 Courtesy *The Pantagraph*. Looking southwest from the corner of Front and Center. Telegraph pole in foreground.

66-7 MCHS.

68 a. MCHS.
b. MCHS. Photo ca. 1860.
c. Printing press. Courtesy *The Pantagraph*. ". . . the publication was discontinued, probably about June or July 1839. The office material was sold out and removed, it is believed, to Peoria . . ." E.J. Lewis, "History of the Pantagraph," *Transactions of the McLean County Historical Society*, Volume II, 1903.

69 MCHS. Photo by Benjamin Gray, ca. 1868. Note: "Get the Florence" poster on fence refers to a brand of sewing machine. A new cupola was built in 1852, and the brackets under the eaves may have been added at that time. The two brick wings were added about 1860.

70 a. MCHS. photo by Bradley and Rulotson, San Francisco, Cal., ca. 1875. ". . . The only elevator connected with photography in the world . . ." (from back of photo.)
b. MCHS. Photo 1903. (See p. 64-5. The Allin cabin was weather-boarded and considerably enlarged and re-modeled by Gridley and a later occupant, Dr. George Stipp.)

71 a. MCHS. Daguerreotype, ca. 1850. 2-1/2 x 2-1/4.
b. MCHS. Original 1836 plat (by Pettit?)

72-3 MCHS. Copy, ca. 1870 from original Daguerreotype, ca. 1860. This is the earliest known photograph of a brickyard in operation. The flag pole expressed Van Schoick's patriotic sentiment.

74 a. Wood engraving, ca. 1855. Published in *The Illinois Wesleyan Story 1850-1950*.
b. Carte-de-visite, ca. 1873. Photo by Prof. Milton Swick.

75 a. Courtesy ISU. Engraving, ca. 1856.
b. Courtesy ISU. Photo ca. 1865.

76 a. MCHS. Photo by R. Fenwick, 1899. Later re-modeled in Queen Anne style. Occupied by Stewart's Music Store, later United Photo Shop. Burned about 1975.
b. MCHS. ca. 1872.

77 a. MCHS. Advertising cuts, *McLean County Directory*, 1859-60. Published by J. Bailey, Chicago.
b. Photogravure. Published in *Bloomington Illustrated*, H.R. Page & Co., 1889.

78 a. From *Weekly National Flag*, Bloomington, October 19, 1855. Col. Samuel Pike, editor.
b. MCHS. Photo ca. 1862. Fire company no. 1, the "Prairie Bird" company. Planks in the street are a pedestrian crosswalk. (Note: it is believed the name "Prairie Bird" was derived from the pumping handles on either side of the engine. When in use they would give it the appearance of a bird flapping its wings.)

Page

79 Courtesy Illinois Bell Telephone Co. Copyright 1967. Painting by George Parrish.

80 a. MCHS. Daguerreotype, ca. 1855. 3-1/4 x 4-1/4 in. "40" on plate.
b. MCHS. Photo ca. 1893. Southeast corner East and Monroe. Church was built in 1856 by contractors Hayes and Evans.

Chapter 4. The War.

81 MCHS.

82 MCHS.

83 a. MCHS. Carte-de-visite, ca. 1860. Photo by P. Butler, Decatur, Ill.
b. Drawing by C. Eugene Asbury. (Note: arched headers on second story windows were introduced in 1872 after fire destroyed the third story.)

84 MCHS. Flag was saved by Carico from Confederate capture at battle of Lexington, Mo. by concealing it under his uniform. He was paroled and, upon his arrival at Bloomington, was photographed with the flag.

85 MCHS. Poster printed at *Illinois Statesman* office, Bloomington?

86-7 MCHS. Original painting for McLean County Historical Society by Martin A. Wyckoff, 1979. The west side of square is shown. Osco's building is only one remaining.

86 MCHS. Original newspaper was the last issue of the *Times*.

88 MCHS. Ferrotype, ca. 1863.

89 MCHS. Ferrotype, ca. 1861. George Fifer was killed at Esperanza, Tex. in 1863. Joseph Fifer was governor of Illinois 1889-1893.

90 a. Photo by McCormac, Clarksville, Tenn., ca. 1862. MCHS.
b. MCHS. Homer Wakefield Collection.

91 MCHS. Painting by Elisha Hunt, ca. 1870. Oil on cardboard. Hunt was Bloomington's first artist, arriving in 1839.

92 a. Facsimile published by Ralph Newman, 1968. Original in private collection.
b. Courtesy Illinois State Historical Library.

93 a. MCHS. Copy by United Photo from original. Taken at camp near Rolla, Missouri, late April 1863, identified by Jim Goben
b. MCHS. Carte-de-visite, ca. 1863. Photo by Gardner, Washington, D.C.

94 MCHS. Evans Collection, drawing noted done by artist from *Leslie's Illustrated Weekly*.

95 MCHS. Carte-de-visite, ca. 1865. Rolls was in Co. C, 33rd IVI.

96 a. Dress sword. MCHS, cat. no. 726-82. Scabbard engraved "Col. J. McNulta, 94 Ill. V. I. From the officers of his com^{d} A.D. Oct. 19th 1863." Blade marked "Tiffany & Co. N.Y."
b. Springfield rifled musket. MCHS, cat. no. 726-38. Contract of Parkers, Snow, & Co., Meriden, Conn., 1864. .58 cal.
c. Buckle, MCHS, cat. no. 726-204. Model 1839. Type used during Civil War, worn as late as the 1880s.
d. Remington revolver, MCHS, cat. no. 726-123. Model 1858. .44 cal.
e. Binoculars and case, MCHS, cat. no. 726-257. Marked "A. Bardou, Paris," and "U.S. Signal Day & Night."
f. Field desk. MCHS, cat. no. 786-520. Used by Gen William W. Orme.

Page

97 a. Bayonet and scabbard. MCHS, cat. nos. 806-728 and 796-601. Model 1855 Springfield.
b. Sergeant's cap. MCHS, cat. no. 726-672. General Service buttons. Cap made by Green & Green, Louisville, Ky.
c. Cavalry sabre. MCHS, cat. no. 726-79. Believed used by William McCullough.
d. Officer's uniform. MCHS, 1st lieutenant, U.S. Cavalry.
e. Smith's carbine. MCHS, cat. no. 726-26. Breech loader, .50 cal.
f. Canteen, MCHS, cat. no. 726-197.
g. Cup. MCHS, cat. no. 726-201. Soldered tin.
h. Mess kit on top. MCHS, cat. no. 727-4. "S & E °" hallmark on spoon. Wooden handle.
i. Cartridge box. MCHS, cat. no. 726-195. Marked "R. Neoe, Philad." and "F.A. Sniffen, U.S. Ord. Dept. Sub-inspector."

98-100 Courtesy Bureau County Historical Society. Bryant was an art teacher at ISNU before the war, and a nephew of poet William Cullen Bryant.

101 a. MCHS. Capt. Francis D. Atkins, Co., C. 33rd IVI. Photo by Scibird & Brother, Bloomington.
b. MCHS. Pvt. Cyrus Betterman, Co. B, 33rd IVI.
c. MCHS. Samuel Coy, Co. C, 33rd IVI.
d. MCHS. Robert W. Clarey, Co. C, 33rd IVI. Photo by C. Schon, 61 Summit St., Toledo, Ohio.

102 Map by Dave Mellen, 1982.

103 From *The Soldier in Our Civil War*, Stanley Bradley Publishing Co., N.Y., 1890.

104 Courtesy Illinois State Historical Library.

105 MCHS.

106 a. ". . . This I had drew by I.H. Philips that bunks with me. He is from Fairbury. . ." *Diary of James T. Ayers*.
b. Courtesy Illinois State Historical Library. Photo ca. 1862.

107 MCHS, Lewis Collection.

108 MCHS. Photo by Joseph H. Scibird, April 16, 1865. Looking southeast from southwest corner of Center and Jefferson.

109 a. MCHS. Ferrotype. Brass mat, black ribbon.
b. MCHS. Worn at Lincoln's funeral in Springfield by members of the "Prairie Bird" fire company.

110 a. MCHS. Camp McCullough was on west side of Bloomington, bounded by Market, Stillwell and Washington.
b. MCHS. Hat insignia of Post 146, the William T. Sherman Post, Bloomington.

110-111 c. MCHS. Reunion of the 94th Illinois Infantry, Miller Park, 1885.

112 a. MCHS, Sinclair collection, M.G.M./U.A. photo.
b. Courtesy M.G.M./U.A. From United Artists publicity package.

Chapter 5. Urban Growth.

113 MCHS. (Partially edited)

114 Courtesy *The Pantagraph*.

115 a. MCHS. Taken at C & A Shops, ca. 1885.
b. From Bloomington *Daily Leader*, July 4, 1881. Semi-centennial edition.

NOTES

Page

116 a. *Gould's City Directory for 1880-1 for Bloomington-Normal.*
b. MCHS. C & A locomotive repair shop, 1886. Man in foreground, William Wilson, superintendent of motive power. Center, unidentified. Rear, George Gregg, general foreman.

117 a. Car shop. Published in *Bloomington Illustrated*, H.C. Page & Co., 1889.
b. MCHS. C & A locomotive repair shop, 1886.

118 a. MCHS, cat. no. 728-2.
b. From Bloomington *Daily Leader*, July 4, 1881.

119 a. MCHS, Cheney Collection.
b. MCHS.
c. From Bloomington *Daily Leader*, July 4, 1881.

120 a. MCHS. Van Schoick Pork Packing Co. employees, ca. 1890.
b. MCHS, Cheney Collection.

121 a. MCHS, Homer Wakefield Collection.
b. Southwest corner, Division and C & A tracks. Published in *Bloomington Illustrated*, H.C. Page & Co., 1889.

122 a. Higgins Marble Works, built ca. 1885. East Front St. George Miller, architect. Higgins's employees probably did the stone carving on the building. Published in *Bloomington Illustrated*, H.S. Page & Co., 1889.
b. MCHS. Higgins, Jung & Kleinau Marble Co. employees, ca. 1885. Front row, third from left, J. Phillip Jung. Fifth from left, Charles Siebert. Men with mauls are carvers. Jung holds a lettering rule. Man in center takes care of tools. Men with blocks are stone polishers.

123 a. From "A Landmark of Days Gone By." Photo ca. 1885. Schmidt home called "Wilhelmshohe" or "William's Heights" after the Kaiser's residence in Germany. Schmidt lived on West Market Street Road, west of I-74.
b. From *Bloomington's Deutsche in Wort und Bild (Bloomington's Germans in Word and Picture)* 1893.

124 a. From *Bloomington Illustrated*, 1889. 315-319 South Main St. George Miller, architect, 1883.
b. From *Bloomington's Deutsche in Wort und Bild*,, 1893.

125 MCHS. Moses Montefiore Temple, southeast corner Prairie and Monroe. George Miller, architect, 1888-9. J.W. Evans & Sons, contractor. August Laufer, mason.

126 a. MCHS. Ferrotype, ca. 1885.
b. MCHS. Carte-de-visite, ca. 1885.
c. MCHS. New Year's Day calling card. Moody and Sankey were prominent evangelic revivalists.

127 a. From *Bloomington Illustrated*, 1889. Built by Hayes and Evans.
b. MCHS.
c. MCHS. Copy from original.

128 MCHS. Standing: Richard Carrell, Fred Hartley, John O'Neil, James Stone, Chas. Joy, Elliot S. Miller, John Kopp, H.D. Kuhlman. Seated: Jesse Butler, G. Boyce, Mayor Benjamin Funk, James Bailey, Wm. McGraw.

129 a. Courtesy Mrs. Karen Strebe. Marguerite O'Hara Kane and Daniel "Stick" O'Neill. 710 North Lumber St.
b. Courtesy Gummerman Printing. From printers supply catalog, ca. 1905.

Page

130 a. MCHS. Rudolph Richter, architect. Hayes and Evans, contractors.
b. From *History of Holy Trinity Parish*, Rt. Rev. Msg. S.N. Moore, 1952.

131 a. From *Transactions of the McLean County Historical Society*, Volume II, 1903. George Miller, architect, 1884. J.W. Evans, Sons, contractors. Northwest corner Center and Locust.
b. Courtesy Mrs. Anthony Koos.

132 a. Courtesy Mrs. Karen Strebe. Taken December 28 or 29, 1877. Draped in mourning for the funeral of engineer James O'Neill, who was murdered.
b. Courtesy Mrs. Karen Strebe. Ferrotype, ca. 1885.

133 a. MCHS. Photo by Bush and Kadgihn, 402 North Main St., Bloomington. ca. 1885.
b. *Holland's Bloomington City Directory*, 1870. Western Publishing Co., Chicago.

134 MCHS.

135 a. Courtesy Mrs. Karen Strebe. Southwest corner Chestnut and Lumber.
b. MCHS. Behr Collection. ca. 1910, Robert Empson at front.

136 a. Courtesy Mr. and Mrs. Dean McCrossin. Albert Ploense in center.
b. MCHS, cat. no. 778-84.

137 a. MCHS. Taken March, 1898.
b. MCHS.

138 a. MCHS. 106 North Main St., May 28, 1894. Left to right:
1. Horse
2. J.W. Rodgers
3. Ella L. Greenlee
4. B. Frank Hosler
5. Otto A. Hensel
b. Courtesy Mrs. Karen Strebe. Left to right:
1. Unkown
2. Nellie Greenlee
3. Will Schell
4. Unknown
5. Charles Gaede
6. Frank Hosler

139 a. MCHS. 306-8 West Front St. Photo by Alfred Marton. P.H. Twomey, second from right.
b. MCHS, Homer Wakefield Collection.

140 a. Courtesy R.W. McKinney.
b. Courtesy R.W. McKinney.

141 a. MCHS. 113 West Front st. Originally stereoscopic view.
b. MCHS, Kirkpatrick Collection.

142 MCHS. ca. 1887.

143 a. MCHS.
b. MCHS. Photo by R. Fenwick.

144 a. From *Bloomington Illustrated*, 1889. G.W. Bunting, architect.
b. MCHS. W.L. Moore in background.

Chapter 6. The Prairie Settled.

145 MCHS, Wilson Collection. Pencil sketch from *The Daleite*, No. 11, Vol. III (newspaper format diary.)

146 a. MCHS.
b. Published in *Belleflower, 100 Years 1871-1971*.
c. MCHS. Block 6, Original Town of Chenoa.

147 a. Courtesy *The Pantagraph*.
b. MCHS. Taken June 1910, one to three miles west of Bentown. Kickapoo drainage ditch, Old Town twp.
c. Courtesy *The Pantagraph*.

148 MCHS. Stereoscopic view, ca. 1915. Keystone View Co., no. H295-(V18443)

149 a. Courtesy *The Pantagraph*.
b. MCHS. Photo by Swick and Briggs, Bloomington, ca. 1878.

Page

150 a. MCHS. F.W. Douglas, delineator, Pantagraph Stock Printing Co. From *Some of the Horses That Made Normal Famous*, Jesse M. and Roy H. Dillon, 1936.
b. Ibid.
c. MCHS.

151 a. MCHS, Dillon Bros. catalogue, 1891.
b. Ibid.

152 a. MCHS, Brigham Collection.
b. From *Atlas of McLean County and the State of Illinois*, Warner & Beers, Chicago, 1874.

153 MCHS, Brigham Collection.

154 a. MCHS, Brigham Collection. Photo taken July 1918.
b. MCHS.

155 a. Courtesy *The Pantagraph*. Photo by Frank Bill, ca. 1935.
b. Photo by C.U. Williams, ca. 1910.

156 a. Courtesy *The Pantagraph*. Photo by Frank Bill. 1931 State Corn Husking Championship.
b. Courtesy *The Pantagraph*. Photo by Frank Bill, 1939.

157 a. Courtesy *The Pantagraph*. Photo by Frank Bill, ca. 1935.
b. Courtesy *The Pantagraph*. A.V. Kinsinger with shovel. Taken on Hans Miller farm, southwest of Carlock.

158 a. Courtesy *The Pantagraph*. Photo ca. 1908.
b. Courtesy *The Pantagraph*. Photo taken 1938.

159 MCHS, Brigham Collection.

160 From *Plat Book of McLean County*.

161 Northwest Publishing Co., Philadelphia (?), 1895.

162 a. MCHS.
b. MCHS. Taken February 25 or 28, 1900. Both this and the above view are looking west on Lincoln Street, Block 54, Town Council Survey.

163 a. MCHS. ca. 1880.
b. Courtesy Delmar D. Wyckoff, Photo ca. 1913. Front row:
1. Irene Nixon
2. ______ Kuhling
3. Delmar West
4. ______ Kuhling
5. Carlton West (?)
6. Grace Vinson
7. Unknown
8. Verna Eberhardt
9. ______ Sigler
Back row:
1. Emma Fowler, teacher.
2. Harlan Wyckoff
3. Delmar Wyckoff
4. Raymond Curtis
5. Roy Vinson
6. Dwight Fenstemaker
7. Elmer Eberhardt
Ad for insurance company of Frank C. and Canby A. Barley, LeRoy. School in NE 1/4, sec. 4, West twp.

164 a. From *Atlas of McLean County*, 1874.
b. MCHS, Brown Collection. ca. 1900.

165 a. Courtesy *The Pantagraph*.
b. MCHS. (Partially edited)
c. Courtesy *The Pantagraph*. Originally Methodist church, built 1867. Sold and moved, used as an implement store, later town hall.

166 a. MCHS.
b. Courtesy Helen Meadors. Photo ca. 1905.

167 a. MCHS.
b. Courtesy *The Pantagraph*.
c. MCHS.

168 MCHS.

NOTES

Page

169 a. Courtesy *The Pantagraph.*
b. MCHS, Brigham Collection. Taken 1917, "the last day of school." SW 1/4, sec. 1, Dry Grove twp.

170 a. MCHS, Brigham Collection.
b. MCHS, Brigham Collection. Ferrotype.

171 a. MCHS, Brigham Collection.
b. MCHS, Hutton Family Collection. On back of Award of Merit given to Linus Hutton, ca. 1880.
c. MCHS, Brigham Collection.

172 a. MCHS, cat. no. 779-161. Used by Mrs. Myrtle Ballard Ketchum near Chenoa, 1905.
b. MCHS, Catherine Rowlands Collection. "Number One" school, May 10, 1911.
c. MCHS, Brigham Collection. May Day, Pleasant Ridge school, no. 184, 1898. Sara Hall Forsyth, teacher.

173 a. MCHS, Rowlands Collection.
b. MCHS, Hensel Collection.

174 a. MCHS, Harvey Collection. ca. 1910.
b. MCHS, Kirkpatrick Collection. Col. J.H. Kirkpatrick at center on platform.

175 a. MCHS, Breen Collection.
b. Courtesy *The Pantagraph.* Photo taken 1932.

Chapter 7. The Age of Elegance.

177 MCHS. Present site of Consistory. Built for J.R. Mason, ca. 1875. In the doorway, W.R. and Mrs. White. At far right, J.F. and Lucy White.

178 a, *Bloomington Illustrated*, 1889.
b. Courtesy Bloomington Public Library. Home built 1859.

179 Courtesy Bloomington Public Library.

180 a. Courtesy Martin A. Wyckoff. From Miller family album. Photo by R. Fenwick.

181 *Artwork of Bloomington, Illinois*, 1904. Gravure Illustration Co.

182 Both images from *Bloomington Illustrated*, 1889.

183 *Up-to-date Homes*, Cornbelt Printing & Stationery, Bloomington, 1899.

184 a. MCHS.
b. MCHS, Frances Pillsbury Collection. Daisy Hill on left. Photo by Strauss of St. Louis, 1892.
c. MCHS. Photo by Coles, Delavan, Ill. Richard Henry Little in center, James Southard at upper left. Little was born in LeRoy, Ill. He was a graduate of LeRoy High School and Illinois Wesleyan University. He was a war correspondent in the Russo-Japanese War, 1904-5, and in later years wrote the "A Line o' Type" column for the *Chicago Tribune.*

185 a. MCHS, Frances Pillsbury Collection. Photo of Frances Pillsbury.
b. Courtesy Martin A. Wyckoff. Unknown group, ca. 1885. From George Miller family album. Bush and Kadgihn, photographers.
c. MCHS. Ad, ca. 1885.

186 a. MCHS. ca. 1895. Mary Clark Hodge, Mrs. Rosney, Julia F. Hodge, Mrs. A.E. DeMange, Paul DeMange, Mrs. Loudon.
b. MCHS. John Sterling residence on North Main St. at the southeast corner of Emerson. Sterling was later a congressman and was killed in an auto crash during World War I. Left to right: Charlotte Sterling, Louis William Masters, Horace Sterling.

Page

187 a. "Camp Bohemia" was on the Kankakee River in northern Illinois. MCHS, Merwin Collection. Photo by Charles E. Voss, Kankakee.
b. MCHS, Merwin Collection.

188 Calling cards. MCHS, Jackman Collection.
b. MCHS. Northwest corner, McLean and Washington. Home of J.N. Ward, present site of LaFayette Apartments. Photo taken 1882.

189 a. MCHS. Unidentified costume party, 1901.
b. MCHS. Ewing Scrapbook.

190-1 MCHS. Northwest corner, Jefferson and Madison, ca. 1890. Building on right old Baptist church, present site of Pantagraph Printing and Stationery.
Back row:
1. William V. Evans
2. Harriet Fyffe
3. Jessie Davis
4. Owen Reeves
5. May Fitzwilliam
6. William V. Dinsmore
7. Will Fitzwilliam
8. Lucy Smith
9. Fred Evans
10. Letitia Scott
11. Rachel Crothers
12. Edward Perrigo

Seated on court:
1. Grace Cheney
2. Kate Harwood
3. Frank Funk
4. Lottie McLean
5. Frank Bates

192 a. MCHS, Tay Collection.
b. MCHS. Photo by Bush & Kadgihn, Bloomington. Botton: Will Matern, Clarence Fisher. Middle: Ed Perigo, W.B. Read, Charles E. Dodge, Ellis Dunn, Billy Loomis, Ben Fell. Top: Dan Warner, Bob Otto, Eugene Blake. Captain was C.E. Dodge; Secretary, W.B. Read; Treasurer, Dan Warner.

193 a. MCHS. Cast included Daisy Hill (left front), L.B. Merwin, R.E. Williams, Rachel Bauman, Aubrey Royce, Bert Eddy, Owen T. Reeves, Ed Van Schoick, Laura McCurdy, Dudley M. Smith, Melvin Dodson and Wallace Bruce Amesbury.
b. MCHS. Stereoscopic view, October 25, 1878.

194 a. MCHS. Theatre program, 1899.
b. From *Illustrated Bloomington and Normal*, 1896. Exterior and interior of Grand Opera House, north side of the 100 block, East Market St.

195 a. MCHS. Theatre program, 1899.
b. From *Up-to-date Homes*, Paul Moratz, 1899.
c. From *Art Work of Bloomington, Illinois*, 1904. Northwest corner, Front and Roosevelt. Paul Moratz, architect.

196 a. MCHS cat. no. 780-115; communion service used at Blooming Grove Christian Church, 1880-1950.
b. From *Art Work of Bloomington, Illinois*, 1904. Northwest corner, Prairie and Jefferson.

197 a. From *Art Work of Bloomington, Illinois*, 1904. Southeast corner, East and Monroe.
b. MCHS.

198 a. MCHS. Ewing Scrapbook. Stationery letterhead, Democratic First Voters' Club, 1892.
b. Courtesy *The Pantagraph.*

199 a. MCHS. Stevenson Collection.
b. Standing, from left: Richard J. McDonald, John J. Caroll, E.E. Pierson, Dr. Frank Fielder, C.T. Merriman, unidentified, Mr. Lock, Sam Nicherson, L.C. Hay, Guy Karr, Aaron Livingston, Albert Wochner, Lee Rust, Harvey Karr, Harvey Rust, Thomas Blake and Thomas J. McGrath. Seated, from left: Unidentified, J.C. Mahoney, unidentified, Andrew Lyon, W.T. Toohey, unidentified, Lawson Bradley, Erley Moore, Clayton Hutchinson, G.A. Ensenberger and James Costello. Mr. Ensenberger was club treasurer.

Page

200 From *Bloomington Illustrated*, 1889. Alfred H. Piquenard, architect, 1870. Although the Illinois State Historical Society describes the building as the "Italian villa" style, it is actually a prime example of the Second Empire style and is illustrated as such in *Identifying American Architecture* (p.52) by John J.G. Blumenthal.

201 MCHS. ca. 1880 Copy by A,M. Marton, ca. 1915.

202 a. MCHS. Photo ca. 1888.
b. MCHS. Campaign ribbon, 1888 or 1892, printed on silk. Pantagraph Printing and Stationery.

203 a. From *Portrait and Biographical Album of McLean County*, Chapman Bros., Chicago, 1887. Lithograph.
b. MCHS. Majority of members from Pontiac, several from Chenoa. The group is typical of militia units of the period. The officers' swords probably date from the Civil War era.

204 From *Bloomington Illustrated*, 1889. Cochran and Piquenard, architects. Heafer and McGregor, contractors. View southwest from Jefferson and Main. Note iron horse trough in foreground.

205 a. MCHS, Scott Collection. Stationery letterhead. Brown, Pettibone & Co., Chicago.
b. MCHS. Photo by A.M. Marton, 220 North Center St., ca. 1890.
c. MCHS. Pen was the "Congress Quill Pen" manufactured by E. DeYoung Co., New York, ca. 1855, and belonged to Scott. Scott used quill pens exclusively until his death in 1898.

206 a. MCHS. Photo by *Illinois College of Photography*, Effingham, ca. 1895.
b. MCHS.

207 a. MCHS. Photo by R. Fenwick, ca. 1895.
b. MCHS. No. 3 School, present site of Irving School. Photo taken 1876 for Illinois school exhibit, Centennial Exposition, Philadelphia. G.W. Bunting, architect.

208 a. MCHS, Scott Collection
b. MCHS. Photo by Funk and Klauer, ca. 1892.

210 a. MCHS, Scott Collection.
b. From *Art Work of Bloomington, Illinois*, 1904. Reeves and Bailey, Peoria, architects.

211 a. MCHS. No. 4 School, Mrs. Ella Price, teacher.
b. MCHS. Photo ca. 1880. Copied from original by A.M. Marton, ca. 1915.

212 MCHS. First two stories built in 1875. Third story and rear section attributed to architect George Miller, added 1887. The tower was removed or destroyed between 1896 and 1903.

213 a. From *Souvenir* of the 29th annual encampment of the Illinois Grand Army of the Republic, 1895. Pantagraph Printing and Stationery.
b. MCHS. Photo ca. 1900. A "ceramic oleograph" by A.M. Marton of Bloomington, printed on porcelain. Marton developed this process, which he claimed was the most permanent form of photography, in regard to fading of the image.

214 a. MCHS. Photo ca. 1900. Torn down in 1907 for YMCA building. Present

NOTES

Page

site of Bloomington Federal Drive-in facility. Note similarity in form to Pantagraph Building.
- b. From *Just For Fun*, a portfolio of cartoons published in the Daily Pantagraph, 1914. The drawings are attributed to Owen T. Reeves, Jr.

215 a. From *Souvenir* of the 29th annual encampment, Illinois G.A.R.
- b. Ibid.

216 From *Bloomington Illustrated*, 1889. Northeast corner, Washington and East. George Miller, architect.

217 a. Courtesy Bloomington Public Library. Photo taken July 7, 1911 at Miller Park by C.U. Williams. Left to right:
1. Mrs. Parham
2. Miss Parham
3. Mrs. Lange
4. Alma Lange
5. Miss Stewell (?)
6. Mrs. Webb
7. Nellie (?) F. Webb
- b. Courtesy Martin A. Wyckoff. Book is a catalogue of exhibits at the Philadelphia Centennial Exposition.

218 a. From *The Story of the Pullman Car*, Joseph Husband, A.C. McClurg & Co., Chicago, 1917. Photo ca. 1875.
- b. Courtesy *The Pantagraph*. Photo taken during the A.R.U. strike, 1894.

219 MCHS. Stereograph no. 1402-M from series published by the Centennial Photographic Co. of Philadelphia, 1876.

220 a. MCHS. Photo ca. 1895. Note that this is a composite photo made by exposing the same plate twice. Viewed horizontally is it a camping scene. Viewed vertically, as the caption indicates, it is a picture of a balanced rock. The picture was taken at Pike's Peak.
- b. MCHS. Photo ca. 1895.

221 a. MCHS. Photo ca. 1910. Vesta ____ and Daisy Hill on the beach at Atlantic City, N.J.
- b. MCHS. Photo ca. 1895. The circular format indicates the picture probably was taken with a very early Kodak box camera. The film was developed and printed by a professional photographer, T.P. Garrett of Bloomington. This was before drug stores offered such services.
- c. MCHS. Photo by H.H. Bennett, ca. 1895.

222 a. MCHS. Photo ca. 1910.
- b. MCHS. Ewing Scrapbook.
- c. MCHS. Photo ca. 1910. Woman in chair is Mrs. Dr. William Hill, not Queen Victoria.

223 a. MCHS. Ewing Scrapbook.
- b. MCHS. Photo ca. 1910. Daisy Hill at left. Captioned by her, "Me all so pious."

224 a. MCHS, Tay Collection. Photo by Centro Artistico, Manila, 1899.
- b. MCHS. Photo taken from northeast corner Monroe and East.

225 a. From *History of the 8th Illinois U.S. Volunteers*, E.F. Harman Co., Chicago, 1899.
- b. Ibid.

226 a. MCHS.
- b. MCHS.

227 a. MCHS, Brigham Collection. This particular parade is unidentified.
- b. From *Illustrated Bloomington and Normal*, 1896.

Chapter 8. The New Century.

228-9 MCHS. Photo by Spafford & Cable.

230 a. MCHS. Brigham Collection.

Page

- b. MCHS. Photo by Spafford & Cable.

231 a. MCHS. Photo by Spafford & Cable.
- b. MCHS. Photo by Spafford & Cable.

232 a. MCHS. Photo by Spafford & Cable.
- b. MCHS. Modern print from original glass negative.

233 MCHS. Photo by unknown woman photographer employed by C.U. Williams.

234-5 From *Art Work of Bloomington, Illinois*, 1904.

236 a. From *Views of Normal*, The Normal Improvement Assn., C.A. Burner, 1913.
- b. From "Bloomington and Normal Railway & Light Company Report," Stone & Webster, 1911.

237 Ibid.

238 Ibid.

239 a. From "Bloomington Mfrs.' Exposition and Merchants' Festival Souvenir Program," 1911.
- b. From "Bloomington and Normal Railway & Light Company Report," 1911.

240 a. From *Telephone Topics*, The Gary Group Operating Telephone Companies, November, 1947.
- b. From "Bloomington Mfrs.' Exposition Program," 1911.

241 a. From Bloomington Central Union Telephone Company directory, 1900.
- b. Ibid.

242 a. MCHS, Society receipts.
- b. MCHS, Iseminger Collection.

243 From Bloomington and Normal Illinois city directory, 1915.

244 a. MCHS, Iseminger Collection.
- b. MCHS. Photo taken June 14, 1903. Among those gentlemen are (roughly left to right): A.L. Wood, W. Greenough, Chas. Diets, A. Wochner, Wm. Courey, H. Thobro, S.P. Irwin, I.N. Phillips, Chas. Cooper, Chas. Stevenson, E. Martens, H. Humphreys, J. Crawford, Fred Verry, J.A. Beck.

245 a. MCHS, Hutton Family Collection. The garage is believed to have been in the Arrowsmith vicinity.
- b. MCHS, Iseminger Collection.

246 MCHS, Brigham Collection. Photo by Underwood & Underwood. Original is stereoscopic view.

247 a. From *Nature Study Review*, February, 1915.
- b. From "Quinquennial Report of the Public Schools of Bloomington 1900-05," J.E. Burke & Co., 1905.

248 a. Ibid.
- b. MCHS.
- c. From "Quinquennial Report," 1905.

249 a. From "Sextennial Report of the Public Schools of Bloomington, Pantagraph Printing and Stationery, 1911.
- b. Ibid.

250 MCHS.

251 a. MCHS, Wakefield Family Scrapbook.
- b. Courtesy *The Pantagraph*.

252 a. MCHS.
- b. MCHS. Women and men used separate ballot boxes.
- c. MCHS, Bloomington Board of Election Commissioners Collection.

253 MCHS.

254 a. MCHS. "Labor Conquers All".
- b. MCHS.
- c. From *Picturesque Bloomington*, 1907.

255 a. MCHS.
- b. MCHS.
- c. MCHS.
- d. MCHS.

Page

256 Courtesy Wayman AME Church.

257 a. From "Bloomington Mfrs.' Exposition Program," 1911.
- b. From "Souvenir of Bloomington, Illinois," Commerce Club, Frank I. Miller, ca. 1912.
- c. From *Bloomington Record*, June 11, 1910.

258 a. MCHS, Kirkpatrick Collection. Photo by C.U. Williams.

259 a. MCHS.
- b. MCHS. Photo by Art Foto Shop.

260 MCHS, Brigham Collection. Jacob Hasbrouck in foreground.

261 MCHS.

262 a. MCHS. Original is postcard, ca. 1915.
- b. Courtesy Pearl Funk. Photo by Fred Hitch.

263 Courtesy Marion McClure.

264 a. MCHS. Photo may have been taken at Atlanta, Ill. Fairgrounds.
- b. MCHS.

265 a. MCHS.
- b. MCHS.

266 a. MCHS.
- b. MCHS, courtesy Dean McCrossin. Photo by Arnold.

267 a. MCHS.
- b. MCHS.

268 a. MCHS. George Miller, architect.
- b. MCHS.
- c. MCHS.

269 a. From *Illustrated Bloomington Illinois*, 1916.
- b. MCHS, Wakefield Family Scrapbook. Taken at Interurban Depot, southwest corner Madison & Jefferson.
- c. From *Illustrated Bloomington Illinois*, 1916.

270 MCHS. Photo by Underwood & Underwood. Original is stereoscopic view.

271 a. MCHS.
- b. MCHS. Left to right: John H. Burnham, George P. Davis, Milo Custer, Fourth figure is unidentified. Photo by J.G. Melluish.

272 a. Washington Street, courtesy Martha Miller.
- b. Button, MCHS.
- c. Parade, courtesy Martha Miller.
- d. North Main, courtesy Martha Miller.

273 Concert, courtesy Martha Miller.

274 Courtesy *The Pantagraph*.

275 a. MCHS, Brigham Collection.
- b. MCHS, Brigham Collection.

276 Courtesy Martha Miller.

277 a. MCHS.
- b. MCHS.

278 a. Courtesy James Adams.
- b. From Bloomington-Normal City Directory, 1919.

279 a. Courtesy James Adams.
- b. From *Illustrated Bloomington Illinois*, 1916.

280. a. From *McLean County School Era*.
- b. MCHS, Brigham Colleciton.

281 a. MCHS, Brigham Collection.
- b. MCHS, Brigham Collection.

282 a. Courtesy William O'Hara. Photo by United Photo.
Back row:
1. Dave Kane
2. Bobby Lynch
3. Art Kane
4. Henry Ryan, manager
5. ____ Irwin
6. Bill O'Hara

Front row:
1. Bill Ryan
2. Dave Conroy
3. "Mush" Ryan
4. Pat McGrath
- b. MCHS, Hutton Family Collection. Left to right:
1. Charles Thompson
2. Howard Ritchie

NOTES

Page
3. Bill Wilkins
4. Abby Arbogast
5. Roy Evans
Standing, coach, name unknown
282 a. MCHS, Home Bureau Collection.
b. MCHS, Home Bureau Collection.
284 a. MCHS, Photo by C.U. Williams.
b. MCHS. Copy by John Hayter.
285 a. MCHS.
b. Courtesy Ruth Hamm.
286 MCHS, Illington Collection.
287 a. MCHS, Illington Collection. Program from Chicago production.
b. MCHS, Illington Collection.
288 MCHS, courtesy Mrs. Elizabeth S. Ives.
289 MCHS.
290 MCHS.
291 MCHS.
292 a. Courtesy *The Pantagraph*. Front St. viaduct over C & A tracks in background.
b. Courtesy *The Pantagraph*. 100 block, South Main St. Buildings left to right:
1. Miller-Davis Building.
2. Royce Hall, built 1857.
3. Oberkoetter Buildings, built 1876. George Miller, architect.
293 a. From *McLean County in the World War 1917-18*, McLean County War Publishing Co., Bloomington, n.d.
b. MCHS.
c. MCHS.
294 MCHS.
296 a. MCHS. Photo by Moore.
b. MCHS, Brigham Collection.
297 a. From *McLean County in the World War*. Front St. viaduct at rear.
b. Courtesy *The Pantagraph*.
c. MCHS. Located on North Center St.
298 a. From *McLean County in the World War*.
b. MCHS.
299 a. From *History's Greatest War*, E.T. Townsend, 1920.
b. MCHS.
300 a. Courtesy Illinois State Historical Library.
b. Courtesy Julia Scott Vrooman Estate, David Wilson, Trustee.
301 MCHS. Probably a parade to mark the dedication of the McBarnes Building.

Chapter 9. Return to Normalcy.
302 a. Harding button. MCHS.
b. Debs button. MCHS. Debs had been imprisoned on charges of draft evasion.
c. Courtesy Steven Scalzo. Photo by R.V. Mehlenback, Peoria. Building at center of block being removed for new Ensenberger Building.
303 a. MCHS. Courtesy Judith Spear. Second from left, Henry Hitt.
b. Courtesy Catherine Koos. Aljo located at 623 North Main St., Bloomington.
304 a. From Montgomery Ward & Co. catalogue, Spring and Summer 1926.
b. MCHS, Goforth Collection.
305 a. MCHS, Goforth Collection. Photo by Art Foto Shop.
b. MCHS, Vanderwater Collection.
306 a. From *Blue Book of the State of Illinois*, 1923-4.
b. Courtesy *The Pantagraph*. Photo ca. 1935.
c. Courtesy *The Pantagraph*. Photo ca. 1935.
307 a. Courtesy *The Pantagraph*. Photo ca. 1916.
b. Courtesy Steven Scalzo. Photo by R.V. Mehlenbeck, Peoria.

Page
308 a. MCHS. Photo by George Goff. Airplane owned by Leo Jackson and Ferdinand Schad; Walter Young and Archie Baldridge pictured.
b. MCHS. Photo by George Goff.
c. Courtesy *The Pantagraph*. Photo by "Scoop." The Pantagraph pioneered aerial photography for newspapers.
309 a. MCHS. Courtesy Catherine Henson.
b. MCHS. Courtesy Catherine Henson.
c. MCHS. Courtesy Catherine Henson.
310 a. Courtesy Delmar D. Wyckoff. Photo taken at Streid's filling station and restaurant, Chenoa, 1930. Delmar Wyckoff, salesman.
b. From *McLean County Courier*, 1950.
311 a. Courtesy *The Pantagraph*. Photo of evidence taken at county jail.
b. Courtesy *The Pantagraph*. Probably West Hovey Ave., Normal.
c. Courtesy *The Pantagraph*. At the county jail.
312 a. MCHS, Home Bureau Collection. Clara Brian's first car, purchased for Home Bureau by the Kiwanis Club.
b. MCHS. Bloomington Market House, built by B.F. Hoopes in 1867. Caused anti-monopoly suit. Home of the *Daily Pantagraph* in the late 1860s. Later the state militia armory and the second home of State Farm Insurance. National Register eligible.
313 a. MCHS, Home Bureau Collection.
b. MCHS, Home Bureau Collection.
314 MCHS, Fifer-Bohrer Collection.
315 MCHS, ISSCS Collection. From *The Institution Quarterly*, 1925.
316 a. Courtesy Dr. Robert Price. Left to right: Dr. Harlan Hart, Elaine Strayer, Dr. J.K. Hawks, and Dr. Edson B. Hart.
b. Courtesy *The Pantagraph*. Building located in Normal's Fairview Park. Photo by United Photo.
317 a. Courtesy Dr. Robert Price. Standing, left to right:
1. Unknown
2. Dr. Leroy Yolten
3. Unkown
4. Dr. Gerald Cline
5. Unknown
6. Dr. Norman Elliott
7. Unknown
8. Dr. Ferd C. McCormick
First row, no cap, Dr. E.M. Stevenson.
b. Courtesy *The Pantagraph*.
318 a. MCHS. Program, 1929.
b. Courtesy Bloomington Consistory.
319 a. MCHS. Photo ca. 1922.
b. MCHS. Photo by Eldo Moore.
320 a. MCHS, Centennial Collection.
b. Courtesy *The Pantagraph*. Note the familiarity of these never-built buildings.
321 a. Courtesy Ken-Way Studio, see page 377 for whole image.
b. Courtesy *The Pantagraph*.

Chapter 10. The Great Depression.
322 Courtesy *The Pantagraph*.
324 a. Courtesy *The Pantagraph*. View taken at 1939 Durley Building fire. Very likely the ancient steam pumper was also used at the 1932 fires.
b. Courtesy *The Pantagraph*. Dance pavilion was built over the water. Present site of State Farm Park.
325 a. Courtesy *The Pantagraph*. Western Union delivery man in foreground. The same building is illustrated on page 210.

Page
b. Courtesy *The Pantagraph*. The interior of the same building is illustrated on page 130.
326 a. Courtesy *The Pantagraph*.
b. Courtesy *The Pantagraph*.
327 a. Courtesy *The Pantagraph*. Corner Jefferson and East, looking west.
b. Courtesy *The Pantagraph*.
328 Courtesy *The Pantagraph*. Corner of Madison and Jefferson.
329 a. Courtesy *The Pantagraph*.
b. Courtesy *The Pantagraph*.
330 Courtesy *The Pantagraph*. Man at left in straw hat is "Uncle Billy" Shelper. Taken at ICRR tracks south of Grove St.
331 a. MCHS, Breen Collection.
b. MCHS, Breen Collection. Some of this scrip was in circulation as late as 1935.
332 a. Courtesy Anthony Koos. National Liquor Store window, 1938.
b. Courtesy Anthony Koos. Alan Sycle on phone.
c. Courtesy John Baldini. Left to right: "Zip" and Ralph Goetske.
333 a. Courtesy *The Pantagraph*. October 13, 1936.
b. Courtesy Richard Middleton. MCHS. Sign hung in A & P Store window on Front St., Bloomington.
334 a. Courtesy *The Pantagraph*.
b. Courtesy *The Pantagraph*.
335 a. Courtesy *The Pantagraph*. Workmen pictured are either mining gravel or landscaping Highland Golf Course.
b. MCHS.
336 a. Courtesy *The Pantagraph*.
b. Courtesy *The Pantagraph*.
337 a. From *Five Golden Decades*, McLean County Farm Bureau, 1965.
b. MCHS. Farm Bureau photo. Site of present bulk plant, 1 block west of Main St. at junction of ICGRR and Sugar Creek in Normal.
338 Courtesy Catherine Koos. William O'Hara on tractor near Hudson, 1938.
339 a. From Funk Seed catalogue, 1931.
b. From Progress Edition, *Daily Pantagraph*, April 1936.
340 a. MCHS, Home Bureau Collection.
b. Courtesy Catherine Koos. Southeast corner Main and Jefferson.
341 a. Courtesy Catherine Koos. Restaurant in basement.
b. Courtesy Catherine Koos. Mrs. White, the proprietor, in foreground.
c. MCHS, Home Bureau Collection.
342 a. Courtesy Bloomington Public Library.
b. Courtesy Bloomington Public Library.
343 a. MCHS. Photo by George Goff, ca. 1934. Plane in rear is Amelia Earhart's.
b. Courtesy *The Pantagraph*.
344 a. MCHS. Photo by Acme. Mrs. V.L. Womeldorff and Cora Lee of Decatur.
b. MCHS. Photo by Acme. Legion commander Art Kane with overseas cap.
345 a. Courtesy Catherine Koos. Bridge over GM & O tracks at northeast edge of Normal.
b. MCHS. Photo taken Augut 6, 1937. Practicing for strafing.
c. MCHS. Left to right: Donald Kent, Don Karr, Richard Terry. Denim was worn to save "wear and tear" on regular uniforms.

Bloomington in 1867